MOLIÈRE

MOLIÈRE

An engraving from the portrait by Pierre Mignard

MOLIÈRE

The Comic Mask

BY

D. B. WYNDHAM LEWIS

EYRE & SPOTTISWOODE

22 HENRIETTA STREET · LONDON

FIRST PUBLISHED 1959
© D. B. WYNDHAM LEWIS 1959
PRINTED IN GREAT BRITAIN BY
THE SHENVAL PRESS
LONDON, HERTFORD AND HARLOW
CATALOGUE NO. 6/2383

TO

DOUGLAS AND MIA
WOODRUFF

'*A narrative means that
not to have him replace him
and not to have him have him replace him*'

GERTRUDE STEIN, *How to Write*

Wolfe should read Humbert

ould read scenarios.

n should read . . . made by
their literary idol Mlle de

should read . . . at this

hould read . . . to

t.
et tout

Plutus.
read 'in

d William

ould read alone.
arrayed.
ould read nuit.
d Bossuet
présent
. . . Et
lieu du

Pope

ère's
of 1682.

Introductory

One rainy autumn night in Paris when Jacques Copeau was playing Alceste at the Vieux-Colombier, against a background of three tall chairs and a spread of tapestry, it may be that more than one of his audience received the *coup de foudre*. One had 'done' Molière at school, like most people. One had listened, hypnotized but unmoved, to these same alexandrines rolled out at the Comédie-Française, so expertly, so rhythmically as to recall the scrolls curving from the mouths of personages in medieval woodcuts – I think the shrug is Alphonse Daudet's. Now the play had come instantly alive. At the first impact of Copeau's voice, throbbing (one was certain) with the veritable pain of Molière himself about to meet his torment Armande on the stage of the Palais-Royal on June 4, 1666, it was evident that in ranking the sad and noble comedy of *Le Misantrope* with Seville Cathedral as one of the chief achievements of the human spirit a good judge of our own day erred not at all.

Morbleu! faut-il que je vous aime!

Is there any other satiric piece written for any stage which holds the spectator spellbound for two hours or more with no dramatic tricks at all, no 'action' in the accepted sense, no cloak-and-sword heroics, no plot to speak of – a piece of pure and timeless psychological conflict, ending moreover, as high tensions so often end in life itself, in the air? Blind and deaf to all persuasion after a final clash with Célimène, Alceste stalks savagely off to seek a refuge from the entire human race. 'We must find some way of stopping him', says the faithful Philinte in effect to Éliante, and the curtain falls. It is a connoisseur's piece, a comedy written almost literally in heart's blood, a byword with the box-office, from Molière's day to this recognized as caviare. He might well have repeated the feat. Being a harassed actor-manager with many livings to earn, he never even tried.

Copeau being dead, and having taken his magic with him, Alceste must perforce move and speak henceforth for many, the fine later reading of Jean-Louis Barrault notwithstanding, in print alone. To no other of Molière's creations belongs one single voice, fondly remembered. Good actors are plentiful and the plays rarely flag. The buffooneries are still fresh and funny, which cannot be said for some of Shakepeare's; the characters still vital, the satire dated, no doubt, like its targets – though Harley Street afforded Shaw considerable new scope for naughtiness – but still sparkling, the craftsmanship still a pleasure to contemplate, though for carpentry Molière has nothing to equal the cabinet-work of a Sardou or a Pinero. Both these masters of the 'well-made play', today nearly as unactable as unreadable, would have blushed to be charged with some of Molière's peccadillos – the sketchy climaxes, for example, the indifference to the curtain-line which should end every act with a neat click, the shameless bustle-technique, recalling Dickens', with which final loose ends are sometimes scrabbled together, the placing, very often, of the *scène à faire*. But Molière knows his trade as well as any Pinero or Sardou. He is, in the phrase of Jacques Audiberti, a 'total athlete of the theatre'. Ninety per cent of his comedy-scenes remain perennially and obstinately hilarious, which cannot be said for those of his contemporaries, though Congreve is wittier and Calderón has more grace. And his dialogue, at least in prose, remains for the most part flexibly faultless, as any actor will agree. His 'free verse' matches the best of La Fontaine. On his alexandrines the purists differ. They are normally vigorous and muscular, with a steady beat. Some have been criticized as over-clogged with metaphor, enigmatic, occasionally incoherent. Nobody was more aware of his shortcomings than Molière.

To match him with Shakespeare – it has been done – seems excessive, all poetry apart. Molière's squaretoed Parisian shoes are planted firmly on the earth, wherever his head may be, and he does not work in gossamer. The young lovers in *Le Sicilien*, that most charming and airy of soufflés, all song and dance and laughter, would not be at home with Lysander and Hermia in the enchanted wood. Virginal and vital and graceful as his young girls invarably are, they are each and all practical little misses of the French upper-middle class who know exactly what they want; namely marriage and a family with the young man of their choice. For an uncritical nineteenth century to rank Molière with Racine, again – not to mention Corneille – appears equally unrealistic. He does not touch the heights or depths of human experience like a fellow-genius of whom the late Hubert Wolfe admirably remarked that Racine 'draws restraint upon restraint closer and closer about him till in his greatest moment he glitters, like a mailed knight, in the shining armour of his superb self-mastery'. Even in *Le Misantrope* there is no tirade liable to cause the sensitive to swoon in their seats, as happened by all accounts to Alfred de Musset on hearing Phèdre's great cry of agony from the lips of Rachel.

Such things are not Molière's concern, and even if they had been, his way of life militated against much traffic in the higher emotions. Labouring for the most part at top speed at the beck of an imperious young King, ordered regularly to produce something new and amusing at the last possible moment, racked by chest-trouble and unrequited passion and well-founded jealousy, burdened with all the daily business of a theatre, suffering the blackest depressions to which artists and epicureans are liable in their pursuit of

> Beauty that must die,
> And Joy, whose hand is ever at his lips,
> Bidding adieu; and aching Pleasure nigh,
> Turning to poison while the bee-mouth sips,

Molière reacted with desperate and enormous vitality against what Pascal calls man's most secret misery, his inability to endure the sight of himself. 'Laughing at my troubles and cocking a snook at all the world' – like Figaro the true comic artist in every age is primarily concerned with alleviating his own megrims, and only incidentally with distracting mankind at large. It may be that Nanny, whose function he shares to some extent, is doing the same when she forestalls uproar in the nursery by making those funny faces. But Molière enjoys an inestimable advantage over most of the world's nannies. His grimaces have for the most part remained funny for over three hundred years, and continue to remind us in the oddest way of people we know.[1]

How far *ce rigoureux censeur des grands canons*, in Bossuet's contemptuous phrase,[2] wasted the weapon of ridicule on trivialities may be judged as we proceed. Assailing fopperies in dress or the grimaces of the *précieuses* is undoubtedly more in Molière's normal line than attacking hypocrisy, a process of which he makes something of a botch. His moral outlook is that of the average middle-class Parisian of his time, and perhaps others: a cool, banal, prudent, time-serving assessment of ethical values of which the ultimate essence might be anglo-modernized as 'Whatever you do, keep in step with the Joneses'. In the matter of the eternal verities he is more or less indifferent. It is customary to attribute this partly, or even chiefly, to his having been in late adolescence a pupil of the celebrated Abbé Pierre Gassendi, who attempted to reconcile Epicurus with Christianity. If so, young Molière was not the only one of his fellow-pupils to develop their tutor's theories too heartily in the wrong direction. Chapelle and Cyrano de Bergerac did so all their lives with exemplary verve, and the profession Molière chose for himself hardly clashed with the same predilection. *Epicuri de grege porcum* – doubtless Horace's precedent was often toasted in bumpers. But Horace, as all the best authorities agree, was joking, and the metaphysics of all three may have grieved Gassendi in his old age.

No champions of enthusiasms, then, spiritual, moral, or any other kind. The only spontaneous act of chivalry in any of his characters is Don Juan's rush to rescue a stranger from brigands in the play of that name. *Dom Juan* is not one of Molière's triumphs, and it is rarely if ever revived. It certainly demonstrates its creator's limitations, representing one of two dives into waters too deep for one lacking the proper equipment all too visibly. The eminent Guillaume de Lamoignon,

[1] 'Satyre is a sort of Glass, wherein Beholders do generally discover Everybody's Faces but their own; which is the chief Reason for that kind Reception it gets in the World.' (Swift, *The Battle of the Books*.)

[2] *Maximes et Réflexions sur la Comédie*, 1694. *Canons*, usually of rich lace, were the trimmings attached to the kneebands of the breeches of contemporary men of fashion, hanging to midway down the calf.

First President of the Parlement of Paris – Lord Chief Justice, so to speak, of France – spoke drily and to the point after the temporary interdict on *Le Tartufe* in 1667. 'You are a comic genius, M. de Molière. You are an honour and a glory to France. But it is not the theatre's business to dabble in religion.' There was no answer to that as there was, in one way, to Bossuet's charge of specializing in trivia, had it been made in Molière's lifetime. A single nod in the direction of the box-office was a sufficient reply to Messire Jacques-Bénigne; every showman knows that what the public wants is laughs, not instruction. It seems a little peculiar of Bossuet nevertheless to cite *Le Malade Imaginaire*, together with Corneille's *Le Cid*, in his indictment of the immorality of the contemporary French theatre. The Dauphin's ex-tutor could have found something much more to the point in *Amphitryon* or *La Princesse d'Élide*.

By and large, however, Bossuet was not talking through his mitre. In Molière's time the Church's agelong accusation against the stage was justified enough. While an edict of Louis XIII ensured decency at least in the two 'official' theatres, the Hôtel de Bourgogne and the Marais, outrageous obscenities in speech and dumbshow were offered the public in the *parades* at the great Parisian fairs, and the Italian comedians often lapsed into skulduggery, in their vivacious way.[1] For such standard reasons the stage-players of France were held *ipso facto* excommunicate unless and until they abandoned their naughty trade and sought absolution, as the large majority took good care to do before it was too late; as Molière's old comrade and mistress Madeleine Béjart did, distributing large charity and dying an exemplary death; as Molière himself would have done, it seems, had he had time, which likewise failed the celebrated Adrienne Lecouvreur, over whose un-consecrated grave a century later so many indignant tears have been shed. It was a situation recognized and accepted by every French player, in whom excommunication pro tem. naturally tended to increase that jaunty, slightly self-conscious defiance of the conventions which even today attaches to this province

[1] The strictures of the Parlement of Paris in the preceding century were partly xenophobic, it is conjectured.

of Bohemia and might be called the Rogue-and-Vagabond complex. One thinks of Mr Chitterlow dazzling the innocent Kipps with revelations of life as it was lived in Number One – was there ever a Number Two? – touring companies in the golden age of Edward VII; 'a quite amazing jungle of inter-woven "affairs" it appeared to be, a mere amorous winepress for the crushing of hearts'. But when the (late) Illustrious Theatre company takes the road with Madeleine and Molière in 1645, it will be seen how little else this troop has in common with the turbulent scallywags of Scarron's contemporary *Roman Comique*. Molière had what we call today 'contacts', and he and his comrades will at times achieve almost official status in the South. If, between whiles, they suffer the customary hazards of bad roads, weather, food, and lodgings, and the proximity of brawlers, Boeotians, bugs, and possibly brigands, it is all part of a time-honoured theatrical noviciate, from which Molière will draw profitable farce-material; though, on the whole, curiously little. Perhaps the gypsy life was not so amusing as they say.

Anyone desirous of getting a clear view of the man in his prime has the choice of several aspects. None of the official portraits, Mignard's included, is to be trusted, we are assured; least of all Houdon's late eighteenth-century bust, now dominating the foyer of the Comédie-Française so regally. Equally untrustworthy, the best authorities agree, is the memory of an old actress, Mlle Poisson, who described Molière in 1740 from childhood-impressions. He was not physically the matinée-idol of her dreams. He was not 'more tall than short'. His carriage was not 'noble'. He had no leg comparable with Sir Willoughby Patterne's, or even 'fine'. Contemporary drawings show a shortish swarthy figure, somewhat squat and thin-shanked, with a large head, a prominent, broad-flanged nose, a wide, sensitive, sensual mouth, and dark eyes, more small than large, set far apart. The eyebrows are thick, eloquent, and dark, the flowing hair and trim moustache dark likewise. Altogether the alert, intelligent, whimsical, sardonic features are those of a born comedian, lined and worn, like Garrick's, by fifty thousand grimaces a year; a mask at once rubbery with perpetual muscular play and leathery from perpetual paint, aptly recalling the masks of the ancestral Commedia dell' Arte and the far-off Atellanae of pagan Rome. The illusion, not uncommon with comic actors, that he was a born tragedian lasted a long time, and was proof, apparently, even against provincial hisses and a shower or two of rotten apples. In the eyes of one of the Mignard portraits may be discerned nevertheless, without much difficulty, the authentic hint of melancholy. 'Laugh, clown, laugh!' – it was to be a couple of centuries before romantic novelists, following the lead of the Goncourts, invaded the circus and everywhere discovered the breaking heart behind the spangles.

Molière's case at least is fully documented. Far more than all other cares the torment of being enslaved by a spoilt coquette twenty years his junior accounts for those long glum silences at tavern suppers in the company of Boileau, Racine, Chapelle, La Fontaine, and other wits, as perhaps for those irritable outbursts at home which a natural generosity and good-humour could not restrain. Envy, hatred, and calumny pursued Molière also, no less and no more than they do any other favourite of the public. The charges of incest and sodomy have not been completely explained to this day. They may be merely tokens of professional esteem. He certainly suffered abominably from Armande, to whom a stylish and venomous pamphlet of 1688 called *La Fameuse Comédienne*, undoubtedly the work of some gifted sister-artist, awards a string of lovers, including a couple of insolent Court rakes who may well have sat for her husband's vengeful etching of Don Juan. 'La Molière', a leading lady with attractions, was doubtless capable of using her tongue *en ville* as skilfully as the late Mistinguett, whose exchange with a malicious elderly rival greeting her at an evening party in the 1920's is still quoted in Parisian stage circles as a model for aspirants.[1] And doubtless Armande could use it at home as well.

Thus it might be said that Molière's most poignant comedy was the one he starred in for eleven years and never wrote,

[1] 'Mother darling!' – 'Surely some mistake, Mademoiselle? I'm a married woman.'

7

though some of its pain is distilled in *Le Misantrope*. *Non iam illud quaero* – the refrain of most of his married life is the long excruciated cry of Catullus,

> I beg but balsam for my bleeding breast,
> Cure for my wounds, and from my labours rest.

They were the years of his most brilliant foolery.

Contemplating the enormous mass of Molièriana which has piled up since the master's death, one is relieved to think that relatively little of it is essential to read. Half a dozen contemporaries supply sufficient authority for most of Molière's life. The contribution of the actor Charles Varlet de la Grange, his devoted *jeune premier*, whose miraculously-surviving register of the company makes a national treasure beyond price, is a model of sober, factual brevity. Gallois de Grimarest's *Vie de Monsieur de Molière* (1705), imparts much information derived from the actor Baron, the young protégé of Molière's declining years, and is much wider in scope, if slightly less dependable. Essential also are Donneau de Visé, founder of *Le Mercure Galant* and father of all gossip-columnists, Le Boulanger de Chalussay, whose anti-Molièresque comedy *Élomire Hypocondre* is full of libels, insults, and information, and the younger Montfleury, whose *Impromptu de l'Hôtel de Condé*, undertaken on behalf of an actor-father parodied in the *Impromptu de Versailles*, is as spitefully illuminating as could be desired. Among later studies, the *Molière* of the well-graced playwright Maurice Donnay (1911) and Émile Faguet's *En Lisant Molière* (1914), a useful corrective to over-adulation, seem to me to express between them, so far as can be ascertained by a foreigner, the attitude to Molière of the flower of the cultivated French of our present age. A prefatory remark by M. Donnay, whose work began as a lecture-sequence, suggests that for anyone wishful to find something new to say about Molière, by far the most sensible thing to do is to confine study to the plays. Without taking this *boutade* too seriously, or being meant to, one may recognize the soundness at its core. From a score of biographers one may discover nothing new about the trials of a great, rich, weary actor-manager-dramatist suspecting himself to be a cuckold, but there is

8

always something new about any genius to be found in his works. The edition of the plays used for this book is Jouaust's *Théâtre Complet de J.-B. Poquelin de Molière*, a replica (1925) of the 'definitive' edition of 1682, with La Grange's preface and the most agreeable minimum of notes by Monval. It may be permissible to add that an intermittent acquaintance with the world of the comedy-stage and a perpetually fascinated, even hypnotized, interest in its remarkable fauna continue to make the entire *milieu* of Molière seem as alive to me as if I had had an apartment in the Place du Palais-Royal. It would be too much, perhaps, to hope that the reader will find himself at times in the same condition.

There are no contemporary English renderings of Molière worth mentioning. Voltaire makes hay of some seventeenth-century native hack prefacing his version of *L'Avare* with 'I may say without vanity that Molière has lost nothing in my hands' (Fielding a century later adapted and embellished the same play very creditably, apart from turning *Le Tartufe* into a No-Popery manifesto). From what Wycherley makes of Alceste of *Le Misantrope* naturalized as Manly of *The Plain Dealer*, one may judge that any lesser Restoration attempts on Molière must be even more distressing. In our own day Mr Miles Malleson has made graceful amends with *The Would-Be Gentleman*, among other versions produced by the late Nigel Playfair with impeccable taste. For the translations offered in these pages one may claim no more than that they are guiltless of 'a chimerical insolent Hope of raising and improving their Author',[1] and strive merely to follow the text. The alexandrine with which Molière brought off some of his best effects has no English equivalent, and since the best French critics still disagree over the use or abuse of the metaphor with which he so frequently decorates or disfigures his verse, it is hardly the business of the outsider to express any opinion at all.

> Les poëtes font a leur guise;
> Ce n'est pas la seule sottise
> Qu'on voit faire à ces messieurs-là.[2]

[1] Pope, Preface to *The Iliad*.

[2] Poets do as they please; nor is this the only kind of foolishness one catches these gentlemen at (Prologue to *Amphitryon*).

Book I

CHAPTER ONE

Jean-Baptiste Poquelin, who later took the stage-name 'Molière', derivation unknown, was born in Paris in January 1622, date undiscoverable, at his parents' house in the Rue St Honoré, position uncertain.

So much for the efficiency of Clio. There is, fortunately, no doubt about Molière's baptismal certificate, which in the registers of St Eustache, his parish church, is dated January 15th. Since infants were normally baptized at this period a day or two after birth, and since Master Jean Poquelin married Marie Cressé on April 27th, 1621, a reasonable date for their first child's birth would seem January 13th or 14th. The question of his birthplace is more difficult. In Paris at the moment two plaques – one at 96 Rue St Honoré, one at 31 Rue du Pont-Neuf, not far away – claim to establish the site.

Failing a Gallup Poll, there seems a slightly stronger case for No. 96. Even if Molière were not actually born on this site, here was certainly the abode of his childhood. A plan survives. It was a steep-gabled, three-storeyed, half-timbered, diamond-paned house of the fifteenth century. A corner-pillar carved with a sequence of gambolling apes and other 'anticks', in the cheerful medieval manner, gave it its name – 'Pavillion des Cinges', a very suitable address for a sucking comedian. It was situated likewise in an excellent position for surveying the human comedy, standing opposite the Croix du Trahoir and facing the entrance of the Rue de L'Arbre Sec, then one of the busiest and most fashionable streets of the Parisian 'West End'. Here on the corner flourished and declined into inevitable bankruptcy the *rôtisserie* of the amiable Cyprien Ragueneau, Apollo's own pastrycook. We shall meet Ragueneau in due course as a down-at-heel utility man in Molière's company, worse actor than poet.

A more serious tradesman was Master Jean Poquelin. At the birth of Jean-Baptiste he had not yet acquired a patrician clientèle and a considerable if fleeting prosperity. But like his father he already held the minor Court appointment of *valet-tapissier du Roy*, and was a liveryman of the Corporation of Merchant Upholsterers of Paris, the equivalent of one of the twelve 'Great Companies' of the City of London. A solid burgess, therefore. Combined with his house in the Rue St Honoré was what contemporary estate-agents undoubtedly described as 'commodious business premises', comprising a shop and a workroom. What the upstairs parlour (*grand' chambre*) looked like in 1632, when Madame Poquelin died, may be judged from an inventory. It was a spacious apartment, hung with Rouennais tapestries. A large Venetian mirror and five paintings also adorned the walls. The tall carved chairs were upholstered in *petit-point de Hongrie*. The contents of the linen-closet, with those of Madame Poquelin's wardrobe and jewel-case, testify equally to the sober middle-class elegance of the child Molière's background, which he could have used in later life for many of his plays.

Whether he stored up much observation of the chattering smart women whisking their trains round the shop downstairs, which dealt in all kinds of luxurious furnishing stuffs and adjuncts of expensive interior-decoration, seems doubtful. With no particular interest the child may have glanced at the Dorantes and Acastes poised stork-like on tall ebony canes in the background.

> C'est Tircis, et c'est Aminte,
> Et c'est l'éternel Clitandre . . .

Such visions, elegantly immobile or languidly combing tall elaborate wigs and tapping gold snuff-boxes – such sublimities, bedizened with falling lace at neck and knee, exhaling powerful essences of Araby, beautiful in their tight-waisted brocades and coloured velvets as fine preposterous birds, or the petulant beauties they escorted, must have been a constant. Master

Jean Poquelin's shop, like so many of Bond Street status figuring in contemporary prints, was undoubtedly a rendezvous for gallantry. Many years before Molière began to study the species seriously the *marquis ridicule* would have been a common object of his landscape.

Infinitely more alluring to little Jean-Baptiste, as to his two younger brothers, as to any boy, would be his father's work-room and the banter and gossip and song of the operatives and apprentices at their looms and benches; perhaps a dozen at least, not counting porters and odd-job men. Familiarity with the workroom would be tacitly conceded to the Poquelin nursery, one may assume. The Corporation of Master Upholsterers was as selective as any other guild of its standing. Apprentices had to be of legitimate birth and approved upbringing. Their masters were pledged to treat and lodge them accordingly, and unmarried journeymen usually 'lived in' likewise. Yet apart from one or two agreeably shrewd and saucy maidservants ('*Il n'est bon bec que de Paris*', laughed Villon), the urban working-class is not represented in the plays at all. Molière seems not to have been aware of the Parisian proletariat, so turbulent and at times so terrifying. Nor, of course, was his public, or at least that part of his public which mattered most, the Court.

The city glimpsed by the child Molière through the bottle-glass panes of the Pavillon des Cinges was the city of Louis XIII and Richelieu. Though Molière's name stands high among that glittering galaxy surrounding Louis XIV, he was seventeen years older than the Sun King, who came to the throne at the age of four, when Molière, so far as can be estimated, had left the Collège de Clermont to be tutored by Gassendi. Realization of the gap between their ages may make it necessary to revise the mental picture of their grouping, so to speak, which one usually retains from the textbooks. The Molière we may picture at the dawn of his fame is a brilliant *farceur* of nearly middle age bent double before a patron young enough to be his son, by the scale of the period. This fact will have some significance when we come to the production of *La Princesse d'Élide*, if at no other time. Their friendship, as with due regard to hierarchic distances it may be correctly described, was based on something more than the frequent bond between kings and their clowns, of which a typical instance is Henry VIII's genuine affection and esteem, until the day when his beloved Court fool described Queen Anne Boleyn, publicly and accurately, as a whore, for Will Somers. Molière not only amuses his King and abets his pleasures but assists the Crown in policy. This may be summed up in the words of Lucien Romier. Once free of the shadow of Mazarin, Louis XIV 'not only subjected to the service of the Court men and women of the world or a body of dignitaries, but made it the microcosm of the values of his kingdom. He succeeded thus in making the authority of the Monarch at once the inspiration and the beneficiary of a complete civilization, in itself admirable.' Hence the incense ascending from Molière's dedications, prologues, and ballets; hence the sweeping bows his Muse pauses ceremonially to make in the King's direction now and again in the course of stage-business. It was not servility, it was part of the national *mystique*.

Any Frenchman born in Molière's year or thereabouts could reflect with gratification that he had seen the golden *Grand Siècle* actually in the making, the France which Louis XIII and Richelieu left behind them being already the strongest and best-governed state – relatively speaking, and disregarding inevitable discontents – in the world. Two powerful menaces to internal peace and prosperity had been dealt with in Molière's early childhood. In 1628, Richelieu wrested La Rochelle after a bitter siege from the Calvinists, and their British allies, and a year later gave them equality with the 90 per cent Catholic majority; with which, though they were vehemently demanding recognition of an armed Calvinist state within the State, they had perforce to be content. The other menace, that of the turbulent grandees of France, in a perpetual fever of intrigue and revolt against the Crown, was dealt with by Richelieu and the public executioner just as energetically, if with less permanent success. The nobles of the Fronde will begin creating trouble again on Louis XIII's death in 1643, five months after that of his Minister, and the barricades will rise.

There were no alarms or upheavals in Paris during Molière's boyhood and adolescence save for a passing panic in 1636, when the Spanish forces in the Low Countries invaded Picardy, occupied Corbie, and threw out scouts as near the capital as Pontoise. The Thirty Years' War had begun in 1618, though Richelieu's disastrous foreign policy, among the direct results of which were to be the rise of Prussia in the eighteenth century and two world-wars in the twentieth, was not in full operation against the Hapsburgs of Austria and Spain till some twenty years later. The Spanish menace of 1636 probably failed to excite the Parisian intelligentsia as much as Richelieu's final bequest to France, a year earlier, the foundation of the Académie Française. The names of some of France's first Immortals were perhaps recited less respectfully by the schoolboy Molière and his playmates than by the awed citizen in *Cyrano de Bergerac*:

> Voici Boudu, Boissat, et Cureau de la Chambre,
> Porchères, Colomby, Bourzeys, Bourdon, Arbaud . . .
> Tous ces noms dont pas un ne mourra, que c'est beau![1]

At least no favourite of the Muses among the forty Founding Fathers was obliged, in his speech of reception, to eulogize the predecessor in his seat. This ritual, which has been the fount of so much dismay, and even horror, was to be established later.

But for the Cardinal's death shortly after its foundation the Academy would have found itself nobly lodged for all time in a rectangle of uniform *pavillons doubles* enclosing the stately new Place Ducale, which was to have risen between the Porte Richelieu and the Porte Saint-Roch. If this project lapsed, there was plenty of impressive new building in the Paris of the 1620–40's to continue the planning-schemes of Louis XIII and Henri IV; the Pavillon de l'Horloge and other classic additions to the Renaissance Louvre, for example, and the handsome town houses of the nobility round and near it; the Palais d'Orleans, since called the Luxembourg; Richelieu's

[1] Final line: 'All these names, not one of which will ever die! – how splendid!' (Act 1, Sc. 1.)

14

own Palais-Cardinal, rechristened Palais-Royal after his death. New quarters were created, more and more gardens were being laid out as public promenades, stretches of the old ramparts on the Seine and elsewhere turned into boulevards, and churches and public monuments wrecked or damaged in the wars of religion were restored and rebuilt, with a score of new convents and religious houses rising as well, mostly for the vigorous new Orders of the Counter-Reform.

The Parisian theatre was beginning to assume increasing importance about this time, though Paris still had only two recognized playhouses, both to be intimately connected with Molière's future – the Hôtel du Marais, where the eminent Corneille presented *Le Cid* in December 1633, a landmark in theatrical history, and the more famous Hôtel de Bourgogne, of which a fragment of medieval building remains in the Rue Étienne-Marcel near the Halles. One might call it at this time the Drury Lane of Paris.

Here by all accounts the child Poquelin was frequently taken by his maternal grandfather, Master Louis Cressé, retired upholsterer and a fervent playgoer, to enjoy the gambols of the Hôtel's trio of stock comedians, known as Gros-Guillaume, Gaultier Gargouille and Turlupin, in the farce which invariably ended the afternoon's bill, whether the main piece was heroic tragedy, comedy, tragicomedy or pastoral. It seems likely, and perhaps desirable, that a great deal of these three clowns' gags and backchat passed over little Jean-Baptiste's head. Gros-Guillaume, a character deriving from the Pedrolino of the Commedia dell'Arte, had been created by an enormously fat actor named Robert Quérin and remained so. His hat was red, his shirt white, his swagging belly enclosed by an iron belt, and his huge moon-face heavily powdered and grimacing violently. Gaultier Gargouille, a Gallic version of Pantaleone of the Commedia, is described in *Masques et Bouffons* by Sand, an authority of the 1860's, as an emaciated, thin-shanked buffoon with a long nose, a moustache like a cat's, and a short pointed beard resembling Pantaloon's. His doublet and breeches were black, with a skullcap of the same colour, and he wore a large dagger, a large pouch and large hornrimmed spectacles. Turlupin descended from the rascally Brighella of the Commedia. He was apparently disguised in the same kind of half-mask, wore a plumed hat, and specialized in puns and double-meanings known as *turlupinades*. Enraptured and possibly, as he grew a little older, edified by these delights, Jean-Baptiste Poquelin is assumed by many biographers to have imbibed his love of comedy and of the theatre at large from many holiday excursions with his grandfather; who was extremely fond of him, says Grimarest.

Meanwhile (the account is Grimarest's) Master Jean Poquelin was casting no favourable eye on these junketings. The boy's mother having died in 1632, as we may recall, his father had shortly afterwards married again. What Jean-Baptiste's stepmother, *née* Catherine Fleurette, a tradesman's daughter, was like we do not know; she died in childbirth in 1636, and there is no clue to her discernible in the only two stepmothers in the Plays, Béline of *Le Malade Imaginaire* being a harridan and Elmire of *Le Tartufe* a charmer. Whatever the domestic situation, Master Jean turned on his father-in-law one day and asked him sharply: 'Do you want to make the boy an actor?' To which old Master Cressé retorted with some spirit: 'I wish to God he could turn out as good a comedian as Bellerose!' naming one of the brightest stars of the Hôtel de Bourgogne. No further exchange is recorded. Master Jean Poquelin probably grunted contempt and walked away. He was not, it seems, a very attractive character. A tradesman first and last, his interests centred almost exclusively on his moneybags. Though there is no reason to believe that he inspired his son's portrait of Harpagon in *L'Avare*, he is said to have indulged in small-scale moneylending 'on the side'. The inventory at his first wife's death moreover reveals a trifle of actual sharp practice. Master Jean Poquelin had to be compelled by the notaries to disclose a sum of 2,000 livres missing from his declaration and stowed in a chest in the small country house at Saint Ouen which the Poquelins shared for holiday purposes with the Cressés. Such a thinker would naturally suspect Master Cressé of attempting to turn the heir to the family business into a prodigal.

He did his duty by his eldest son, at any rate. For the past half-dozen years – we are now approaching 1636, the year of a considerable change in his prospects – the boy Jean-Baptiste Poquelin has been receiving the elementary education suitable to his station at the nearest parish school. These schools were under the general direction of the Precentor of Notre-Dame, who nominated the teachers of both sexes. A revised curriculum was issued in 1626. It embraces reading in French and Latin, writing, arithmetic, ciphering, grammar, the A.B.C. of plainsong, and, of course, religious instruction and preparation for first Communion. Pupils attended from eight to eleven in the morning and two to five in the afternoon, and from every teacher were required, before appointment, testimonials to his or her Catholicity, general character, and qualifications from three 'persons of honourable condition' and his or her parish priest. Such an education, at a very modest fee, was held sufficient for any Paris tradesman's son, as, by and large, it was. In the upholstery trade, as in others, he would complete it by learning the business as an apprentice. The procedure was normal and traditional. Why, therefore, Master Jean Poquelin suddenly decided to give his eldest son the education of a son of the nobility or the high bourgeoisie is not recorded, but Grimarest's version may be authentic. Perceiving young Jean-Baptiste, who had just returned from the theatre, to be sunk in deepest gloom, his father one day asked the reason and got, as they say, the whole packet. His eldest son loathed the shop, the workroom, the hereditary Court post of *valet–tapissier*, which would soon be duly passed on to him – it required attendance at Court on a roster at stated intervals, to assist the Household flunkeys in the service of the Royal bedchamber – and the upholstery trade *in toto*, and longed for a better education and fairer prospects. His grandfather, there present, warmly supported him. Master Jean Poquelin at length gave in. Some time in 1636, probably in October, Jean-Baptiste was entered as a day-boy at the Collège de Clermont, which might be called the Eton-cum-Stonyhurst of seventeenth-century France.

Still flourishing, with restorations and additions, and under other auspices, in the Rue St Jacques, and now called the Lycée Louis-le-Grand, the Collège de Clermont represented in Molière's time the triumph of Jesuit education over the Sorbonne.

Not quite a century earlier the irruption of the new Society of Jesus into the University quarter, brandishing a scientific Renaissance recipe for producing 'the complete man', had been met with opposition so vigorous and so venomous from the Sorbonne dons, the heads of fifty-odd colleges, the lawyers of the Parlement of Paris, and the whole jealous academic horde that, as Fülop-Miller remarks, the best efforts of Elizabeth Tudor's army of spies, *agents-provocateurs*, and priest-hunters in England seem amateurish by comparison. By 1636 opposition had long since evaporated. Round about the time of the fourteen-year-old Poquelin's entry, the College was educating two thousand day-boys (*scolastici*) and three hundred and thirty boarders (*convictores*), including the sons of half the nobility and gentry of France and three 18-carat princes: Armand de Conti, Henri de Lorraine, and Henri de Savoie. In that age of rigid social distinctions, with their attendant advantages, it is unlikely that the boy Poquelin had any contact with the boy Conti, his future patron. The princes, attended by their 'governors' and lackeys, would study and take their recreation apart from the mass of the school, segregated even in the lecture-room. When allowed to mingle with inferiors they would naturally turn to that contingent of their fellows borne on the College books in Renaissance style as *pauperes*, 'the poor'; what are now called bursars, or scholarship boys, educated free and distinguished by the wearing of a dark smock. As has often been remarked, sympathies and friendships readily engendered between the social extremes are extended less readily by either to the middle element. Armand de Conti, nevertheless, was to be an admiring friend, for a space, to his bourgeois ex-schoolmate in the provinces.

18

The Rector and headmaster of the Collège de Clermont at this time, it appears from the registers, was Father Jacques Dinet, assisted by Father Julien Heyneufve, the undermaster, who succeeded him, and, in the familiar phrase, 'a large and well-qualified staff'. Fees not stated, but doubtless up to modern public-school standard. Latin was spoken in form exclusively. The curriculum preserved the Classico-Renaissance-Humanist phraseology which still remains a link with education for service of the State under the Roman Empire. The lower forms were and are labelled 'Grammar', 'Syntax', 'Poetry' and 'Rhetoric', respectively. Command of language attained, the higher forms turn to the study of thought and are still known as 'the Philosophers'. Those preparing for the Church and, today, for science begin here as well. The 'complete man' was further developed by such recreations as music, dancing, fencing and theatricals. Ballets of a grave and dignified kind were frequent at Jesuit prizegivings, or 'Academies', of this period. Clermont, like others of their colleges past, present and future, had a properly-equipped theatre, with all appurtenances; one of the first performances outside Spain of a moral drama on the Don Juan theme was given at the Jesuit College of Ingoldstadt in 1615. It would seem only right and proper, therefore, for Jean-Baptiste Poquelin, *dit* Molière, to have acquired his first taste of the art of acting at a school where end-of-term productions of Terence, Plautus, and Seneca regularly entertained polite and glittering assemblies, which might include Richelieu or the King himself. But it seems that at Clermont only the boarders took part in the plays, no doubt because it was easier for the producer to assemble and rehearse them. One may lawfully visualize a pair of glowing eyes and flushed cheeks in the crowd of boys at the back of the auditorium. Subsequent criticism over the supper-table in the Rue St Honoré would wax in quantity and quality alike as the voice of Jean-Baptiste grew less falsetto and finally broke for good.

He spent six fruitful years at Clermont, and may be viewed without much difficulty going to and fro; a stocky, dark, wide-shouldered boy in the squaretoed buckled shoes, ample breeches, and linen-collared doublet of the period, his flowing untidy locks crowned by a wide-brimmed felt hat, with or without a feather and worn askew, his alert dark eyes fixed from afar on the frieze of gesticulating figures against the balustrade of the Pont-Neuf. Here in sunshine or in rain, and liberally splashed by the infamous Paris mud, he would loiter to the last possible moment, fascinated always, as we know, by the line of quacks, mountebanks, jugglers, balladmongers, and quick-fingered spellbinders of many kinds whose special pitch this noble bridge had been since the time of Henri III. The chanted patter of the quacks (*charlatans*, or *opérateurs*) will be reproduced in one of the ballet-interludes of *L'Amour Médecin*. It celebrates the popular specific known as *orviétan*, guaranteed to cure

> Tous les maux que sur nous l'ire du Ciel repand:
> La gale,
> La rogne,
> La tigne,
> La fiévre,
> La peste,
> La goute,
> Verole,
> Descente,
> Rougeole:
> O grande puissance de l'Orviétan![1]

Rowdy backchat and byplay with his attendant zanies, stooges, or Jack-Puddings was a feature of every charlatan's performance. In the vicious anti-Molière broadside called *Élomire Hypocondre*, Le Boulanger de Chalussay will a few years hence invent a quarrel between Molière and Madeleine Béjart during their provincial tour in which she accuses him of being so mad to get on the stage that he was on the verge of hiring himself as a buffoon to two of the leading Pont-Neuf quacks, Bary and L'Orviétan. 'At that', says Madeleine

[1] '... every ill with which Heaven's anger afflicts us – itch, ringworm, fever, plague, gout, pox, rupture, measles – O, the mighty power of Orviétan!' It was an electuary invented by Dr Geronimo Ferrante of Orvieto early in the century, and originally combined fifty-four drugs and herbs, including a tiny percentage of opium. Its popularity soon became international.

scornfully, 'we took pity on you'. A libel, undoubtedly, yet some indication that the spell must have lasted long after Molière's schooldays. If gaping at such riff-raff was hardly a worthy pastime for an ex-Philosopher of the Collège de Clermont, steeped in the Humanities and familiar with the poetry and drama of the golden age of pagan Rome (he seems not to have been on the same terms with the Greeks, likewise on the Clermont curriculum), it was equally so for a disciple of the celebrated Abbé Pierre Gassendi, among whose private pupils we find Jean-Baptiste shortly after leaving Clermont, in 1642–43. There seems no good reason for rejecting this tutelage, though it has been done.

Another generous impulse, for which, given his admitted closeness with money, he deserves every credit, had conquered Master Jean Poquelin. The learned Gassendi, priest, philosopher of the Baconian school, chemist, physicist, musician, and astronomer, took few pupils and no doubt charged accordingly. Jean-Baptiste had achieved one more ambition, this time through his ex-schoolmate and lifelong friend Chapelle. Chapelle was the illegitimate son of a high civil servant and man-about-town, Pierre Luiller, *Maître des Comptes*, who happened to number Gassendi among his more serious friends. In 1642 we find Gassendi tutoring young Chapelle in Luiller's Paris house, where he was a guest for some time.

Three other fellow-pupils had preceded young Poquelin. Two of them, Hasnaut and François Bernier, are of less interest than the third, Cyrano de Bergerac, born Savinien de Cyrano, aged twenty-one: a personage of future notoriety, differing in several ways from the lovelorn lyrical Rodomont of Rostand's play. The veritable Cyrano's aquiline beak, for example, was not a public spectacle, nor was he a Gascon from Bergerac in the Dordogne, but a Parisian by birth, the son of Abel de Cyrano, Seigneur de Bergerac in the Chevreuse, near Versailles. Forced to abandon a military career after being severely wounded with his Guards regiment during the taking of Arras from the Spaniards in 1640, enjoying a reputation even now as a swordsman, Cyrano was to become a Parisian celebrity, one of Grub Street's noisiest brawlers, scribbling books and a play or two and living more or less on quarrels. The memoirs of the musician Charles Coypeau d'Assoucy, that attractive old blackguard, give a tantalizingly brief glimpse of the aftermath of an argument between the two in d'Assoucy's lodgings over a roast fowl, during which d'Assoucy escapes being pistolled (he avers) only by skipping downstairs and running as far as Italy. Why the blusterous Cyrano took the fancy in 1642 to sit at the feet of Gassendi with three youths still in their teens may be gathered to some extent from his chief literary work. He was all his life fascinated by astronomy, and his *Histoire Burlesque d'un Voyage Dans la Lune* owes his tutor a great deal. Though none of his fellow-pupils seems to have cared much for him, Jean-Baptiste Poquelin *dit* Molière will do Cyrano the honour some years hence of stealing a scene from his comedy *Le Pédant Joué*.

Himself a model cleric, Gassendi was perhaps not entirely to blame if some of his young pupils misconstrued his teaching. He was quite clear about it in his own mind. His idol Epicurus, as every person of intelligence is aware, is neither an epicure nor an epicurean in the vulgar sense but an apostle of frugal sobriety, holding that man's goal is a calm happiness derived from complete harmony of body and soul. Therefore, and atomic determinism and the indifference of the gods notwithstanding, Epicurus seemed to Gassendi as qualified for Christianization, relatively speaking, as an Aristotle or a Plato. A not untenable thesis, with proper reserves and safeguards, it brought the Abbé Gassendi no trouble from ecclesiastical authority. But it certainly involved skating over some very thin ice, and the master's exegesis seems to have gone over the heads of at least three of the young men seated before him, adoring 'the divine Gassendi' as a second Socrates. Having taken leave of him, at all events, they will devote themselves henceforth to the practice of Epicureanism as the world, not the Abbé Pierre Gassendi, translates it. Each will indulge himself in his particular pleasures, Bergerac in scepticism and brawls, Chapelle in boozing and loose loves, Molière in such self-indulgences as the life of an actor-manager offers and the mood directs.

Un homme de morale assez basse, is the verdict on the later Molière of the austere Émile Faguet, adding that to take France's greatest comic poet for one's director of conscience would be a quite deplorable error of judgment. Such a directive seems to have been necessary forty years ago.

CHAPTER THREE

The time arrived for Master Jean Poquelin to cast up his accounts and demand some return for his money. His eldest son had nothing to suggest at the moment but the law, his true ambition being ripe but as yet unavowable. During and since his year under Gassendi he had been 'shown the Town', as the saying was, by ruffling Cyrano de Bergerac, who knew all the best cabarets and had the entrée backstage to the theatres. A fair amount of youthful riot may be deduced, no doubt. At the Théâtre du Marais young Poquelin had seen *Le Cid* and other stately tragedies of Pierre Corneille, with comedies by the same illustrious hand; at the Hôtel de Bourgogne were the comedies of Rotrou and the full-blooded farces already mentioned. Pieces by hacks like Tristan, Du Ryer, Mairet and Alexandre Hardy doubtless gave him a lesson or two in what to avoid.

For a born satirist the ranting at the Hôtel de Bourgogne and the awful majesty of its leading actor, Montfleury – by all accounts a most imperial 'ham', his future butt and enemy – would yield recurring diversion. Young Poquelin can more often be seen at the Petit-Bourbon, alert and intent. At this theatre Giuseppe Bianchi's Italian company had been playing, at Louis XIII's invitation, since 1639. Their principal comedian, Tiberio Fiorillo, the famous 'Scaramouche', protégé of kings and cardinals and destined not many years hence, to be Molière's model and intimate, may have begun already to qualify for the description under his portrait by Vermeulen:

> Il fut le maître de Molière,
> Et la Nature fut le sien.[1]

[1] 'He was Molière's master, and Nature was his own.'

What Molière owes to the Commedia dell' Arte is visible almost everywhere in his works, as anyone may perceive. From the *parades* at the long-established fairs of St Germain and St Laurent he was to learn something as well; the one, held on ground owned by the Abbey of St Germain-des-Prés, extended from February 3rd to Palm Sunday, the other, on a site now covered by the Gare de l'Est, occupied the month of July. Duchartre has sufficiently recalled their atmosphere in the seventeenth century:

> The fairs drew great crowds of people belonging to every station in life. There were great lords, marquises, lackeys, pages, rogues, honest and solid bourgeois, pretty ladies, and adventurers of all kinds who thronged to see the marionettes of Brioche and the two-headed cow; they danced to the rigadoon and applauded Gertrude Boon, called *La Belle Tourneuse*, for her sword-dance. Vendors went about selling Marseilles soap, Siamese bonnets, all sorts of Greek and Italian wines, and hot cream-cakes at two *liards* (a quarter of a sou, figuratively a farthing). Tooth-extractors blew horns to attract customers and sharpers fooled the gullible with loaded dice. The air rang with the sounds of fights, disputes, laughter and singing.[1]

Duchartre oddly omits a dancer at the Fair of St Germain as popular as Gertrude Boon and much more noteworthy, since she turned into a considerable actress and Molière, Racine and Corneille all three adored her. She was a magnetic minx in her teens named Marquise de Gorla, daughter of a quack, outside whose booth she danced on a trestle-stage to fiddle music. Without doubt young Jean-Baptiste Poquelin and his friend Cyrano were more than once among the crowd acclaiming her act. It ended in a whirl of skirts affording a lightning glimpse of long silk stockings attached to a pair of neat velvet knickers, and was, in fact, the equivalent of the modern American fan-dance. Some ten years hence Marquise de Gorla was to marry the actor René du Parc[2] and to become one of Molière's three leading ladies; likewise to wring from the ageing and aggrieved Corneille at Rouen those *Stances à La Marquise* which have

---

[1] *La Comédie Italienne*. Paris, 1929.
[2] Being excommunicate, French players qualified for marriage by describing themselves as musicians.

misled not a few into assuming that some lady of quality had been wilfully toying with that illustrious, ever-susceptible, heart.

> Marquise, si mon visage
> A quelques traits un peu vieux,
> Souvenez-vous qu'à mon âge
> Vous ne vaudrez guere mieux . . .[1]

Another noticeable débutante, whom Jean-Baptiste Poquelin must have seen tripping through a tragicomedy or two at the Marais, was destined to play a considerable part in his career. She was four years older than himself, red-haired, bonny, vivacious, shrewd, highly intelligent, not overburdened with virtue, and professionally what is still called a 'good trouper'; Madeleine Béjart by name.

So, for the moment, Jean-Baptiste elected to appease Master Poquelin, his fuming parent, by agreeing to the most respectable of professions, and profitable withal. To qualify in civil law at this period was not very difficult. Any properly equipped aspirant with a smattering of the elements could get a diploma without much trouble from the Law Schools of Orleans, the only university in France, with that of Poitiers, empowered to grant them. The Orleans diploma at this time was a professional joke. It is inevitable to quote the brief ceremony described in the memoirs of Charles Perrault.[2] Arriving at Orleans from Paris late one night, Perrault and two fellow-students knocked up the porter at the Law Schools and bribed him to wake three of the resident professors. Satisfied at length that this was what would be called in modern business circles *une affaire sérieuse*, the learned men descended, yawning, in dressing-gowns, wearing their doctoral birettas over their nightcaps. After a few routine questions and answers, humanized by the counted chink of gold, the examiners returned to bed and three qualified lawyers, after a merry night, to Paris, waving a diploma apiece.

---

[1] 'Marquise, if my features betray a few signs of age, reflect that on reaching my years you yourself will be a prize worth hardly more . . .'

[2] Author of, among other and more serious works, the nursery classic, *Contes de Ma Mère l'Oye*.

Since Jean-Baptiste Poquelin likewise qualified at Orleans, after a little necessary coaching of which there is no record, one may not unlawfully assume such the same procedure. Once more his father paid the bill.

But Jean-Baptiste was never to draw up a will or address a court of law. Some little time beforehand Master Jean Poquelin had insisted on passing on his Court charge as *valet-tapissier*. In the spring of 1642 Jean-Baptiste was duly warned for three months' duty in the Roussillon, where Louis XIII was directing counter-operations to the recent Spanish invasion. It may well be, as most reliable authorities believe, that during this Pyrenean interlude Jean-Baptiste first met Madeleine Béjart, then attached to a touring company which played before the King at Mongrin, near Eaux-Bonnes, in that year. If so, any further projects of Master Jean Poquelin to detach his heir from the Bohemian life were a waste of time. A pair of large bright eyes had settled everything.

On his return to Paris Jean-Baptiste, now twenty-one and not yet legally of age, returned his Court patent – he was to resume it years later – to his father and suggested that one of his brothers might like it. At the same time he demanded his share of his mother's estate and got it, or at least 630 livres of it. There seems to have been a heated family scene. Master Jean Poquelin's worst premonitions were fully confirmed. Rejecting the law and the business together, Jean-Baptiste announced his fixed intention of not only going on the stage but directing his own company forthwith. The Parisian tradesman's reaction to this proclamation of social and probably financial suicide may be imagined. Grandfather Cressé ('Your people! . . .') probably came in for his due share of abuse. At length, having given in yet again, Master Poquelin made one final despairing attempt to reclaim the young fool by inducing a respectable notary of his acquaintance, Georges Pinel by name, to reason with him. The sequel is comic enough to have been used in one of the youth's future farces. Some time between 1641 and 1642 this Master Pinel, a somewhat unstable character, had been engaged by the elder Poquelin to give Jean-Baptiste a course in accountancy. Engaged again to exhort his ex-pupil to commonsense and business-method, Master Pinel the notary found himself offered the 'pedant' roles in a theatrical company now in process of assembly, discarded inkhorn and calculating-tables with a pirouette, and took to the stage with avidity. His signature appears on the articles of association we are about to contemplate.

On June 30th, 1643, at the house in the Marais of Marie Béjart, *née* Hervé, widow of Joseph and mother of Madeleine, Jean-Baptiste Poquelin signed a legal document, with nine others, founding a new theatrical company calling itself, with no false modesty, *l'Illustre Théâtre*. The other signatories were his co-director Madeleine Béjart, her sister Geneviève, her brother Joseph, Georges Pinel, Denys Beys, Clérin, Bonnenfant, Madeleine Malingre, and Catherine des Urlis. The Rubicon was crossed. Jean-Baptiste Poquelin, soon to style himself 'Molière', had become a naturalized Bohemian.

The Béjarts were a slightly raffish family of the Marais, lounging, as it were, on the fringe of respectability in dressing-gowns and curl-papers, shabby and clamorous and poor. The late Joseph Béjart had been a harassed minor Government official, a bailiff in the Department of Eaux et Forêts. Comely red-haired Madeleine, one of the four of his eleven children who went on the stage, was the first to strike out for herself. By 1636, at the age of eighteen, being as capable in money matters as she was a good actress, she had managed by dramatic or other art to put aside some 2,000 livres, £500 at least in modern money, and was living in a smart little house, with garden, near the Place Royale in the Marais quarter. The generic term *demoiselle du Marais*, then current, is not without significance. To some extent the quarter was to seventeenth-century Paris what St John's Wood was to Victorian London, a retired, elegant, leafy, a-moral paradise where men-about-town kept odalisques and life began after dark. There were big houses of the nobility and the upper bourgeoisie in and round the handsome Place Royale, and dwellings in less genteel nooks and corners suitable for people of the Béjarts' standing. Since about 1636, Madeleine Béjart had been the mistress of Messire Esprit-Rémond de Modène, chamberlain to 'Monsieur', the King's brother. The *collage* lasted on and off for some years; a daughter was born to the pair in 1638. M. de Modène, a married man, later living mostly in the provinces, was an easy type and apparently had no objection to sharing Madeleine with her fellow-director of *l'Illustre Théâtre*. It was after all a matter of routine, like the traditional obligation of any ambitious drama-student at the Conservatoire to please her professor. Madeleine's relations with Jean-Baptiste Poquelin will be in any case a business connection first and foremost. He must soon have been forced to admit, like M. de Modène, whose finances she also supervised, that having such a capable *femme d'affaires* at call was not every lover's good fortune.

It has been suggested that what feeling for Molière she had was mostly maternal, which seems likely enough considering her temperament and her four years' seniority. Her own affair had run lately kim-kam, as John Aubrey would say. Appointed deputy-governor of Charleville in Champagne in 1639, mixed up subsequently in the anti-Richelieu activities of the Duc de Guise and others, and wounded in the skirmish at La Marfée, M. de Modène was now pardoned, reclaimed by his elderly wife, and recuperating at his château in the Comtat, seemingly for good. Madeleine's return to the stage for an indefinite period was therefore imperative. It was certainly she who organized the formation of the Illustrious Theatre, reserving in the deed of association the right to choose her own roles as leading lady. Undoubtedly Madeleine was producer as well as business manager. The others were stage-struck amateurs, with which species the Marais at this time swarmed, it seems.

CHAPTER FOUR

The Illustrious Theatre was, in later stage-parlance, a total flop, *un four noir*.

Was it the fault of their first premises, a tennis-court, hastily converted, near the Porte de Nesle, on the present Quai Conti? Or that of their second, another converted tennis-court called the Croix-Noire?[1] Or that of their repertoire, chiefly tragedy supplied by authors like Du Ryer, Magnon, Desfontaines and the slightly more notable Tristan l'Hermite? Or was it due to the unfortunate illusion of their co-director and leading man, now calling himself 'Molière', that he was a born tragedian? Whatever the reason, business was bad from the beginning, and debts increased to such an extent that on August 2nd, 1645, we find J.-B. Poquelin, *dit* Molière, held in the Châtelet prison for a 298-livre debt, 'goods supplied', at the suit of a chandler, a draper, and a moneylender. He was soon bailed out; not by his father but by an honest contractor, one Léon Aubry, who had paved the entrance to one of the Company's theatres and may not have seen his money yet, like other creditors. We may glimpse Master Jean Poquelin, in the background, grimly rubbing his hands. He did not recoup Aubry till three years later. His eldest son's relations with him had not been very agreeable for the past year or so, but in his prosperity Molière will remember obligations and help the old man in his decline. On the other hand nearly every father in Molière's plays is more or less close-fisted and Harpagon of *L'Avare* is a pathological case. If Master Poquelin contributed to any of these portraits he only partially deserved it, perhaps. His son was certainly no slave to money.

Meanwhile the Illustrious Theatre had faded away. During the late crisis five of the company, including the ex-notary Georges Pinel, had packed up and scarpered, as they would say today. The survivors, Madeleine, Molière, and the two other Béjarts soon decided that the only procedure was to recruit again and try their luck in the provinces. Molière will be away from Paris for the next fourteen years.

Fourteen years' vagabondage in seventeenth-century France by a company of strolling players should supply plenty of

---

[1] These were of course 'real tennis' courts, *jeux de paume*, resembling hangars; roofed, floored, possibly provided with a gallery, and capable of holding an audience of a couple of hundred at least. The theatre called the Hôtel de Bourgogne was a hall in what remained of Duke Jean the Fearless' medieval town-house, partially demolished in 1543; it is represented as an ex-*jeu de paume* in the opening scene of *Cyrano de Bergerac*. A surviving tower is visible in the Rue Étienne-Marcel.

picaresque adventure; rather disreputable, slightly noisy, full of swaggering triumphs and ignominious flights, of kisses and brawls and boastings and jealousies and loves and feuds, all intense, all temporary, all enhanced by dramatic art; an extension of the day's work, a carry-over of nervous fluid, an urge to exhibitionism so native to Thespian genius that the actor hardly knows if he is acting or not. There will be only a few authentic glimpses of Molière's company on the road, unfortunately. Every now and again they are lighted up clearly for a moment, then the curtain falls for a long interval.

How the lowest-grade travelling theatre-troop of the period – about fifteen are known – fared on the road may be gathered from Paul Scarron's novel of 1651, *Le Roman Comique*, a less amusing work than one would expect, and as an exercise in the picaresque not comparable in any way with *Gil Blas*, its brilliant near-contemporary. However, we see Scarron's mummers trudging the highroad with their ox-cart, piled with a pyramid of baggage and properties and rolls of scenery, on which reclines enthroned the leading lady. Most of the men are armed with large guns or long swords, some are weighed down with bass-viols and drums; their costume, less impressive than their bearing and gestures, is mudsplashed and shabby. As they enter a town and encounter the Provost's men trouble almost invariably ensues. More entertaining are the tribulations of d'Assoucy on his way south with his two disreputable *pages à musique*, and Chapelle's celebrated account of his jaunt with Bachaumont. No doubt there were periods when Madeleine and Molière and their company, now recruited to necessary strength, suffered the hazards of the road like humble rivals; arriving after sunset, dusty, muddy, weary, at the same bad inns, playing that night in barns or outhouses, jostled, admired, insulted, bored, sitting down to infamous suppers, sleeping in straw, or beds much less clean and comfortable, and moving on next day. The women of the troop were pestered by the same small-town gallants. The men no doubt frequently faced the dawn haggard and broke after a night's gambling, and perhaps a brawl, in the local *tripot*. The usual amorous permutations and combinations within the company provided the usual flare-up of quarrels and reconciliations. Loving or hating, weary or brisk, drunk or sober, the nightly business of the stage had to be gone through: the heroic spoutings, the stampings, the exhortations and implorations and tirades, the laughter and the tears.

One need not waste many tears on Molière and his troop. They must have suffered relatively little on the road, their tour having been well organized, obviously by Madeleine Béjart. We hear of them at Easter 1646, at Agen, Albi, Carcassonne, and Toulouse, playing for some time before the Duc d'Epernon, governor of Guyenne; under the ducal patronage, merged or alternating with the troop of Charles du Fresne, then in his service, and benefiting largely from the ducal extravagance. Later they are glimpsed at Nantes, where an entry in the civic registers records the passage of 'le sieur Morlierre'. At Narbonne a baptismal-certificate testifies that 'Magdalaine de Baisar', a native of Paris, stood godmother to the offspring, presumably, of one of the troop. In the autumn of 1650 they were at Pézenas for the *États* or provincial assembly of Languedoc, then in session. In this hilly little town all the nobility and gentry of the province had gathered for the debates and the entertainments with which they traditionally relaxed themselves. They spent freely and would be delighted to give supper-parties for these well-groomed players from Paris, the ladies of the company especially. One sees them in the candlelight, clustered round the sprightly Madeleine, while Molière, chatting at the other end of the table with some titled *aficionado*, catches her eye with a humorous flicker of the lashes. He was still believing himself to be a tragedian, but it may be that the farce which concluded the programme was what most of his audiences waited for. During a season at Lyons in 1653, when they were giving Corneille's *Andromède*, we at last discern some of the present players. Four can be identified; the historic roll will not be complete with the names of La Grange, Brécourt, Du Croisy, and the others till Molière is established in Paris. Among those already in the troop are the enormous comedian René du Parc, as yet not married to Marquise de Gorla, the lean, quarrelsome, alcoholic De Brie and his attractive wife Catherine, and, a long way down, the one and only Ragueneau (Cyprien), late of the Rue de l'Arbre Sec, Paris.

Alas for the Muses' own pastrycook, alas for the Restaurateur-by-Appointment to Apollo! The celebrated grill and *confiserie* which had so long been a home from home for a gallimaufry of more or less reputable poets, philosophers, pamphleteers, playwrights and others of the Muses' favourites, flocking *chez* Ragueneau to extol their host's execrable verse, to swallow his excellent food and wine, paid for chiefly in epigrams, sonnets, or complimentary tickets, to borrow his money, patronize his chefs, and insult his customers – this Liberty Hall for the intelligentsia was now closed for ever. *Quo, Musa, tendis?* Inevitable bankruptcy had overtaken a vain, fatuous, kind-hearted little Maecenas with a wife and family to support. To quote the grinning d'Assoucy, who probably owed Ragueneau more money than any of them, it was 'a black day for the poetic gentlemen' when the Provost's men descended early one winter morning on the Rue de l'Arbre Sec, expelling the last of the Old Guard ('one met them after dawn up and down the streets, wiping their noses'), and arresting their host at the cry of a mob of creditors.[1] It was a blacker day still for Ragueneau, who finished it in a debtors' cell.

On emerging from prison a twelvemonth later the unfortunate ex-pastrycook piled what remained of his belongings on a baggage-ass and left Paris, with his wife and their daughter, Marie, for the south. In Languedoc a strolling troop gave him a job as *valet de comédie*, or utility man. Not long afterwards he achieved contact with Molière, an old acquaintance, and Molière took him and Marie into his company; an act of pure charity, since Ragueneau had swiftly turned out to be an even worse actor than he had been a poet. After several trials and disasters Molière amid the general relief appointed 'Monsieur de l'Estang', as Ragueneau professionally styled himself, official candle-snuffer to the theatre, which seems to have been his true artistic vocation. He died in August 1654, at Lyons. Marie Ragueneau, a mediocre small-part actress, and apparently,

[1] *Les Avantures de Monsieur d'Assoucy.* Paris, 1677.

a thoroughly nice woman, married into the company in 1672, becoming Mme Charles Varlet de la Grange, and is no more heard of.

No easier to rule than any other collection of temperamental extroverts, Molière's full company must obviously have been, by and large, what the Navy calls 'a happy ship', though for the public's benefit he will damn them all heartily in the *Impromptu de Versailles*:

MOLIÈRE: I think these types will drive me crazy.
  (*Enter Brécourt, La Grange, and Du Croisy*).
  Well, for God's sake! So you want to make me furious today, gentlemen?
BRÉCOURT: What can we do about it? We don't know our parts. You're making *us* furious, trying to get us to work like this.
MOLIÈRE: Phew! These actors! What perverse brutes to handle!

But he is smiling, whatever paroxysms of rage and vengeance they may drive him into at rehearsals. Tantrums there are in any case traditional. A play of which the producer did not rave, hoot, roar, weep, curse, tear out his hair, and gnaw the backcloth at every rehearsal would not get produced at all. It may be taken on the evidence of La Grange's registers alone that insofar as one actor or actress can like another, M. de Molière's company managed so to do, and to include their tyrant as well.

The comedian Du Parc brought a valuable new recruit into the fold round about 1653 by marrying Marquise de Gorla, the fairground dancer whom we have already met. She was much more than a dancer; she proved a captivating actress, whose unique destiny, remarks Donnay, was to make three of the greatest men of the age fall in love with her. As observed already they were first Molière, then Racine, finally the elderly Pierre Corneille. Molière and Corneille were unsuccessful. Not so Racine, and if it is a shock to find the austere and classical Jansenist in such a galley, the Racine of *Phèdre*, and *Athalie*, and the paraphrased Roman Breviary hymns, it is needful to recall that this happened in Racine's gay-dog days, long before his conversion.

It was the warm-blooded Molière's destiny in this year,

1653, to become entangled with three of his actresses simultaneously – Du Parc, De Brie and Madeleine, still more or less sharing his intimacy. Grimarest reports that Madeleine faced the situation as such a woman would:

> Since she perceived there was no help for it, she took the best way, which was to console herself by maintaining over Molière the authority she had always exercised.

In the commercial phrase, it was she who made him; taking charge of his and the theatre's finances and, as documents show, making contracts and investments, subscribing to public loans, making private ones, borrowing on good terms, taking legal action to recover debts. She had, it turned out, nothing to fear from Marquise du Parc, who happened to be in love with her husband and put her director firmly in his place. He had more success with Catherine de Brie, his mistress for some years. And if his life became automatically more complicated, the situation was extremely useful to a commencing playwright on the brink of success.

For to Molière in this same year, 1653, came a piece of great good-fortune and the overture to fame. Among the notables at Pézenas during the late session of the États of Languedoc was one of his lordly ex-schoolmates at the Collège de Clermont, who had an estate just outside the town. As already observed, it is hardly likely that he and Armand de Bourbon, Prince de Conti, ever exchanged a glance at Clermont. The tints of the Old School Tie are nevertheless clearly discernible in the pattern of events to follow. Conti had an imperious mistress, Mme de Calvimont, installed at La Grange-des-Prés. Mme de Calvimont adored the theatre. The Prince's chaplain, the Abbé de Cosnac, was accordingly instructed to order Molière's company over. In the meantime a rival impresario, one Cormier, got in first with a suitable present to Mme de Calvimont, who adored money. A day or two later Molière arrived at La Grange-des-Prés with company and baggage-wagon to find the Cormier troop in possession, and all smiles.

At once Molière lodged a respectful protest with the Prince, asking for at least his travelling expenses. In an irritable mood

Conti waved this away, whereupon De Cosnac, acutely embarrassed, offered Molière a thousand crowns of his own for a performance at Pézenas. At this Conti, *a grand seigneur* not without equity or grace, ordered a performance forthwith. It charmed all present except Cormier and his actors, Mme de Calvimont, notoriously a silly, vapid creature, and the Prince her slave. A second command-performance charmed all save Cormier and his troop. They were dismissed next day and Armand, Prince de Conti, took Molière's company into his service and Molière himself into his cordial intimacy.

Under such auspicious patronage they played at Montpellier towards the end of 1654, again during a session of the États of Languedoc. In 1655, at Lyons, they presented a new piece, a five-act comedy in verse, from the Italian – 'for the first time on any stage' – by M. de Molière, their director, It was his first full-length work, entitled *L'Estourdy* ('The Scatterbrain'). Though his Parisian début with this same piece was not to be made till the November of 1658, Molière the playwright had arrived.

Book II

Since there are few rules, if any, applicable to playwriting, an art on which many treatises are available, it does not seem very important that Molière by contemporary standards was a rather late arrival at the age of thirty-three, his predecessors Corneille and Rotrou having stormed the theatre successfully in their early twenties. Age appears to matter as little in this field as experience. Relative schoolgirls have been known to capture the town overnight with a maiden effort. At the other end of the scale a venerable British drama-critic woke up one morning towards the end of his life after a nightmare and turned it into a melodrama which to his own astonishment made him a small fortune; his first play and his last. With fourteen years' experience of the theatre behind him Molière had therefore no more and no less chance of success at thirty-three, barring genius, than anyone else. While touring the provinces he had scribbled a few short farces, some no more than revue-sketches, and chiefly from the Italian. The only two which have survived are stuffed with puns and horseplay and of no great moment. They filled a gap and they brought the laughs in 'the Sticks'. Molière himself thought nothing of them, except to preserve a few good lines for future use, and never bothered to print them. But for a virtuoso of the early eighteenth century who happened to possess the manuscripts and sent them to an editor in 1734, *La Jalousie du Barbouillé* and *Le Médecin Volant* would not be in print today.

The success of *L'Estourdy*, then, owed little or nothing to its author's long familiarity with the mechanics of his trade. But in 1655 a new voice had spoken.

He had not yet found himself. *L'Estourdy* is a long and complicated business, derived from Nicolò Barbieri's *L'In-*

avvertito, with a glance or two at Luigi Groto's *Emilia*. The burden and heat of the fun is borne by one of those rascally valet-tricksters of whom the Italian contemporary theatre was so fond. Mascarille of *L'Estourdy* comes in fact straight out of the Commedia dell' Arte and is the first expression of a standing debt. His direct ancestor, like that of all Molière's valets, is Mezzotino, himself a descendant of Scapino and Brighella. In Paris the character was annexed once for all, round about 1688, by the comedian Angelo Constantini of Verona, to whose livery the striped waistcoats of French menservants remain a lingering memorial. Molière may well have seen earlier impersonations.

To unravel the plot of *L'Estourdy* is tedious, but the main bones of the piece may be indicated. The scene is Messina. It is the task of the valet Mascarille to devise, on behalf of his young master Lélie, a sufficient sequence of stratagems and ruses to enable Lélie to defeat his rival Léandre in their contest for the heart of Célie, a beautiful slave. Obstacles to Lélie's success apart from Léandre are Trufaldin, Célie's aged and formidable master, Pandolphe, Lélie's father, another mean, angry old man, and above all Lélie's own amiable gift for bungling, which checkmates Mascarille's every move, to some extent because Lélie is never informed by his valet beforehand which trick is on the tapis. Hence for Mascarille in his impudent way to be perpetually scolding his master for being a blundering ass –

LÉLIE: Qu'est-ce donc? qu'ay-je fait?
MASCARILLE: Le sot, en bon françois.[1]

– seems hardly reasonable. Realizing this objection, Molière with sprightly insouciance forestalls it by putting it into Lélie's mouth:

LÉLIE: Je ne m'estonne pas si je romps tes attentes;
    A moins d'estre informé des choses que tu tentes
    J'en ferois encor cent de la sorte.
MASCARILLE: Tant pis.[2]

---

[1] Lélie: What's the matter, then? What have I done?
Masc: In plain French, made a fool of yourself.
[2] Lélie: I'm not surprised if I spoil your games. If I'm never told what you're up to I'll probably spoil a hundred more.
Masc: Too bad.

37

In the eyes of some purists this is not playing the game. Whether Molière's audiences cared one may well doubt.

Like Figaro a hundred years later, Mascarille (Sp. *mascarilla*, a little mask, or masquerade) displays more wit and intelligence than his master; a superiority lacking any ideological implications for an age in which, though there was no babble about Democracy, the Pepys' maid would join them for evening games and music as the normal issue of her day's work. Every servant in Molière's plays is emphatically one of the family, and as free-tongued as any of them. Mascarille has apparently, we note, had a classical education; his exulting cry of '*Vivat Mascarillus, fourbum imperator!*' links him, perhaps designedly, with the comedy-slaves of Terence and Plautus.

No other character in *L'Estourdy* save Lélie, the hero, has much individuality. In the style Voltaire discerned weaknesses and negligences. Other critics point out solecisms and obscurities. For the defence Donnay remarks that the play was probably conceived afoot or on horseback, along the highroad, and dashed down on paper at odd moments in a wayside inn. The comedy 'business' is as yet simple and tentative. In that brightly-variegated age, before the entire world had taken to bowlers and reach-me-downs, the humours of dressing up like a Turk or a Swiss and murdering the French language ('*Mon foy, pien choly!*') were obvious and plentiful. But the distinctive Molièresque hallmarks of fresh, frank, eupeptic good-humour and a swinging vivacity are already there. Nothing could be more dexterous moreover than the author's self-extrication from a very awkward situation – the discovery by Andrès, a presumed Egyptian, a few moments before the final curtain, that the beautiful Célie, with whom he has fallen deeply in love, is his sister. Turning to her with hardly a pause, the resourceful youth declaims:

> Qui l'auroit jamais crû que cette ardeur si pure
> Peust estre condamnée un jour par la nature?
> Toutefois tant d'honneur la sceut tousjours regir,
> Qu'en y changeant fort peu je puis la retenir.[1]

[1] Who could ever have believed that this pure ardour of mine could be condemned one day by Nature? But it was ruled always by such regard for honour that I can preserve it, now, with hardly a change.

A brisk bustle-technique has now sorted everything out. 'My daughter!' cries old Trufaldin to Célie when Mascarille has finished rattling off his revelations. 'Father!' cries the lovely slave. The proper lovers are united, their beaming parents bless them, and the curtain falls. Célie's bedazed cry a moment earlier, as Mascarille ends his patter, is the cry, perhaps, of not a few modern readers of *L'Estourdy:*

> Je demeure immobile à tant de nouveautez![1]

Being of tougher fibre than we and being accustomed to imbroglio derived from the Italian, Molière's provincial audiences would delight in such games of cats'-cradle, the longer and more intricate the better.

CHAPTER TWO

At this point we may pause a moment, Molière and his comrades being profitably engaged in the service of Armand, Prince de Conti, to contemplate one of the most amusing blackguards of the period, now descending on *Messieurs les Béjars* at Lyons for a stay of some months.

No one acquainted with that diverting ragbag of impressions, indiscretions, and digressions which compose the all-too-brief memoirs of Charles Coypeau, self-styled Sieur d'Assoucy and Emperor of Burlesque, can fail to recognize in this deboshed seventeenth-century musician a striking reincarnation of Eumolpus in Petronius, even to his prevailing vice. His memoirs, a symphony of belches and comic oaths, grumblings and grievances, sudden hoots of loud laughter, rattling dice, crashing glass, giggles, screams, the plucking of lutestrings, the clash of blades, the thud of flying feet, could have come out of the *Satiricon* almost anywhere. In 1655 d'Assoucy was fifty years old, which in those days was the brink of old age; as featherbrained, hilarious, debauched, and occasionally penitent a buffoon as ever. He of course knew Molière and the Béjarts well, being himself an intimate of

[1] All these novelties strike me numb.

Cyrano de Bergerac and Chapelle and an habitué, in former days, of Cyprien Ragueneau's *rôtisserie*, to the fate of whose proprietor, recently deceased, he will devote a long serio-comic threnody.

But who could better authenticate such authentic folly (he has been discussing an eccentric Parisian lawyer-poet) than my poor departed Ragueneau? – Ragueneau, known to all Parnassus, Ragueneau, beloved by all poets and cherished by all comedians, that Ragueneau, in short, who cocked a snook at all the cooks of Paris as he toiled ceaselessly with his six acolytes before the ever-blazing fires of a highly-profitable grill? Our Ragueneau, our illustrious confectioner, who rained down forcemeat-pasties on Parnassus, that foster-father of the Muses – what has become of him, alas, after nourishing those ungrateful daughters so well? I ask you, De Beys; you who infected him with the madness of versifying; you, De Beys, who ravished from us the finest pastry-cook in Paris to turn him into the worst poet in the universe; you who (etc., etc., etc.).

At the time of d'Assoucy's entry into Lyons poor Ragueneau had not yet snuffed his last candle for Molière, and could join in the hilarity at the supper-table as d'Assoucy embroidered his burlesque adventures so far. Sped down the main corridors of France by, apparently, a whole series of such, d'Assoucy was on his way from Paris to Turin, where he had hopes of appointment as master of the music at the court of Charles-Emmanuel II of Savoy. Preceding him along the highway paced a baggage-ass carrying a cofferful of lutes, theorbos, songs, epigrams and sonnets, and escorted by Valentin and Pierrotin, a pair of enigmatic youths, singers or 'music-pages', dressed in black and wearing short, tight cloaks with imitation silver-lace furbishings; more accurately, by-no-means enigmatic youths, since everybody in Bohemian Paris knew their em-ployer's pastimes. The rear of the little caravan was brought up by d'Assoucy, 'a fearful man' like the Babu in *Kim*, alertly scanning the landscape for bandits, himself unarmed. As he explains to his readers, any sword or pistols he might carry would be of far more value to the enemy. In Chapter X of the *Avantures* he comes to his pleasant memories of Lyons:

What charmed me there most of all was to meet Molière and the

Béjarts. Such are the charms of the Comedy that I was loath to quit these delightful friends. I accordingly stayed three months at Lyons amid all the jokes, the play-acting, and the feasting . . .

A rambling digression intervenes, concerning two current discords in a perfect harmony. Having accompanied Molière and his troop by boat up the Rhône to Avignon, where they had an engagement, d'Assoucy got into a gambling-den in the Jewish quarter of the city and was fleeced. On a previous occasion, a few leagues beyond Paris, a Gentile pig-dealer had performed the same operation. This time 'a big, pale, long-nosed Jew called Melchisedech took my money, Horny Moses (*Moyse-le-Cornu*) nabbed my ring, and Simon the Leper, having swiped my cloak, gave me the poxy itch'. Another current worry is the increasing malignancy of the page Valentin, a 'little dragon' jealous of his comrade's voice. After going into these matters at some length, d'Assoucy resumes:

However, since a man is never poor so long as he has friends, and since I enjoyed the esteem of Molière and the friendship of the whole Béjart family, I found myself, despite the Devil, Dame Fortune, and the whole Hebrew race, richer and happier than ever; for these hospitable folk, not content to assist me as a friend, received me like a relative. Ordered to attend the États, they took me with them to Pézenas, and I can scarcely count up the favours I enjoyed from the whole company. They say the best kind of brother tires of keeping a brother more than a month. These people, more generous than any brothers, did not tire of seeing me at their table for a whole winter. Indeed I might say –

And he burst forthwith into verse of a sort, saluting his gay and kindly hosts and the excellent table, with its seven or eight courses, kept by Music and Comedy.

A cette table bien garnie,
Parmi les plus frians muscats,
C'est moy qui soufloit la rostie,
Et qui beuvois plus d'ypocras.[1]

In fact, d'Assoucy adds, returning to prose, he was completely at home with them all, whatever he did. At length, having succeeded in extracting money from '*Monseigneur le*

---

[1] 'At this well-furnished table, amid the fruitiest of muscat wines, it was I who put away the roasts and drank most of the hippocras.'

Prince de Conty' and one or two of his entourage, and having to find a page to replace the sinister Valentin, who after an unsuccessful attempt to drown Pierrotin in the Saône had taken to his heels, d'Assoucy accompanied the Molière troop to Narbonne and left them there to continue his journey south. His subsequent adventures and mishaps in France and Italy will not concern us until the end of 1672, when d'Assoucy will be (he thinks) all-but-commissioned to write the incidental and ballet-music for *Le Malade Imaginaire*. Meanwhile we may take leave of the old rascal in the sardonic lines of Chapelle, rejecting what seems to have been an offer of the most obliging and Assoucian kind:

> De votre page qui vous suit,
> Et qui derrière vous se glisse,
> Et de tout qu'il sait aussy,
> Grand'mercy, monsieur Dassoucy,
> Monsieur Dassoucy, grand'mercy![1]

CHAPTER THREE

So d'Assoucy goes his raffish way, having yielded us one of the few glimpses available of Molière in the provinces. In December 1656 the troop was again at Béziers for the États, presenting Molière's second full-length comedy, *Dépit Amoureux* ('Lovers' Tiffs'); another five-act piece, again in verse.

Cut to two acts, as it is when played today at the Comédie-Française – Act I being untouched, Act II composed of the six opening lines of the present Act II, Sc. 3 plus Sc. 4 in its entirety, and Scenes 2, 3 and 4 of the present Act IV – it makes highly agreeable entertainment, having become, so to speak, a fugue on the theme of Horace's ode to Lydia (*Donec gratus eram tibi*, III, 9), in two distinct social keys. All that is lost is a painfully-involved imbroglio lifted bodily from Nicolò Secchi's *L'Interesse* and rendered more confusing by Molière himself.

---

[1] '. . . and as for that page of yours who follows and glides behind you, and for all he knows as well – no, Monsieur d'Assoucy, thank you all the same; Monsieur d'Assoucy, no, thanks very much.'

The pattern resultant from the surgical operation of a later age is mainly a sequence of charming love-scenes, quarrels and reconciliations between Éraste and Lucile, echoed in the language of below-stairs between their servants, Gros-René and Marinette.

To follow the original intrigue through five acts is another weariness, with little reward save the discovery that in Secchi's theatre a girl could masquerade as a boy for at least seventeen years without arousing the least suspicion in anybody, her family included. This is what happens in the printed version of *Dépit Amoureux*. The boy Ascagne is actually the girl Dorothée, and, if this is not sufficient, poses as his/her sister Lucile; she, Dorothée-Ascagne, being in love with Valère, who is in love with Lucile, who does not love him. A confidante named Frosine humps the intrigue along with confidential speeches of some length, inspiring in the reader a boredom which, more than one critic has suspected, was shared by Molière himself. Not the least vexing twist of the plot is that Albert, father of Dorothée-Ascagne, has himself been fooled. The boy-child for whom she was substituted at birth by Albert, in order to annex a deceased uncle's fortune, died very young, Albert's wife secretly substituted Dorothée, and Albert never guessed it. Since a seventeenth-century audience swallowed this kind of play like a seven-course supper it is not for us to blame Molière too much, perhaps. He alleviates the burden with a garrulous pedant named Metaphraste, comic in the true Molièresque manner. But Metaphraste has not enough to do.

Dépit Amoureux brought Molière a setback and helped him thereby to a decisive step. An inspiration smacking sweetly of modern business-method was to blame. In the hope of covering production-expenses by a subsidy from the États of Languedoc, then again in session, he deluged the assembly with complimentary tickets and had to take them all back a day or two later by order of the President, being curtly informed at the same time that he need cherish no such hopes. A second setback was coming. Not long afterwards his patron and friend Armand de Conti signified that their association was coming to an end. Like not a few other notables of the period,

Conti had experienced conversion of a very thorough kind, involving the reform of his whole existence and the abandonment of all pleasures not contributory to the spiritual life. His theatrical hobby went the way of his loose loves before he joined a society of clerics and laymen founded in 1630 by the Duc de Ventadour for pious and charitable works, and known as the Company of the Blessed Sacrament. In 1667 Conti published a *Traité de la Comédie et des Spectacles selon les Traditions de l'Église* which more than lives up to the severe promise of its title.

Fortunately for Molière the years of prosperity had arrived. He had money behind him, and he had begun to make a name. Determined to waste no more sweat on the provinces, he prepared to move north. In the summer of 1658, he was in Rouen with his troop and making regular contact with the capital. It turned out that one member of the Royal family, the King's brother, 'Monsieur', Duc d'Anjou, had as yet no theatrical company in his service. Towards the autumn Molière was informed that Monsieur had decided to employ him at the rate of 300 livres annually per member of the company. On October 24th, having been presented by Monsieur to the King and the Queen Mother, Molière gave his first Parisian performance before them and the whole Court.

CHAPTER FOUR

October 24th, 1658. The Salle des Gardes in the Louvre. Scanning through a chink in the curtain the kind of audience assembling behind a row of tall empty gilt chairs facing the stage – the two in the centre, miniature thrones mounted on a shallow dais, awaiting the Queen Mother, Anne of Austria, and twenty-year-old Louis, King of France, must have been reasonably intimidating – Molière doubtless shared to the full the sweating tension behind the scenes.

He had chosen Corneille's tragedy *Nicomède* for the opening piece, followed by a farce called *Le Docteur Amoureux*, since disappeared. During later opportunities of glancing round the auditorium a more unnerving sight than the assembled royalties and a glittering Court would keep drawing his eye. The magnificos of the Hôtel de Bourgogne were all there, watching the show keenly: the men and women of the King's company, Beauchasteau and his impressive wife, Hauteroche, Villiers, the great Montfleury himself; applauding the tragedy, not too vigorously (the new man was obviously a stick), smiling at the farce, not too broadly, and exchanging at intervals inscrutable shrugs, winks, and lifts of the eyebrow.

The second half of this vital evening at any rate went well. The young King was seen to laugh repeatedly and uproariously at Molière's clowning. The farce had been prefaced by a studiously modest *entr'acte* address to the King, spoken by Molière. Bowing low in the centre of the stage, thanking his Majesty profusely for his goodness in excusing his defects and those of his company, he begged him further to accept 'one of those little entertainments which brought me a certain reputation when I offered them to the provinces'.

A day or two later first-night nerves and morning-after forebodings were amply alleviated. By the King's order the new troop was henceforth to share the Petit-Bourbon theatre with the popular Italian Comedians, and having arranged to pay the Italians 1,500 francs a year for this privilege, Molière moved in forthwith.

The Petit-Bourbon, formerly the hall of the fourteenth-century Hôtel de Bourbon, on the south side of the Louvre, was now occupied by the Fiorillo-Locatelli troop, which boasted at least two performers of starriest quality – Domenico Biancolelli, a master-Harlequin, and Tiberio Fiorillo, greatest of all Scaramouches, who was to be over some years, as noted already, Moliere's comic exemplar and his close friend. Fiorillo's Scaramouche wore no mask, substituting face-powder and specializing in such grimaces as had never contorted the features of mortal clown before. In the Old Italian Comedy Scaramouche is a poor gentleman's valet, slippery as an eel, given to ingenious and hilarious intrigue, devoted to women and the bottle, a braggart and a poltroon.[1] Costumed in tradi-

[1] *Scaramuccia* – a small brawl, or skirmish.

45

tional black ('*Le ciel s'est habillé ce soir en Scaramouche*', Hali will say in the nocturnal opening-scene of *Le Sicilien*), Fiorillo enhanced his clowning by considerable acrobatic gifts and a fine singing-voice, for operettas were also on the bill. He could walk into the Royal apartments whenever he visited the Louvre; Louis XIV had laughed at him since infancy. In 1644 the godparents of Scaramouche's second child, baptized in the Royal parish church of St Germain – l'Auxerrois, were the Queen Mother of France and Cardinal Mazarin, her Minister; his first had been baptized by Cardinal Chigi in Rome. Actors in Italy were not under a permanent ban of excommunication as in France, it may be observed in passing. Excluded on principle from the Papal States, the Commedia companies were welcome at all the little Italian courts. One of their most benevolent sixteenth-century patrons, examining and approving scenaries, suggesting improvements, and even autographing some of the scripts, had been the great Cardinal – Archbishop of Milan, St Charles Borromeo.

So Molière was now installed with the Italians in the Petit-Bourbon, playing alternate days and facing the formidable metropolitan public for the first time. To conquer and tame what are often gracefully referred to in later French theatre-circles as *les cochons de payants* the seventeenth-century actor-manager needed more than the right script and skill in his trade. Strong nerves, patience, tact, quick thinking, and a ready smile were essential in a frequent battle for precedence. Almost unendurable at times was the monstrous handicap of being more or less hemmed in by men of fashion on the stage itself, the smart procedure being to arrive late, talking loudly, ignoring or obstructing actors and guards, creating as much confusion as possible. Éraste in *Les Fascheux* ('The Nuisances') will shortly sum up these pests in the person of a bulky turbulent fop bustling in after the play has begun, crying 'Holà-ho! A chair, quickly!', proceeding to stroll about the stage, greeting friends, and finally planting his chair in the middle, where his large back screens the actors from three-quarters of the pit. 'My God!' cries Éraste in despair, 'must we French confirm what all our neighbours say about us?'

Apart from the fops, the gentlemen of the Royal Guards and the *Mousquetaires* were a recurring nuisance, given to arriving late, noisy, drunk, bullying the doorkeepers – they claimed free admission – menacing the spectators, liable to brawl among themselves and draw swords at any moment. Smart women chattered at intervals as in their own drawing-rooms, footmen and pages bickered, girls selling wine, cakes, and fruit flirted and cried their wares, and a restive pit might whistle and howl like a zoo and even pelt the players. Under half a dozen round wooden chandeliers the candle-lit stage was very simply furnished at Molière's début, and for some time afterwards, with stylized scenery and folding screens adapted from the Commedia. More and more elaborate sets and 'machines' will be needed as his productions grow more luxurious, and half a dozen fiddles across the footlights will swell to a sizeable orchestra. New turmoil will be introduced by the distribution before curtain-rise and between the acts of programmes or *livres de ballet*; Molière will turn it into one of the ballet-interludes concluding *Le Bourgeois Gentilhomme*. Where in these pages the curtain is said to rise or fall, this may be taken as a figure of speech. The theatre-curtain of the period was a large and usually decorative tapestry in halves, slid apart at the beginning of the play and together at the end. One essential of every performance must not be omitted – the final crosstalk-act of the 'orator' of the troop announcing the next performance. On his quick wit and repartee much depended. Molière himself will assume this duty for some time, and find his talent for grimaces very valuable.

That the friendship of a portent like Tiberio Fiorillo was of something more than professional advantage to him may well be surmized. Their contemporaries were well aware of the bond between them. Thus an enemy, Le Boulanger de Chalussay, gibing at Molière's alleged efforts to perfect himself in 'the art of rousing laughter':

> Que fait-il, le matois, dans ce hardy dessein?
> Chez le grand Scaramouche il va, soir et matin,
> Là, le miroir en main, et ce grand homme en face,
> Il n'est contorsion, posture, ny grimace

Que ce grand escolier du plus grand des bouffons
Ne fasse et ne refasse en cent et cent façons.[1]

The friendship was genuine enough. 'This great actor',
says an obscure admirer of Molière who supplied librettos for
the Fiorillo-Locatelli troop, 'and this ten times greater playwright lived in close intimacy with the Italians, since they were
all actors and honest folk. There were always two or three of
them (Molière's company) at our supper-table.'[2] A pleasant
comradely picture and a lenitive for fierce enmities elsewhere.

Dropping the tragedy for once, Molière opened his first
Parisian season with *L'Estourdy* and *Dépit Amoureux*. Both
were played before the King as well. Both were a popular
success. A slight reshuffle of the company is reported at Easter,
1659, when the two Du Parcs left Molière for the Marais and
were replaced by two players from that theatre, the popular
low comedian Jodelet and his brother L'Espy. A more important recruit arrived simultaneously from some company
unknown: the faithful, the invaluable Charles Varlet de La
Grange, for the next fourteen years to be Molière's *jeune
premier*, devoted and intimate right-hand man, and registrar,
due to leave behind him a parchment-bound volume now
preserved under lock and key in the archives of the Comédie-
Française like a major relic. Thanks to La Grange's registers,
kept lovingly in a clear, clerkly hand, we know everything that
happened in this theatre from 1659 to 1685; every production,
with its date and the box-office returns, every birth, marriage,
or death within the company itself. La Grange's care and
delight in his task are exemplary. Should an ink-blot occur,
it is licked off at once in schoolboy fashion, as the page reveals.
Nothing is crossed out, and there are no blunders. A series of
marginal symbols illuminates the text – a cross for a birth, for
example, a black lozenge for a death, a blue-tinted circle for a
marriage; for any outstanding first-night success the margin

[1] 'And how does he work towards this daring end, the rogue? By
going to see the great Scaramouche night and day. There, mirror in hand
and the great man before him, not a single contortion, posture, or grimace,
but is copied and recopied in a hundred or more ways by this eminent
pupil of the greatest of clowns.'

[2] Duchartre, *op. cit.*

or the title itself bursts into rays and aureoles and lighted candles of triumph. Himself apparently of a slightly higher social grade than the average actor of the period – his father was 'captain of the Chateau of Nanteuil', which may or may not indicate a concierge – La Grange added to his other excellences that of being a first-class actor. It will be he who takes command not long after Molière's death, co-opts the best of the Marais and the Hôtel de Bourgogne, and founds the Comédie-Française we know today.

So, feeling the wave of success already swelling and rising under him, Molière produced on November 18, 1659, *Les Précieuses Ridicules*, his first comedy of satiric observation; a one-act piece of seventeen scenes in prose, based on a trifle he had scribbled and played in the provinces.

Highbrows are natural meat for the satirist; female highbrows above all. There were no brows in contemporary Europe loftier than those of Catherine, Marquise de Rambouillet, and her clique of poets, philologists, serious fine gentlemen, and earnest ladies of quality, and few targets for satire were more indicated than the smart Parisian salons which aped them, saving always the provincials who aped the Parisians. The habitués of the Hôtel de Rambouillet and their aims were actually by no means risible. Instilling good morals, good breeding, and good taste into the deportment and speech of a decadent Beau Monde was a crusade entirely praiseworthy, and the affectations of Rambouillet were not for the most part ridiculous. It is the jargon of their apes, current long after the Marquise had closed her salon, which arouses Molière's derision, and the cackle of two affected provincials of this species which yields him his comedy. He will make this point in his preface a year later to the printed play. 'True *précieuses* would be wrong to take offence when someone pokes fun at silly creatures who imitate them badly.' And in fact those of Madame de Rambouillet's following, the Marquise included, took no offence to speak of, despite the fun made Molière of their literary idol Mlle de Scudéry, her *Carte du Tendre*, her monumental, interminable romances, and the highflown names of her characters, which the leading *pré-*

49

cieuses had freely adopted. Thus Cathos in the play, protesting to her astonished uncle Gorgibus against his addressing her and Madelon, his daughter, by these vulgar baptismal names:

> Truly, Uncle, any ear with a trifle of delicacy must suffer furiously at hearing such names enunciated! But the names of Polixène, which my cousin has chosen, and Aminthe, which I have selected for myself, wear a grace to which you are bound to submit.

Having anagrammatized her own Christian name into 'Arthénice', Catherine de Rambouillet might justly, with those of her female friends who indulged in such Scuderian whimsies as 'Barthénoïde' or 'Urimédonte', have suspected the playwright's intention, were sauciness from such a fellow worthy of a *grande dame's* resentment.

The background of the play is not particularized. It might be any town Molière had passed through in the South, from Lyons to Pézenas. The plot is simplicity itself. Cathos and Madelon, two small-town *précieuses*, have just rejected two highly eligible young admirers, the Seigneurs La Grange and Du Croisy, for lacking the requisite fine language and *bel air*. La Grange suggests playing a retaliation trick on the ladies. Du Croisy concurs. Their valets, masquerading as the Marquis de Mascarille and the Vicomte de Jodelet, fresh from Paris and primed with the latest jargon, proceed accordingly to fascinate Cathos and Madelon with ease. At the height of the fun their masters appear and inflict a sound drubbing apiece, the ladies are overwhelmed with shame and confusion, nobody is left to pay the fiddles, and the curtain falls.

It is not perhaps a highly civilized play. The gentlemen's vengeance seems a trifle ill-bred. The valets, from the old Italian stable, are all too impudent. The *précieuses* might have been taken down a peg or two less brutally, one feels. However, the piece is gay and quick, and certainly amused the Parisians. '*Courage, Molière!*' shouted a first-night enthusiast from the pit. '*Voila la veritable comédie!*' The anecdote is Voltaire's, and possibly apocryphal, but it represents the public verdict on this little romp with the intelligentsia, and a just one. For the first time Molière had discarded the Italians and trained his hilarious artillery on a topical target. Nor had he omitted, even so early, to score off the pontiffs of the Hôtel de Bourgogne. 'Unless I deceive myself,' says the bogus Marquis de Mascarille to Cathos, 'you have perhaps thrown off some comedy or other? We must certainly see it. Between ourselves I've composed one myself which I'm thinking of having produced.'

CATHOS: Really? Which company are you giving it to?
MASCARILLE: What a question! To the Great Comedians, naturally! Nobody else can give these things their value. The others are all ignoramuses who recite their stuff like ordinary talk. They don't know the way to boom out a line and stop at the right place – yet how is anyone to know a good line if the actor doesn't stop there and let you know it's time to applaud?

It was great fun, and battle with the Hôtel de Bourgogne was joined. But what promised to be a long and profitable run received a smart check from officialdom within a month, when a certain M. de Ratabon, Superintendent of the Royal Office of Works, served sudden notice to quit. The Petit-Bourbon was to be demolished immediately to make way for a new colonnade to the Louvre.

Protests to the King proved unavailing. M. de Ratabon had his orders – possibly, suggests genial Maurice Donnay, a little lady-friend at the Hôtel de Bourgogne as well – and Molière and the Italians had to start moving out. The King, it soon appeared, had something better in store for them. The splendid hall of Richelieu's Palais-Royal was to be their joint new home, and M. de Ratabon was set to work on necessary structural alterations forthwith. Molière filled the interval with a series of performances, *visites*, at great houses, in those days a sideline of considerable value. On October 26th, Monsieur's comedians gave *L'Estourdy* and *Les Précieuses Ridicules* at the Louvre before the King and Cardinal Mazarin, now a sick man in an invalid chair, and earned 3,000 livres thereby. On January 20th, 1661, they opened at the Palais-Royal with *L'Estourdy* and a new farcical comedy of twenty-four scenes in verse by their director entitled *Sganarelle, ou le Cocu Imaginaire*.

In verve and gaiety this piece has been ranked by a perfervid nineteenth-century critic with *The Merry Wives of Windsor*. In calmer mood, perhaps, he tended to revise this comparison. It was certainly a triumph for Molière. As the ridiculous Sganarelle, *bourgeois de Paris*, obsessed with a terror of cuckoldry, he is said to have electrified the town with a wealth of clownings inspired by the art of Fiorillo.

To a modern ear the farce may seem nowadays to creak in every complicated joint. Swooning in a public square, the fair Célie, destined by an unfeeling father for Valère, but in love with Lélie – the master's confusing trick of using the same names over and over again for differing characters will never be completely dropped – is charitably escorted home by Sganarelle. His wife, known throughout the piece for some reason unexplained as *la Femme de Sganarelle*, happens to view all this from a window. She draws her own conclusions, hastens out of doors, and picks up a miniature of Lélie which Célie, providentially for the plot, has dropped by accident. Poring later over this at home, she is discovered and charged with adultery by Sganarelle, and hotly returns the charge. Amid the tangle of misconceptions ensuing Célie is led by Sganarelle to believe that her adored Lélie is his, Sgnarelle's, wife's paramour. Everything is straightened out in the last five minutes by Valère's father, Monsieur Villebrequin, who withdraws from his arrangement with Célie's father, Gorgibus, and allows the lovers to marry. The runcible mechanics of the plot, which were not drawbacks in 1661, are relieved by the deftness of the verse, a considerable advance, connoisseurs agree, on anything Molière had evolved so far. One excellent farcical line among others comes from the craven Sganarelle. Armed to the teeth and hunting everywhere for Lélie, he comes across the blameless youth unexpectedly. 'What are all the weapons for?' asks Lélie in surprise. 'I thought it was going to rain,' mumbles Sganarelle. His final or curtain couplet supplies the moral:

> De cet exemple-cy ressouvenez-vous bien,
> Et, quand vous verriez tout, ne croyez jamais rien.[1]

Owing to the determination of the French to regard cuck-

[1] 'Bear well in mind this present example (of foolishness) and even if you were to see everything, never believe a word of it.'

oldry as an evergreen joke, the rest of Europe having more or less left off laughing at this painful situation at the end of the eighteenth century, *Sganarelle ou Le Cocu Imaginaire* has long since been out-distanced by the invention of succeeding fertile generations of Palais-Royal *farceurs*, and is never revived nowadays. It is nevertheless far more a work of art than Ravenscroft's contemporary piece *The London Cuckolds*, our principal native fantasia on the same homely theme. Molière wrote the *Cocu*, as it is called in stage circles, a year before his marriage. It may be that he found the fear of cuckoldry a topic less provocative of mirth three or four years after it.

Four box-office triumphs in succession were meanwhile followed by a resounding failure. Produced on February 4th, 1661, *Dom Garcie de Navarre* collapsed almost immediately, despite some not uncomely rhetoric, in a storm of hisses.

It is a five-act heroic tragicomedy in verse, in the stately Spanish manner, featuring a sombre Navarrese hidalgo, subject to frenzies of jealousy, who turns out very soon, alas, to be a terrible bore. After fifteen years of the theatre Molière undoubtedly knew as much about the operations of jealousy as the next man, but he chose to orchestrate its subtleties in an unfamiliar key. Skilfully as she probes Don Garcia's case, Molière's muse is very far from being at home in the city of Astorga in the kingdom of León. Her climax moreover is highly unconvincing. 'Your malady is worthy of pity,' says gentle Donna Elvira, surrendering to Don Garcia at length after suffering abominably from his tantrums and injustices. 'But jealous or not jealous,' she adds, 'my King can give you to me.' 'Heaven!' cries the Don. 'Make my heart capable of supporting its joy!' And the curtain falls on the kingdom of León, amid the distant chime of wedding-bells. There is no guarantee that Don Garcia, the first of Molière's three patho-logical cases, will not break out during the honeymoon and start the drama all over again.

If *Dom Garcie de Navarre* makes heavy reading – it was not printed till after Molière's death – it throws valuable light on its author's susceptibility to Don Garcia's malady. Following his recent exercise on the cuckoldry-theme, it has perhaps a slightly ominous ring as well. The curtain was about to rise on Molière's own drama, in which he is due to suffer no less thoroughly, though more quietly, than his tormented Don.

In the April of 1661, records La Grange, Molière announced to the company his forthcoming marriage and asked for, and was accorded, another share in the theatre. He was nearly forty. His bride-to-be was Armande Grésine Claire Élisabeth Béjart, officially the eighteen-year-old sister (but as some authorities insist, the daughter) of forty-three-year-old Madeleine, and herself an actress of talent.

Book III

CHAPTER ONE

Exquisitely of the theatre is an early passage in *La Fameuse Comédienne*, that anonymous broadside of 1688 against a leading Parisian actress known to the playgoing public and Court circles as 'La Molière', which is so venomously diverting:

> She is the daughter of La Béjart, lately deceased, a provincial comedienne who provided a good time for a number of the young gentlemen of Languedoc at the period of the happy advent of her daughter. Amid such a whirl of gallantry it would be fairly difficult to name the father; all I know is that her (Armande's) mother used to assert that in her gay days she could never, if one excludes Molière, endure anybody but a man of quality, and that for this reason her daughter was of very noble blood . . . She (Armande) has been thought to be Molière's daughter, though he later became her husband. However, nobody knows the actual truth . . .

Et voilà, ma chère! Almost certainly, as has been conjectured already, this must be the work of one of 'La Molière's' comrades of the stage, dipping a dainty quill into the finest vitriol. She is not alone in making Armande the daughter of Madeleine, at least. Grimarest does the same. Racine, the great Racine, for some time one of Moliere's bosom friends, seems to go even further in a letter to one of his acquaintances:

> Montfleury has drawn up a memorial against Molière and addressed it to the King. He accuses him of having married the daughter after sleeping with the mother. But Montfleury has no voice at Court.

And again, there is Brossette, the Boswell of Boileau, another of Molière's intimates:

> M. Despréaux (Boileau's full name was Nicolas Boileau-

Despréaux) tells me that Molière was formerly in love with La Béjart, the actress, whose daughter he married.

And once more there is the acid Le Boulanger de Chalussay, who makes a cautiously oblique reference to the scandal in *Élomire Hypocondre*. Apropos the misfortune of the elderly Arnolphe of *L'Escole des Femmes*, who brings up Agnès from infancy as his future wife, only to have her stolen from him by a blade her own age, Élomire – Molière reflects that Arnolphe left things too late; he should have begun before Agnès was in the cradle, 'as somebody or other did':

> Arnolphe commença trop tard à la forger,
> C'est avant le berceau qu'il y devoit songer,
> Comme quelqu'un l'a fait . . .

One might imagine that three official documents discovered in the last century would settle this matter, but for a number of authorities they do not. In the marriage-contract, in the marriage-certificate, and in a document involving a debt-ridden heritage Armande figures as the daughter of Madame Marie Béjart, *née* Hervé; that is to say, as Madeleine's sister, born twenty-five years later. To this evidence the recusants reply vigorously that it is no evidence at all if Madame Béjart had assumed the responsibility for Madeleine's child before birth; a not infrequent happening even nowadays where some family scandal is imminent, and a happening extremely possible among a Bohemian tribe like the Béjarts.[1]

So the question remains in suspense. We may note that although Molière took prompt action against *Élomire Hypocondre*, which was judicially suppressed,[2] neither he nor Armande ever made any reply to an accusation which was the talk of the town, and that Louis XIV showed his own opinion of the story by standing godfather to their first child. Two things seem possible. Madeleine herself may not have known who Armande's father was. And again, Molière might have discovered the truth only after marriage.

[1] Joseph Béjart the elder, Marie's husband, died in 1643, which possibly just qualifies him as a candidate for the paternity of Armande.
[2] It was republished in 1672, probably clandestinely.

They were married, at any rate, on February 20th, 1662, in the Royal parish church of Saint Germain-l'Auxerrois near the Louvre, Armande bringing her husband a dowry of 10,000 livres, officially provided by Madame Béjart, but actually, it is suspected, by Molière or Madeleine, or both. For young women like nineteen-year-old Armande, no breathtaking beauties by Hollywood standards, the French have a consecrated phrase – *pire que jolie*. Her portrait will be sketched by a still-infatuated husband eight years onward in *Le Bourgeois Gentilhomme*. It comes in a charming piece of dialogue between Cléonte, in love with Lucile, and his man Covielle. Lucile has recently cut Cléonte dead. To console his bitterly-wounded master, and at his order, Covielle begins cheerfully running her down. 'Firstly, her eyes are small', he begins.

CLÉONTE: Yes, that's true; she has small eyes. But they're full of fire – the most brilliant and lively eyes in the world, and the most moving you could ever see.

COVIELLE: A large mouth.

CLÉONTE: Yes, but it has a charm you don't see in other mouths. It's a mouth which, when you look at it, inspires desire – the most seductive, the mouth most made for love in the world.

COVIELLE: As to her height – she's not very tall.

CLÉONTE: No. But she has poise, and she's well-made.

COVIELLE: She puts on a listless air whenever she moves or speaks.

CLÉONTE: That's true, but there's grace in it. Her ways are so engaging that a sort of fascination steals into your heart.

COVIELLE: Her talk –

CLÉONTE: Her talk is charming.

COVIELLE: She's always serious.

CLÉONTE: What do you want? Bursts of sprightliness and joy all round? Do you ever see anything more tedious than women who will laugh at anything?

So they come to something important:

COVIELLE: Well, to finish up, she's as capricious as any woman in the world.

CLÉONTE: Yes. I agree she's capricious. But everything suits a woman with beauty – you can stand anything from a beauty.

57   E

COVIELLE: Since it's like that, I can see you're just yearning to love her always.

And so he is. *On souffre tout des belles*, and Molière was certainly to suffer from Armande. As the saying is, she was a born actress; the slightly rude word *cabotine* suits her perfectly. If it is correct to identify her, as most good authorities do, with a child-actress billed as 'Mlle Menou', who had been brought up in Languedoc and appeared with Molière's troop in *Andromède* at Lyons at the age of ten, Armande had very little of her trade to learn when she married. They had of course known each other for years. Since his return to Paris Molière had been living with or, at any rate next door to, the Béjarts in the Place du Palais-Royal; a cheerful, slovenly existence, no doubt; plenty of laughter and quarrelling and bursts of song, with tirades and gesticulations and meals at all hours. Armande may well have grown up with some affection for the *ami de la maison*, apart from his value as a rising power in the theatre. According to *La Fameuse Comédienne*, Madeleine pushed the girl at length into Molière's arms. Grimarest says the exact opposite; it was Madeleine's furious nagging, having divined and detesting Molière's intentions, which ultimately drove Armande practically to chisel an offer of marriage out of him, and a terrific domestic upheaval ensured. Both versions may be right. Good fat parts were involved for all three principals.

Early in his betrothal, Molière produced a new three-act comedy in verse, *L'Escole des Maris* ('The School for Husbands'), his first subjective play of ideas. Two girl-children, Léonor and Isabelle, have been placed, under their late father's will, in the charge of two elderly brothers, his friends; Ariste being now about sixty and Sganarelle forty. When the girls are of the proper age their guardians may either marry them or dispose of them otherwise, as they think fit; it seems that such extraordinary contracts were possible in seventeenth-century France. The girls are now of marriageable age, and the brothers have differed totally on their upbringing. Ariste, who could run a very expensive and profitable school in the England of 1959, has educated Léonor on the progressive – self-expressive plan which has made not a few lucky pedagogues rich in the modern Anglo-Saxon world; no scoldings, no lectures, plenty of pretty frocks, parties, and indulgence of every girlish whim.

> J'ay souffert qu'elle aie veu les belles compagnies,
> Les divertissemens, les bals, les comédies . . .

Having decided to marry the girl, Ariste will continue to allow her to do exactly as she pleases – *liberté toute entière*. On the other hand Sganarelle has brought up young Isabelle on a plan embracing good plain serge frocks, a sufficiency of daily needlework and domestic chores – for recreation Isabelle has been allowed to amuse herself with knitting stockings – and no step outside the door without proper supervision. One may guess very early that Sganarelle, played for laughs by Molière, is going to get his just deserts ere long, since he too has decided to wed his young ward. One may guess likewise that the marriage of Ariste and his girl-wife is going to be idyllic, *L'Escole des Maris* being an advance-instruction course for Armande Béjart, who played Léonor. So froward Isabelle runs off with young Valère, but Léonor and her sixty-year-old Ariste live happy ever after.

Why Ariste should be sixty years old and not, say, forty, Molière's own age, with a Sganarelle of, say, thirty, is a question which has excercised a few of the thoughtful. It would not have affected the theme to lower their ages a little, and fewer eyebrows would have been raised, especially in later centuries, at the mating of Ariste and Léonor. In the France of 1661 a man of sixty was deemed practically senile. Hence Léonor's rhapsody on returning from the ball, having scorned and rejected all the advances of ardent youth for love of the dear old gentleman at home, may have been a little hard to take even at that time.

> Et moy, d'un tel vieillard je prise plus le zèle
> Que tous les beaux transports d'une jeune cervelle . . .[1]

'Trust her not – she is fooling thee!' the old Spanish ballad comes inevitably to mind. As the curtain falls one's doubts of

---

[1] 'And for myself, I prize the ardour of an old man like this far above all the fine transports of a youthful brain . . .'

Léonor increase by leaps and bounds. Molière was plainly over-playing his hand here. Youth to youth; he reverts to normal with her sister Isabelle, a delightful little schemer, outwitting the ever-watchful Sganarelle in the letter-scene with a trick plainly derived from a tale of Boccaccio.[1] Love laughs at the most complicated burglar-alarms, and the theatre then had no situation more successful than that of the jealous old hunks outwitted by youth and beauty. Wycherley was exploiting it contemporaneously in *The Country Wife*; not that one would for a moment compare a mopsy like little Mrs Pinchwife with the virginal Isabelle, whose objective is entirely blameless.

L'Escole des Maris was received with almost universal acclamation. Produced at the Palais-Royal on June 24th, 1661, it was played a week later before Henrietta Maria, Queen of England, at the château of Vaux-le-Vicomte, where Fouquet, Minister of Finance, was entertaining her with Monsieur and Madame. A little afterwards Louis XIV saw it at Fontainebleau.

This summer of 1661 must have been the happiest period in Molière's life. Deeply in love with Armande, he was on a rising wave of fame and fortune, already a familiar of several of the *gratin* or top-crust. They might not ask him to their houses as yet, but there was a great deal of entertaining at his period in the fashionable cabarets of Paris, and Molière, according to Grimarest, gave and received his full share. Agreeably relaxing after the patronage of the highborn would be the supper-parties at the Croix de Lorraine or the Pomme du Pin with Chapelle and his immediate cronies, Lignon, Broussin, and others; parties often lasting till dawn, with song and laughter. Still more agreeable were the regular appoint-ments with Racine, Boileau and La Fontaine, whose affectionate esteem was undoubtedly worth more to Molière than all the condescension and flattery he got elsewhere. The four had gravitated together like young men of genius in any capital. To keep their symposia select, Boileau had taken an apartment in the Rue du Vieux-Colombier, on the left bank near the Luxembourg. Here they met three times a week to sup and discuss life and letters half the night over their wine. The

[1] *Decameron*: The Third Novel of the Third Day.

site of Boileau's apartment-house has not been identified even
by such a tireless authority on Old Paris as M. de Rochegude,
but in so short a street it cannot have stood very far from the little
famous theatre of the 1920-30's – today, alas, itself a ghost –
where Jacques Copeau was to lend masterpieces by two of
Boileau's guests unforgettable new meaning. It is distressing to
reflect that some authorities dismiss the whole existence of this
brilliant little society as a myth based on a poetic whimsy of
La Fontaine's.

Molière himself was already a recognized portent, and
enmity, not unnaturally, was increasing in volume and cutting
itself fresh quills. Professional vendettas apart, he had infuriated not a few victims of his satire even so far; among them
the mock *précieuses* and the *marquis ridicules* at Court, to be
joined very soon by a section of *dévots* offended by a passage in
L'Escole des Femmes, the vanguard of more formidable religious
opposition still to come. The vengeful fury of the Faculty of
Medicine was as yet below the horizon.

CHAPTER TWO

Six months before his marriage came the first of those 'rush'
assignments which were to be Molière's frequent lot. On the
eve of a spectacular crash Nicolas Fouquet, Minister of Finance
and multi-millonaire patron of all the arts, was about to
entertain Louis XIV and Queen Maria Theresa at his palatial
château of Vaux-le-Vicomte near Melun, still a showplace.
A fortnight beforehand Fouquet ordered from Molière, now
purveyor of comedy by Royal appointment, an after-dinner
divertissement to include music and ballet. The result was *Les
Fascheux* ('The Nuisances'), a kind of revue-sketch in three acts
and eighteen scenes in verse; 'conceived, written, conned,
and played in the space of fifteen days', as Molière ventured
modestly to remind the King, his collaborator, in a subsequent
preface.

This series of piquant character-sketches is strung on the
slenderest of threads. Trying to keep an appointment with

Orphise, his beloved, in the Cours-la-Reine, the fashionable promenade of the moment, a young marquis named Eraste is waylaid and obstructed by a dozen distinct types of bore in succession. Each act ends with a ballet of other obstructive nuisances – bowls and pall-mall players, lookers-on, promenaders, loungers, masks, gardeners and whatnot. Dances by Beauchamp, the Royal ballet-master, music by Péllisson, *décors* by Lebrun, 'machines', nowadays called 'effects', by Torelli.

After the performance at Vaux-le-Vicomte on August 17th, Molière encountered Louis XIV in person in one of the galleries. The King had failed to enjoy a banquet composed by the illustrious chef Vatel, whose cry of 'I have lost my honour!' before rushing away to commit suicide one April night ten years later rings for ever from one of Mme de Sévigné's most vivid letters. This happened after a minor breakdown in the supper-service at the Prince de Condé's chateau at Chantilly. The King had arrived after a day's hunting with a larger retinue than was expected, and one or two tables went short. Despite his employer's attempts to soothe him the distraught Vatel fled to his apartment and fell on his sword, an expiation rare in the culinary world.

There was no contretemps at Vaux-le-Vicomte in August 1661, but the King rose from table in slightly petulant mood. Vatel's current masterpiece had been served in thirty-six dozen of massy gold plate – a tactless display, the Royal household plate being silver; nor was his Majesty, a man of taste, anything but bored and irritated by the overwhelming opulence of the château and its surroundings, which had employed 18,000 workmen. The arrest and imprisonment for twenty years, after trial for public peculation, of his too-ambitious host was imminent. The King had nevertheless enjoyed Molière's show, and said so. 'But you've overlooked one of them', he added. The Marquis de Soyecourt, a hunting man famous as a bore of bores, was passing. The King nodded in his direction. When a few days later Molière repeated *Les Fascheux* by Royal command at Fontainebleau, a new caricature was included.

M. de Soyecourt, a genial redfaced Mohock who, they say, having briefed Molière, naturally failed to recognize himself as Dorante, is not the brightest of the galaxy, perhaps. A good stage-bore must bore, or appear to bore, his fellow-characters without boring the audience for a single moment, and is accordingly rare. No hunting-bore has ever figured satisfactorily even on the British comedy-stage. The superb Jorrocks himself would, one fears, fail to arride any but the simplest addict of slapstick. It is largely, no doubt, a question of the jargon. Alcipe, Molière's cardroom-bore, is not excessively diverting either except to piquet players; but as the Court and *le Tout-Paris* were equally piquet-mad Molière had a considerable audience with him to begin with. Five of his bores extend a wider entertainment-appeal: Ormin the economist, for example, whose obsession is turning the entire French coastline into a string of seaports, and Caritidès, the literary bore, who wants to correct the orthography of public signboards, and the two pretty highbrows Orante and Climène, who cannot make up their minds whether a woman wants to be loved more or loved better. The unnamed theatre-pest described by Eraste and the dance-mad Lysandre are sufficiently laughable, and the fire-eating Alcandre, who tries to force Eraste into seconding him in an imminent duel, gives Molière an opportunity for a salute to his King. 'No,' says Eraste firmly, 'I've had fourteen years soldiering and nobody can question my courage, but duelling has been banned by Royal edict.'

> Un duel met les gens en mauvaise posture,
> Et nostre Roy n'est pas un monarque en peinture . . .
> Je me fais de son ordre un supreme loy,
> Pour luy desobeïr, cherche un autre que moy.[1]

At last – one may picture Molière racking his brains to beat the clock with some sort of a finale – Eraste drives off a gang of ruffians attacking an elderly gentleman in the distance who turns out to be Damis, uncle and guardian of his Orphise and hitherto hostile to the match. Avuncular gratitude and blessings

---

[1] 'A duel gets people into bad trouble. Our King is not a painted image . . . I hold his order to be a supreme law. If you want to disobey him, get somebody else.'

for the reunited lovers are interrupted by the entry of a noisy crowd of masks and fiddlers, soon expelled, and the piece ends with a dance of Swiss guards succeeded by a dance of shepherds and shepherdesses. It is highly pleasant after-dinner entertainment, showing, like so much work produced by genius at high pressure, no trace of sweat.

Like a good showman Molière proceeded immediately to capitalize Royal favour in the ensuing preface to the printed play, addressed to the King.

> I must confess, Sir, that I have never written anything with such ease, or so quickly, as that part of it which Your Majesty commanded me to perform. I discovered a joy in obedience which was worth more to me than Apollo and all the Muses. From this I perceive that inspired by such a command, I could produce an entire comedy.

He was to be taken at his word. Meanwhile another full-length piece was taking shape. On December 26th, 1662, ten months after marriage, he produced a resounding success, *L'Escole des Femmes*, a five-act comedy in verse which a clique of brawlers tried unsuccessfully to wreck on the first night.

It is the first of the six great comedies, and it reconsiders the theme of *L'Escole des Maris* from another angle. A girl-child of unknown origin is brought up from the age of four by a rich eccentric designing to marry her. He has taken great trouble to deprive her of instruction of every kind, holding that an ignorant wife is the best safeguard against cuckoldry, of which he goes in mortal terror. As with Sganarelle in the previous play, youth and human nature prove too much for Arnolphe. It is he, not the innocent Agnès, who turns out to be the fool.

Arnolphe's brother Chrysalde, himself happily married to a wife of education and intelligence, tries to laugh Arnolphe out of his obsession. Chrysalde is a satirist with a sense of humour, and a long merry tirade in praise of cuckoldry will eventually mislead the great indignant Bossuet considerably. From the entry on the scene – the entire action, obedient to the classical 'unity of place', passes in a public square in Paris – of handsome young Horace, son of an old friend of Arnolphe, it is evident what the end will be.

Two quaint technical stumbling-blocks are discernible in a play full of charm and beauty. Arnolphe has recently taken the name of 'Monsieur de la Souche'. Unaware of this, Horace makes him, as Arnolphe, the confidant of successive attempts to get Agnès out of old De la Souche's clutches, and is not enlightened. There is also the grotesque scurry of the dénouement. The final scene of Act V is a string of versicles and responses in which Chrysalde and Oronte, Horace's father, newly arrived on the scene with a personage named Enrique, who has spent the last fourteen years in America, explain rapidly to all concerned that the rustic Agnès is actually Chrysalde's niece and the daughter of the said Enrique. Abridged and stripped of the elegance of the alexandrines, the patter runs thus:

CHRYS: By a secret marriage my sister had a daughter whose identity was concealed from the family.

ORON: And who was sent into the country by her husband to be brought up under an assumed name.

CHRYS: Shortly afterwards he was obliged to leave his native land.

ORON: On returning to France he at once sought the woman to whom he had confided his child's welfare.

CHRYS: And this peasant told him frankly that she had placed Agnès in your (Arnolphe's) hands at the age of four (etc., etc.).

Enrique meanwhile stands by dumb as a fish, opening his mouth just before the curtain falls to remark in three lines that he has no doubts about the identity of his daughter, is deeply moved, and consents to her marrying Horace.

Ah! ma fille, je cede à des transports si doux! . . .

Thus does the master in his wilful way, and when it suits him, let dramatic propriety go hang. It does not spoil a delicious play. Agnès, played by Catherine de Brie for nearly fifty years, is one of the most enchanting creations in any theatre. Her awakening to love is invested with a kind of springtime grace, at once tender and playful, which keeps L'Escole des Femmes eternally fresh. Every intelligent high-school girl in France, and still more every débutante at the Conservatoire, knows by heart the scene (Act II. Sc. 5) in which Agnès describes to the glowering Arnolphe how one recent summer evening on the balcony she was saluted by

> Un jeune homme bien fait qui, rencontrant ma veüe,
> D'une humble reverence aussitost me salüe;
> Moy, pour ne point manquer a la civilité,
> Je fis la reverence aussi de mon costé;
> Soudain, il me refait une autre reverence,
> Moy, je m'en refais de mesme une autre en diligence . . .[1]

So the bows and curtsies answer each other as the young man passes, returns and passes and returns again.

> Tant que, si sur ce point la nuit ne fût venüe,
> Toûjours comme cela je me serois tenüe,
> Ne voulant point ceder, by recevoir l'ennuy
> Qu'il me pust estimer moins civile que luy . . .[2]

Prince Charming proceeds to bribe Arnolphe's servants. Next evening he ascends the staircase, glorious and conquering at first sight, and the nightingales tune up, and it seems to these young things, in the exquisite phase of some forgotten old French poet, as if a slice of the moon had fallen into their love. And Arnolphe listens grimly to wide-eyed Innocence relating the wonder:

> Il juroit qu'il m'aimoit d'une amour sans seconde,
> Et me disoit des mots les plus gentils du monde,
> Des choses que jamais rien ne peut égaler,
> Et dont, toutes les fois que je l'entends parler
> La douceur me chatoüille et lá-dedans remüe,
> Certain je ne sais quoy dont je suis toute émeüe . . .[3]

At this the old fool winces and mutters aside. What sort of a cross-examination is this, where the examiner suffers all the pain? A very Molièresque bit of comedy follows. 'Did he not

[1] '. . . a good-looking young man, who on seeing me immediately saluted me with a low bow. Not wanting to be behindhand in civility, I curtsied likewise for my part; whereupon he immediately made me another bow, to which I duly replied . . .'

[2] '. . . So that if night had not fallen just then I'd have still been there, not wanting to give in, and hating the idea that he might think me less polite than he was . . .'

[3] 'He swore he loved me with a love above all others. He said the loveliest things in the world to me – things that nothing can ever equal. Every time I hear him say them sweetness thrills me and stirs something in me, I don't know what, which completely shakes me.'

take something from you, Agnès?' The girl blushes and hesitates. With suspicion and anger increasing every moment, Arnolphe presses his question. After considerable fencing she owns up. Yes, Horace did take something from her. What, then? What? What? Eh? What was it? Agnès confesses at length. 'I couldn't help it. He took the ribbon you gave me.' And Arnolphe recovers and mops his aged brow.

One other passage may demonstrate the power with which a cynical elderly man of the theatre (if Molière may not unjustly be thus described) has divined and transmitted the tremulous candour of virginal first-love. Agnès has contrived to send Horace a letter in prose:

> Since I'm just beginning to understand that they've brought me up to be completely ignorant, I'm afraid of saying something which may not be proper, and saying more than I ought to. The truth is I don't know what you've done to me, but I do know that what they're making me do to you hurts me to death. I shall have all the trouble in the world to do without you, and I should be only too happy to be yours. Perhaps it's wrong to say this, but anyway I can't help it . . . Tell me frankly what the truth is (i.e. whether he is sincere or not), because I am very sincere myself. You would be doing me the biggest wrong in the world to deceive me, and I think I should die of misery.

The end is inevitable, and in the last act, with cruelly irresistible logic, Agnès points this out to Arnolphe. 'Is it my fault if I can't love you? Why didn't you make yourself lovable, like him? I never tried to stop you, so far as I know.' 'I did my utmost,' growls Arnolphe, and a peal of silvery laughter can be heard in Agnès' swift riposte:

> Vrayment, il en sçait donc là-dessus plus que vous,
> Car à se faire aymer il n'a point eue de peine.[1]

There is excellent comedy in *L'Escole des Femmes*; the frenzy of Arnolphe, the leg-pulling by Chrysalde, an absurd notary babling in legal jargon, a saucy maidservant named Georgette, first of an engaging line. The piece was vehemently applauded and vehemently attacked, with pen and tongue, by a minority

---

[1] 'Obviously, then, he knows more about these things than you do, because he had no trouble at all in making himself loved.'

which included a rigorist company of *dévots* denouncing a passage in which Arnolphe reminds Agnès that wives breaking solemn vows of fidelity taken before the altar in the sacrament of marriage may qualify for hell. Spoken by a comic old ass threatening the girl with boiling cauldrons, *chaudières bouillantes*, the lines might well be offensive to others than the wholly-pious. They will be remembered against Molière quite soon, when he will select a buffoon of a valet to defend Christianity, in a fashion, against the atheism of Don Juan, and again when he comes to take religious hypocrisy for his theme in *Le Tartufe*. The comedy-stage, as France's leading lawyer was to remind him, is not the place for such diversions.

Within six months Molière replied to attacks on his latest success with a one-act conversation piece in prose, *La Critique de l'Escole des Femmes*, produced at the Palais-Royal on June 1st, 1663, to run – oddly enough, seeing that though amusing enough, nine-tenths of it is artistic 'shop' – for thirty-one performances. In a Parisian drawing-room six ardent playgoers are taking *L'Escole des Femmes* to pieces. They are Élise and Uranie, women of breeding and intelligence, Climène, a featherbrained *précieuse*, a cackling ass of a marquis, unnamed, Lysidas, a rival author, and the Chevalier Dorante, Molière's mouthpiece. It may be easily gathered that the favourable critics, Élise, Uranie and Dorante, get the better of the opposition before the end, and during the process Molière the show-man seizes the opportunity to hand both ends of his discerning public, the Pit and the Court, a bouquet apiece. The most entertaining contribution comes from Lysidas the literary gentleman, decently reluctant to knock a brother-artist but stricken to the heart for Art and his country's sake. Thus Lysidas, mourning in mellow tones the ascendancy of *toutes ces bagatelles* over the true drama:

> Everybody goes for these things nowadays, everybody rushes to see nothing else. You see great works played in frightful solitude, whereas these bits of nonsense draw the whole of Paris. I confess it sometimes makes my heart bleed. It's a shameful thing for France.

Tu parles, coco! The voice is indeed familiar. It drew furious counter-attacks from the current hireling of the Hôtel de

Bourgogne, Edmé Boursault, who detested Molière and saw himself, possibly correctly, as Lysidas, and from Donneau de Visé, another enemy. But De Visé's *La Critique de la Critique* and Boursault's *Portrait du Peintre* alike served chiefly to confirm Molière's utter superiority.

Meanwhile Molière had still to answer the malicious gossip about his private life circulating in Paris. This was not an easy task, some of it – for example, that relating to Armande's capriciousness – being based on truth. Directed at length by the King to reply to the traducers, Molière produced a light comedy-sketch entitled *L'Impromptu de Versailles*, eleven scenes in prose, at Versailles on October 14th, 1663, and at the Palais-Royal on November 4th.

The theme is what is nowadays called 'backstage'. The curtain rises on a desperate situation. A royal order a week beforehand for something new has taken Molière and his company unawares. On the fatal day, with the King and his entourage due to arrive very shortly, Molière's troop have still to know their parts, and their director rends his wig in traditional fashion. The company having at length drifted on the stage, grumbling loudly – Mlles Molière, Du Parc, De Brie, Béjart, Du Croisy, and Hervé, with MM. Brécourt, De La Grange, Du Croisy, La Thorillière, and Béjart – rehearsal begins.[1] Armande, 'La Molière', who played Élise in *La Critique*, is cast for a *satyrique spirituelle*, Molière for a *marquis ridicule*.

The rehearsal itself being the play and merely a vehicle for swipes at the enemy, he swiftly gets to work on the portentous ornaments of the Hôtel de Bourgogne first of all. He was a superb mimic. The imitations of Montfleury (*'excellent acteur'*), Beauchasteau and his wife, Hauteroche, and Villiers, offered to his company as models for the right way to speak verse, must have been excruciatingly funny except to the colleagues concerned, some of whom may have been present. Thence, after some general reflections on the arts of comedy and tragedy (which highly displeased Corneille), and some attempt to get on with the matter allegedly in hand, itself a play about the

---

[1] The two Du Parcs had returned to Molière after the recent death of Jodelet.

theatre, Molière proceeds to tackle Boursault and his fellow-scribblers. Whether the lethal squabbles of actors, authors and others of the Muses' children excite the general public as much as their agents believe is a matter never, perhaps, fully decided. Current onslaughts at any rate afford Molière opportunity for a general declaration on 'this foolish war', and a suggestion that there exists a line to be drawn:

> I shall make no reply whatever to their criticisms and counter-attacks. Let them say the worst possible about my plays, with pleasure . . . Courtesy however has its limits, and there are things which amuse neither the public nor those who provide the topic. With all my heart I offer them (his enemies) my work, my features, my gestures, my words, my tone of voice and my way of speaking, to do with these and say about them whatever they please, if it gives them any advantage. I have no objection whatever, and if it amuses the public I shall be delighted. Granted all this, they should have the grace to leave me the rest, and not to touch on such themes as, I am told, they exploit to attack me in their comedies. And this boon I very civilly beg of the honest gentleman (Boursault) who dabbles in writing for them. This is all the reply they will get from me.

To which Molière's enemies might suggest that (*a*) he was possibly wrong about what amuses the public, and (*b*) he had made no reply worth mentioning, and least of all to scandalous rumours about his *ménage*. A sufficiently concrete reply was Louis XIV's bestowal on him, at the Easter of 1663, of an annual pension of 1,000 livres, the contemporary equivalent of a Legion of Honour cross. In addition, his distinguished friend Boileau, the rising pontiff of contemporary verse, had recently printed a compliment to *L'Escole des Femmes:*

> En vain mille jaloux esprits,
> Molière, osent avec mépris
> Censurer ton plus bel ouvrage . . .[1]

which was itself a decoration. Enmity was now sufficiently answered.

The *Impromptu de Versailles* ends, as it should, with a reprieve. Joseph Béjart, Molière's present utility-man, enters hurriedly

[1] 'In vain, Molière, a thousand jealous spirits presume scornfully to censure your finest work . . .'

at the last moment to announce that the King of his bounty is agreeable to the postponement of the new production in favour of any convenient play at hand. 'Sir, you give me back my life!' breathes Molière, and on his grateful acknowledgment the curtain falls.

CHAPTER THREE

Not long after the *Impromptu* the King took Molière at his word. Like Queen Victoria's consort, whom he otherwise does not greatly resemble, Louis XIV was a good dancer and devoted to this exercise, treading a saraband or a coranto with natural dignity and grace. Modern fiddlers playing the stately dances of Lully, the Couperins, or Rameau, all with the same exquisite tinkle of melancholy in their minor cadences, can still raise the *Grand Siècle* from the dead in a flash. Towards the autumn of 1663, Molière received the order for something new and amusing, with a ballet. In the third entracte of *Le Mariage Forcé*, duly produced at the Louvre on January 20th, 1664, his Majesty took part with the Marquis de Villeroy and two Court ladies in a *pas de quatre*, all four in Egyptian costume.

The King was in his twenty-fifth year, and in full enjoyment of youth and splendour; a true Bourbon in generosity of mind and perpetual susceptibility to women, a man of breeding at all times. Louis' qualities and defects are very fairly balanced in Saint-Simon's well-known pen-portrait fifty years later. But for the handicap of his neglected and unhappy upbringing Louis might have been a much greater man. He took kingship seriously. His celebrated punctuality and his table of degrees for the raising of his hat to subjects of all ranks from the palace charwomen to princes of the blood exemplify his exactitude at all times. Louis XIV may be seen at this moment as a well set-up young man of medium height, with imposing rather than handsome features; a commanding Bourbon nose, a gracious air; cultivated, eminently accessible, kindly, often charming; polite even in anger, enveloped always by a respect-compelling aura which as he grew older, says Saint-Simon, 'imposed silence, even a kind of fear'.[1]

What Molière and nearly all his great contemporaries in letters owed to Louis need hardly be stated. They were as lucky as the *literati* surrounding Caesar Augustus. It is impossible not to admire this splendid Bourbon, with all his faults, and it is permissible to admire him most at the end of his long and dazzling reign, as the Sun King goes down in a cloudbank of humiliations and he resigns himself to a painful death with, as Lucien Romier says, 'that self-control, that majestic imperturbability which were the admirable sides of his character'.

Divested of his Majesty's performance, *Le Mariage Forcé*, which was produced with eight ballet-interludes by Jean-Baptiste Lully at the Palais-Royal on February 15th, and achieved thirteen performances, is not of compelling interest. Another variation on the cuckoldry theme, its three acts and ten scenes in prose are gay enough, but the best of it is stolen unblushingly from Rabelais. As with Panurge, Sganarelle's perpetual anxious cry is '*Seray-je cocu?*', and a scene with two dancing, teasing Egyptian female fortune-tellers might have been lifted almost verbatim from the Third Book of Pantagruel. Thus, being assured after some byplay that he will marry the charming Dorimène, and quite soon, Sganarelle, played by Molière, comes to the point:

SGANARELLE: Excellent, excellent. But tell me – do I run any risk of being a cuckold?
SECOND EGYPTIAN: A cuckold?
SGANARELLE: Yes.
FIRST EGYPTIAN: A *cuckold*?
SGANARELLE: Yes. Shall I be a cuckold?
(The two Egyptians dance, chanting 'La, la, la, la').
SGANARELLE: Damme, that's no answer! Come here. I'm asking you, both of you, if I shall be a cuckold.
SECOND EGYPTIAN: A cuckold? You?
SGANARELLE: Yes, me. Shall I be one?
FIRST EGYPTIAN: You? A *cuckold*?
SGANARELLE: Yes, me. Yes or no?
(The two Egyptians dance and sing as before and go out.)

[1] *Mémoires*, 1714.

SGANARELLE: Devil take those bitches, leaving me in this state! I absolutely must know how my marriage is going to turn out.

Already, like Panurge, Sganarelle has failed to get an answer out of a couple of philosophers, Pancrace the Aristotelian and Marphurius the Pyrrhonian. Now, like Panurge with the astrologer Her Trippa, he resolves to consult a seer. The play then fades into a comic ballet. Sganarelle is mocked, magicked, and beaten, and young Lycaste carries off Dorimène, which might be considered a happy ending for Sganarelle likewise.

This artless romp was the prelude to an immensely elaborate project to which Molière was ordered to contribute. It flowered in the May of the same year. Louis was deeply in thrall to a new mistress, one of Madame's maids of honour, the exquisite Louise-Françoise de la Vallière, Duchesse de Vaujour, whose subsequent thirty-five years of expiation as Soeur Louise de la Miséricorde, a humble Carmelite nun, were to make, as Bossuet said, one of the *merveilles de la Grâce* of the century. To entertain Mlle de la Vallière in the early summer of 1664, the ardent King ordered a great alfresco entertainment – banquets, the comedy, balls, jousts, hunts, masques, ballets and a lottery – at his beloved Versailles, to last a week.

Molière's share in this scintillating Bank-holiday revel cost him something more than the agonies of a harassed author working against time. At the last moment he had to present his impresario-in-chief, the Duc de Saint-Aignan, a keen balletomane and amateur producer, assisted by M. de Vignari, an Italian specialist in complicated stage 'machines', with a makeshift script. Only the first of the five acts of *La Princesse d'Élide*, the centrepiece of the programme, is in verse. The rest are in prose, though he had time to complete all the verses accompanying the ballets and spectacles, called *Les Plaisirs de L'Isle Enchantée*. This discrepancy probably mattered very little amid a whirl of amusements, lovemaking included, enjoyed by the Beau Monde during this carnival; but the spectacle of Armande as a princess of faery, glittering and irresistible, intoxicated by success, surrounded and flattered by the most dashing rakes of the Court, must have given her husband and lover some bad moments.

In the comedy under the fragrant summer night-sky he played Moron, the Princess's buffoon. As the lovelorn Princess ordered him to serve her passion for Euryale, Prince of Ithaca, his eye may have been glumly searching a dazzling audience for some master-seducer like De Guiche or Lorraine or Lauzun (if, as one or two authorities concerned for Armande's reputation assure us, De Guiche happened to be in Warsaw at this moment, there were plenty of gallants to take his place). It must be admitted that licence was in the air. Molière himself was giving the King's liaison every encouragement. Euryale's grave elderly tutor, Arbate, indeed assures the youth more than once that a gallant young prince cannot make love too early or too often.

> Moy vous blasmer, Seigneur, des tendres mouvemens
> Où je vois qu'aujourd'huy panchent vos sentimens?
> Le chagrin des vieux jours ne peut aigrir mon ame
> Contre les doux transports de l'amoureuse flame,
> Et bien que mon sort touche à ses derniers soleils,
> Je diray que l'amour sied bien à vos pareils . . .
> Et qu'il est mal-aisé que sans estre amoureux
> Un jeune prince soit et grand et genereux.[1]

Agreeable advice, reiterated in song by choruses of *aymables personnes* in the silks and satins of Arcadian pastoral:

> Songez de bonne heure à suivre
> Le plaisir de s'enflamer;
> Un coeur ne commence à vivre
> Que du jour qu'il sçait aymer . . .[2]

With everything in this aristocratic saturnalia playing, so to speak, directly into Eros' hands – the tender, starry, many-scented nights of May, the lights and darks, the mystery of the

---

[1] 'What! Can I blame you, Sir, for those tender emotions to which I perceive your heart is turning now? The peevishness of old age cannot sour me towards the sweet transports of amorous flame, and though my life approaches its end I will affirm that lovemaking is well suited to your peers . . . It is impossible for a young prince to be generous and great without being in love.'
[2] Ditto.

great silent forest, the perpetual violins, near or distant, the brilliance of the entertainments, a gay highborn crowd intent on nothing but delight, the feasting and flattery and frivolity, Royalty and Beauty leading the farandole – with all this one can scarcely blame a professional charmer like 'La Molière' for having her dainty head turned, though Armande may not have had so many lovers in these seven days as her friends in the theatre averred.

Performances of *Les Fascheux* and *Le Mariage Forcé* were also given during the week. On the last evening but one Molière offered the first three acts of an unfinished new play in verse called *Le Tartufe*, exploiting an entirely new comedy character, a religious hypocrite thus named. The King, who is believed to have encouraged Molière when first consulted, enjoyed the piece, as did most of the Court; but it outraged the Queen Mother, Anne of Austria, and many others of the devout. Molière had apparently made little or no distinction between real piety and false. Considering these and other protests, Louis forbade public performance before revision. When finished, he added, the piece must be submitted to persons capable of judging the issues involved.

This check took Molière considerably aback, for his theatre urgently needed a new piece. He begged the King at Fontainebleau to let him produce *Le Tartufe* as it was. Louis refused. As the play stood, the risk of offence was too great to be undertaken by the Most Christian King of France, *fille aînée de l'Église*. A Papal envoy, Cardinal Fabio Chigi, was due imminently at Fontainebleau on a diplomatic mission, and Louis gladly passed the responsibility. Having charmed the Roman diplomat by a performance of *La Princesse d'Élide*, Molière was commanded to read the three acts of *Le Tartufe* to him in the King's presence. It went off perfectly. Possibly Molière skated over thin ice with sufficient skill to deceive a foreign ear? Possibly Cardinal Chigi was not very conversant with any other French but diplomatic? At all events he had no criticisms to make, and Louis XIV judged that Molière might proceed. The completed play in five acts was given before the Princess Palatine and Condé ('the Great') at Raincy on November 20th,

1664, and instantly raised a storm. Suppressed four years previously as an illegal society, the Company of the Blessed Sacrament, which may or may not have been indirectly attacked in *Le Tartufe*, was still able to organize strong opposition, and a pamphlet by a Parisian curé denounced Molière as an enemy of religion. In the face of this the King gave way and lapsed into vague verbal promises with recommendations of further revision. The first public performance of a new version re-titled *L'Imposteur* will take place on August 5th, 1667, with further consequences to be surveyed in their place. We return to 1665.

With the destiny of *Le Tartufe* in the air, and desperately needing something immediate to fill the gap, Molière laid hands on a theme which had already inspired several adaptations all over Europe. Some fifty years earlier a Spanish playwright-monk, Tirso de Molina, in religion Fray Gabriel Téllez of the Order of Our Lady of Mercy, had produced a drama called *El Burlador de Sevilla* ('The Playboy of Seville'), based on a legend long since current in Andalucia. Its popularity soon became international. The Don Juan of Tirso de Molina is a character at times almost comparable psychologically with a Quixote, a Hamlet, or a Faust. A couple of recent and less vital French versions were available by 1664. A burlesque on the theme had been played in Paris by Giuseppe Biancolelli's Italians. Molière had probably seen it.

He produced *Dom Juan* on February 15th, 1665, at the Palais Royal, five acts in prose, and took it off after fifteen performances, for good; seemingly on the King's advice, though public reception had been favourable enough.

It is a breathless, slightly incoherent mixture of comedy and farce, betraying haste in its composition, changing its background in every act, and strewn with loot from predecessors. Molière's Don is a sedulously diabolical character, all of a piece and sufficiently described by his valet Sganarelle in the opening scene:

> ... the greatest villain the world has ever seen, a madman, a dog, a devil, a Turk, a heretic, believing neither in Heaven, Hell, or the Loup-Garou (the traditional bogey of the nursery), living his

life like a real brute-beast; an epicurean swine, a real Sardanapalus, who shuts his ears to every Christian remonstrance and treats all our beliefs as tomfooleries.

The model, it has been universally surmised, was almost certainly one or other, or some half-dozen, of the insolent Court roués who had been laying siege, perhaps successfully, to Armande during the recent Versailles junketings; in which case *Dom Juan* is a work of jealousy and vengeance. There were more than a few of the Juan breed among Louis XIV's courtiers, though he himself was certainly not of their number, as his devoutly penitent will and testament alone may demonstrate. Later in the reign the Black Mass itself would be celebrated behind locked doors by the apostate Abbé Guibourg for Mme de Montespan's satanist clique. Less disgusting were the vagaries of noblemen like De Guiche, Lauzun, Roquelaure, Bussy-Rabutin, de Nevers, the Chevalier of Lorraine and the like, though blasphemous enough. Being of their breed, Molière's Don Juan differs fundamentally from Molina's. *Trivial y realista* is the verdict of a modern Spanish critic, Romera-Navarro, whereas Molina invests his Don with something of a sombre grandeur. In the thick of his villainies the Spanish rake never doubts the justice of God and merely keeps postponing reform; his cry might almost be '*Mañana!*' The last reply of Molière's Don Juan to the implorations of his terrified valet, on the other hand, is to shake his first at Heaven. 'No! No! Whatever happens, no one shall ever say of me that I was capable of repentance!'

For this and other reasons Molina's is far the stronger play, opening dramatically as it does by night on an unlighted chamber in the King of Naples' palace, with the voice of the Duchess Isabela heard in the darkness:

'Duke Octavio, you can go out more safely this way.'

A man's voice answers:

'Duchess, I vow again to marry you.'

But it is not Duke Octavio, her betrothed, it is Don Juan Tenorio of Seville impersonating him, and after the Duchess, discovering this, has frantically called for lights and the guard ('*Ay, perdido honor!*') he leaps blithely over the balcony to resume his diversions elsewhere. Molière on the other hand raises the curtain on Sganarelle, the Don's valet, praising the virtues of snuff and proceeding to describe his master's iniquities to the equerry of Donna Elvira, Don Juan's discarded wife, though to this functionary they could surely be no news. As 'theatre' the monk's opening certainly excels.

To this same Sganarelle, the clown of Molière's piece, falls the task, as already observed, of defending religion against the Don and proving *inter alia* the existence of God, an attempt moving Don Juan and the pit to unrestrained mirth, especially since Sganarelle ends by falling on his nose. This in itself was calculated to produce trouble for Molière, and did. He invited even more by making Don Juan feign conversion, meanwhile praising hypocrisy to his valet in a long tirade.

> There's no shame in it now. Hypocrisy is the fashionable vice. All fashionable vices pass for virtues. The man of virtue is the best of all characters one can assume nowadays, and your professional hypocrite enjoys marvellous advantages . . . How many men do you think I know who have cleverly covered up the slips of their young days with this trick, and turned the cloak of religion into a shield which allows them, in this respectable guise, to be the worst men in the world?

And the Don proposes to avenge himself on his enemies by exploiting his pretended zeal for religion. The basic insinuation, whether Molière intended it or not, is that in the France of St Vincent de Paul and St John Eudes the hypocrites are a majority. It was, and is, the case against the master on this issue that he fails to provide Don Juan with an opponent of equal intellectual calibre. The same will apply to *Le Tartufe*, where wickedness is clever and the good are perfect fools. If he invited trouble by loading the dice in this fashion Molière had only himself to blame, one feels. Maurice Donnay sums up his Don Juan very reasonably. This fantastic egotist and monster of vice has no need to fall back on Nietzsche; he is simply 'a pathological case and a candidate for general paralysis of the insane'. The missing moral to the play may be supplied from Molina's, where the statue of the dead Commander has the last word:

Esta es justicia de Dios:
'Quien tal hace, que tal pague'.

'This is Divine Justice – what one has done, one pays for.'

There is a good, if incongruous, comic interlude between Don Juan and a creditor, the tradesman Monsieur Dimanche, some of which Congreve filched for a scene in *Love for Love*. Viewing the Don in harmlessly playful mood is rather like a glimpse of Donatien Alphonse François, Marquis de Sade, engrossed in a game of spillikins, and evokes the same light grue. A more significant comedy-scene opens Act III. To escape an avenging body of rustics after attempting a couple of light seductions in their midst, Don Juan disguises himself as a countryman and Sganarelle assumes a shabby black gown discarded by a doctor of medicine, jocularly assuring his master that he has already issued a few good prescriptions. 'Why not, after all?' is the Don's comment. 'They've no more share in curing disease than you have.' At which Sganarelle is taken aback despite himself.

SGANARELLE: What, sir? Have you no belief in medicine either?
DON JUAN: It's one of the world's biggest delusions.

The opening shot has been fired against the Faculty of Medicine. As Molière's malady proves less and less curable it will develop into a satirical bombardment on the grand scale, to be more or less continuous till his death.

Sooner or later, no doubt, he would have got around to the Faculty in any case. The Doctor of Medicine from Bologna is a stock standby of the Commedia dell'Arte; a solemn, infallible gaby and – naturally – cuckold in his huge black hat and long gown, gravely stroking his professional beard, muttering incomprehensibilities in pseudo-Latin jargon, and despatching his patients serenely one by one to the grave. At the beginning of 1664 Molière was himself in the Faculty's clutches, thanks to recent overwork and an increasingly worrying chest-cough which forced him in August of that year to hand over his role as 'orator' of the troop to La Grange, now better fitted than he to battle with noisy audiences. Concerning his favourite doctor, Mauvilain by name, a later exchange between Molière and his

King, which would soon be going the rounds of Paris, voices his attitude towards all of them.

'What is Mauvilain doing for you nowadays, Molière?'
'Well, Sir, we discuss things, he orders medicines for me, I don't take them, and I'm getting better.'

Dr Mauvilain was to prove highly useful to Molière in another way, at any rate. He was a rancorous and aggressive type, at perpetual odds with his Faculty, which had twice suspended him, and only too pleased to quote samples of his rivals' ignorance and imbecility for an ever-appreciative auditor. Molière meanwhile was not getting better, and his phsyical condition was not improved by increasing tension at home. In February 1664, Armande bore him a son, christened Louis, to whom the King stood godfather. The child died seven months later, depriving Molière of what may have seemed the only hope of saving their marriage. But he was allowed little time to brood. On Friday, August 14th, his troop became by decree *La Troupe du Roy*, with a 6,000-livre annual retainer, and within a month the King set him to work again. On September 15th, 1665, *L'Amour Médecin* ('Doctor Love') was played at Versailles. A week later the Parisians were flocking to the Palais-Royal to laugh themselves sore at a piece in which the entire Faculty of Medicine is mocked with a verve still fresh and alluring. The doctors will thenceforth need many of their own sedatives and salves.[1]

It is too light a piece to rank among the great comedies, but it bubbles and sparkles with wicked fun, perhaps, more than any. The top brass of the Harley Street of contemporary Paris figures in it, recognisably, under barely-disguised names from the Greek invented for his friend, it seems, by Boileau, and either Dr Mauvilain or one of his predecessors had briefed his patient on the medical circus to good purpose. Four leading specialists have been called in by Sganarelle, a wealthy Parisian

[1] Grimarest, quoting Parisian gossip, has a curious theory for Molière's attitude towards the Faculty. An avaricious doctor's wife from whom the Molières took apartments for a time raised their rent, began a feud with Armande thereby, and had to be turned out of the theatre. It does not seem a convincing reason for an onslaught lasting nearly ten years.

burgess, to examine his daughter Lucinde, who is determined to marry young Clitandre against her father's will and is shamming a mysterious dumb disease accordingly. The consultation scene is inimitable. Having pouched their fees, the four eminent doctors sit for a while in dignified silence, coughing. M. des Fonandrés (from φόνος, murder, and ἀνδρός, man disguising the personality of Dr Élie Desfougerais, physician to the King) then opens the ball.

M. DES FONANDRÉS: Paris is becoming extraordinarily large, With a good practice one has to take in a lot of ground.

M. TOMÈS: I don't mind saying I have a first-class mule for that purpose. You'd hardly believe the amount of road he has to cover every day.

M. DES FONANDRÉS: I've got a marvellous horse, an absolutely tireless creature.

M. TOMÈS: D'you know what my mule has done today? My first visit was down opposite the Arsenal, from the Arsenal to the end of the Faubourg St Germain, from the Faubourg St Germain to the bottom of the Marais, then to the Porte St Honore, from there (etc., etc., etc.).

M. Tomès (τομή, incision) is Dr Dauquin, another Royal physician, famous for his passion for bleeding. Of the two others, Dr Macroton (μακρος, long and τόνος, tone) is Dr Guenaut, the Queen's longwinded physician, and Dr Bahys (βαύζειν, to bark) is spluttering Dr Esprit, another of the Royal medical staff, an apostle of antimony and emetics. Small-talk exhausted, the conference merges at length into an undignified brawl over the treatment of a recent patient. Finally:

M. TOMÈS: Remember the man you sent to his grave not long since.

M. DES FONANDRÉS: Recall the lady you despatched to the other world three days ago.

And the bemused Sganarelle duly receives his money's worth:

M. TOMÈS: If you don't have your daughter bled at once she's a dead girl. (Exit)

M. DES FONANDRÉS: If you have her bled she won't live another quarter of an hour. (Exit)

81

A treacherous colleague had enlightened Molière to some purpose on the great quarrel at that moment dividing the Faculty, the Bleeders versus the Purgers. Following the conference at Sganarelle's house comes an equally hilarious special meeting convened by a certain redoubtable M. Filerin, representing the Faculty, to berate all concerned for quarrelling in the presence of the layman.[1] 'For Heaven's sake,' snaps M. Filerin in effect, 'bear in mind that the power of the profession depends on the majority's chief obsession, and don't let the side down.' One deduces that this is the essence of the Oath of Hippocrates. M. Filerin sums up in a moving peroration:

> Man's chief foible is his love of life. From this we of the Faculty profit with our portentous jargon (*pompeux galimatias*), and we well know how to take advantage of the veneration with which fear of death surrounds our trade. Let us then cherish that degree of esteem which human weakness bestows on us, and act all together, where patients are concerned, in annexing any happy success and throwing the responsibility for all blunders on Nature. And let us not be foolish enough to destroy the fortunate issues of an error which provides so many of us with a living.

The belligerents then make it up, on their own terms. If Tomès will pass Des Fonandré's darling emetics for the patient in question, Des Fonandrés will pass anything Tomès suggests for the next case. M. Filerin benignantly approves, and the scene is over.

It is not too difficult to foresee the dénouement of this merry charade. Presenting himself in disguise as a brilliant young specialist with a new treatment, foreshadowing modern psychiatry ('My method is to heal mind before body'), Clitandre prevails on Sganarelle not merely to approve the mock-betrothal of himself and Lucinde, but to accept the appearance of a notary with pen and parchment as an essential part of the cure. The marriage-contract duly signed and witnessed, Sganarelle learns, too late, that the soi-disant specialist and his charming patient have eloped 'to finish the rest of the marriage'. A ballet-interlude ends each act; a dance of doctors, a dance of

[1] The significance of 'Filerin' has not been established.

charlatans and their assistant *trivelins* and scaramouches, and a final trio sung and danced by the figures of Comedy, Ballet and Music. *L'Amour Médecin* has always been prized as a little jewel-box of wit, fancy and style. The 'Notice to the Reader' prefacing the printed edition is fully entitled to a touch of complacency in addition.

> This is nothing but the merest sketch, a little impromptu which the King was good enough to want for his diversion. It is the most hurried of all the pieces his Majesty has commanded of me, and when I say that it was proposed, written, conned and played in five days, I speak nothing but the truth . . .

Five days! It amused Paris for twenty-six consecutive performances, a highly successful run of the period, and has continued to amuse numbers untold for three centuries; always, possibly, excepting members of the medical profession, whose looks in 1665 must certainly have matched their gowns. When *L'Amour Médecin* was packing the Palais-Royal there were about 150 doctors in the city of Paris, making, as someone has remarked, enough noise for 1,500. A tight and jealous corporation, as in any age, the doctors of Louis XIV's France swore by the sacred implements of the trade, the lancet, the catheter and the syringe, wrote a variety of fantastic and complicated prescriptions, believed, with their contemporary, the great Van Helmont, that (e.g.) a foul shirt sealed with fermenting grain in a glass vessel at a given temperature will in due course breed live mice, and maintained a terrifying solidarity. They had good memories also. They would not forget their grinning new enemy at the Palais-Royal, and to do Molière justice he was to take great pains henceforth to keep his memory green among *MM. les Médecins*.

He was now working on a supreme and lovely masterpiece inspired by infatuation for a wife who did not love him, and his marriage was swiftly deteriorating. In August 1665, Armande bore him a second child, a girl christened Esprit-Madeleine, the godparents at St Eustache being Messire Esprit-Rémond de Modène and Madeleine Béjart, who had resumed their old easy liaison. Nobody has yet succeeded in explaining the baptismal function of M. de Modène, except that it might have been an attempt to sidetrack slander still busily attributing Armande's origin to Molière. Their new child in any case made no difference. By the autumn of 1665, or shortly afterwards, Molière and Armande had quarrelled for the last time and were living apart – and no wonder, cried half Paris, since she had been deceiving him shamelessly ever since Versailles. This may be exaggeration. The separation lasted five years nevertheless.

CHAPTER FOUR

For the next five years Molière and his wife were to meet only at the theatre, Armande returning to live with Madame Béjart and Molière either to his lodgings in the Place du Palais-Royal or to apartments he had taken in 1664, after the suspension of *Le Tartufe*, in the quiet little riverside village of Auteuil; today part of the smart 16th Arrondissement, then in open country, on the edge of the Forest of Rouvray, of which the remains are known as the Bois de Boulogne.

Here Molière occupied the ground-floor, with access to the park, of a house near the river belonging to the Sieur de Beaufort, a retired official of the Duke of Orleans' household.[1] One room was sub-let to Chapelle for company's sake. Inevitable depressions inflicted on a couple of dyed-in-the-wool Parisians by what Tchehov's fashionable actress in *The Seagull* calls 'this sweet country boredom' ('Oh, what can be more boring?') were mitigated by frequent all-night supper-parties, one of which is described with relish by Grimarest. At this *agape* everybody except Molière, who had had nothing but a glass of milk and had gone to bed hours before, was so drunk, the eminent Boileau included, that towards 3 a.m. they decided to drown themselves forthwith in the Seine, flowing conveniently at their door. At the last moment somebody thought of informing their host, who came downstairs in his dressing-gown and reproached them.

[1] The site is at the angle of the Rue de Rémusat and the Rue Théophile Gautier.

'Drowning yourselves without me? I thought you were friends of mine?'

'He's quite right,' said Chapelle after a pause. 'Come and drown with us, then, Jean-Baptiste.'

'Gently! gently!' said their host. 'Why drown ourselves at night, as if we were desperate or drunk? No. In the morning, towards eight or nine, before breakfast and before the world, we'll all throw ourselves in head first.'

Everybody approved, everybody went to bed, and to-morrow, as the old saying goes, was another day. It seems that Molière not infrequently retired to bed early and sober on these occasions. His moods at home, as at the tavern, varied from voluble gaiety to the blackest of melancholy trances. In one of these latter moods one day, apparently in 1667, as he was musing under the trees at Auteuil, he was moved to discuss Armande with Chapelle. 'I was born,' Molière began, 'with the strongest inclinations to tenderness, and as I believe my efforts in this way could by mere force of habit inspire her with the kind of feeling that time cannot destroy, I overlooked nothing to achieve this.' A curious illusion for a man with such experience of women. He continues:

As she was quite young when I married her I did not notice her plaguy inclinations, and believed myself to be a little less un-fortunate than most men in the same position. Marriage failed to cool my passion, but I found such indifference in her that I began to realize my precautions had been useless, and that the utmost she felt for me was far from what I should need to be happy. I reproached myself with a delicacy which seemed absurd in a husband, and attributed to her moods what was actually the result of her lack of tenderness for me.

He proceeds to describe a violent quarrel over the Comte de Guiche, one of the string of lovers awarded Armande by her enemy of *La Fameuse Comédienne*, and by half Paris. He then resumes his sombre plaint. All his tenderness and patience have not changed Armande in the least, and his sufferings are a matter for pity. He has now come to the point when every-thing in the world has some connection with her in his heart. He is obsessed with her entirely. The mere sight of her throws him into a transport and deprives him of the power to think. He has no eyes henceforth except for her charms. 'Don't you think I've reached the limit of madness?' he asks Chapelle sardonically. He gets nothing but a few vaguely optimistic banalities from his epicurean friend, a frivolous egotist with a total lack of understanding. 'I can see *you've* never loved anything as yet,' says Moliere bitterly at last. The scene rings so true that it is disturbing to find a few suspicious authorities dismissing this talk with Chapelle as a literary tour-de-force by the unknown author of *La Fameuse Comédienne*, its only source.

Grimarest, however, has a confidence-story as well; a later and rival version, in which Molière, discussing Armande with two other old friends, Dr Rouhault and the painter Mignard, lays most of the blame on his own jealous and difficult temperament and leaves Armande practically spotless.

> Being a hundred times more reasonable than I, she wants to enjoy life agreeably, and being assured by her innocence, she disdains to submit herself to the precautions I demand. I mistake this negligence for contempt. I would like a few signs of affection in order to believe she has the same for me, and I could wish there were more propriety in her behaviour. But my wife, being always free and easy in this way (which would be devoid of all suspicion for any man less pernicketty than I am) leaves me without pity to my worries. Being concerned, like all women, with nothing but the need to charm all and sundry, she laughs at my weakness.

Trop de fleurs, perhaps? Grimarest is replying to *La Fameuse Comédienne*, which makes Armande a spoilt, arrogant trollop of the choicest. After the heady success of *La Princesse d'Élide*, for example, she develops a violent passion for the Comte de Guiche, and finding it received with indifference by that haughty rake, flings herself into the ready arms of Lauzun, with a young Guards officer and a few other gallants helping to console her. Meanwhile her current lover, the dissolute *commanditaire* – Abbé de Richelieu, grand-nephew of the Cardinal, has intercepted a letter of hers written to De Guiche, and has been kind enough to show it to Molière. A terrific domestic scene ensues. Armande admits a passion for De Guiche, but swears it has led to nothing, and Molière believes and forgives her. Not long afterwards he is warned by wellwishers that his wife is deceiving him again, and explodes. Armande denies everything furiously, weeps, raves, swoons, and Molière has eventually to beg her pardon. This time she counter-attacks, accusing him of still carrying on his affair with Catherine de Brie; which in fact he is, having returned to her long since for consolation. After a few more dramatic scenes, very good for their art, in which Armande reveals a growing aversion for her husband, the pair decide to separate without legal formalities, and do so.

How much of this spite-inspired farrago is true remains undiscoverable, like the identity of the author. The literary style – especially that of the second half, by a different hand – is quite admirable, for which reason it has been attributed tentatively to either Chapelle, Racine, or La Fontaine; also to a couple of actresses, Mlles Guyot and Boudin, to an actor named Rosemont, and one or two other colleagues of the theatre. Racine, though Molière broke with him in 1665, and La Fontaine may be discounted immediately. In 1688, the year of publication of *La Fameuse Comédienne*, Racine had been out of this kind of world for eleven years, a convert to the most rigid Jansenist piety. La Fontaine, a lax but amiable character, was incapable of stabbing a friend in the back, dead or alive, and never hurt anyone if he could help it. Chapelle remains a possible candidate, but certain graces of expression, and above all the ruthless, exquisite venom of *La Fameuse Comédienne* and its intimate knowledge of the *type cabotine*, point to a feminine and a theatrical hand. Some of it, incidentally, is true.

In these unnerving conditions Molière put the finishing touches to an enduring masterpiece. He had recently, in addition, received a double blow from his friend Racine, his junior by seventeen years, whose first play, *La Thébaïde*, he produced in 1664. A fortnight after his production of Racine's new tragedy, *Alexandre*, Molière to his astonishment found it being played simultaneously at the Hôtel de Bourgogne. Dissatisfied with Molière's production, Racine had simply gone over to the rival company without notice, and, what was worse, had taken his mistress Marquise du Parc, one of Molière's leading ladies, with him. It was an act of treachery impossible in the theatre today, and sufficiently brutal to drive the overburdened Molière frantic. Their friendship was over for good.

A little more bitterness may have been distilled into the closing scenes of *Le Misantrope* thereby. There was a great deal of actuality in it already. Armande, idealized, obviously sat for Célimène. Molière, idealized, is to a very large extent the tortured Alceste. Catherine de Brie is certainly Éliante, his consoler, and Chapelle supplied a fair amount of Philinte. But when *Le Misantrope* opens at the Palais-Royal on June 4th, 1666, it will be perceived that the squalid quarrels of the Molière *ménage* have been transmuted into golden and timeless magic.

Book IV

CHAPTER ONE

Up and down the drawing-room of a Parisian *élégante* a dark-browed man of quality named Alceste is pacing in a rage. He is frequently in a rage. The house belongs to a frivolous and enchanting young widow named Célimène. Alceste is fatally in love with her, ravaged by doubts of her professed feelings for him, savagely jealous of every rival for her hand. He is further handicapped by a rugged and surly virtue perpetually at odds with a world less upright and inflexible than he. A moral theologian could indict him almost at sight for the sin of pride. Like a prototype at Court, the ex-Calvinist Marquis de Montausier, on whom Molière partly drew (the Marquis was highly flattered), Alceste is an object for polite titters. But he is also a figure strangely appealing in his capacity for inviting and enduring pain. Could one, like the tender Éliante, his friend, go so far as to call him *noble et heroïque*? Heroic, at any rate; charging a universe of red rags head down, like a magnificently wrongheaded Miura bull.

As he paces to and fro at curtain-rise his other friend, Philinte, trying to soothe him, is suddenly turned on and accused of being a liar and a skunk. It seems that a moment after embracing a Court acquaintance with protestations of friendship and offers of service, Philinte could not recall his name. 'You should die of pure shame!' snarls Alceste.

> Morbleu! c'est une chose indigne, lâche, infame,
> De s'abaisser ainsi jusqu'à trahir son ame;
> Et, si par un malheur j'en avois fait autant,
> Je m'irois de regret pendre tout à l'instant.[1]

[1] 'My God, it's ignoble, it's cowardly, it's infamous to demean oneself like that, to the extent of betraying one's soul! If I were ever unlucky enough to have done it I'd go out and hang myself in remorse a moment later.'

'It seems no hanging-matter to me' observes the genial Philinte, a philosopher who takes Vanity Fair as he finds it and is no more shocked by egotism and treachery than by

> des vautours affamez de carnage,
> Des singes mal-faisans et des loups pleins de rage.[1]

If you live in society, Philinte points out, you must observe its usages. Another snarl from Alceste. No! Plain speech and total frankness, whatever the consequences! And Philinte raises amused eyebrows. What! Would Alceste risk informing the elderly Émilie, for instance, that her efforts to paint herself young are a public scandal? Yes, Alceste would. Really? And to assure Dorilas that he is the world's biggest bore with his perpetual bragging about his family? Most certainly. 'You're joking!' says Philinte, but Alceste is not.

> Je ne me moque point,
> Et je vais n'épargner personne sur ce poinct.
> Mes yeux sont trop blessez, et la cour et la ville
> Ne m'offrent rien qu'objets à m'echaufer la bile:
> J'entre en une humeur noire, en un chagrin profond,
> Quand je vois vivre entr'eux les hommes comme ils font...
> Je ne puis plus tenir, j'enrage, et mon dessein
> Est de rompre en visiere à tout le genre humain.[2]

By the end of the opening scene we know what to expect of Alceste, on social ethics a perfectionist of almost lunar fantasy, who might profitably have looked up St Thomas Aquinas on the three degrees of the lie.[3] We are prepared therefore in advance for most of his misfortunes in the play. We know he will lose his forthcoming lawsuit, quite unjustly, and with great art Molière does not bother to mention what his lawsuit is about. We know he will very nearly have to fight Oronte,

[1] '... vultures starving for carnage, malevolent apes, and raging wolves.'
[2] 'I am not joking in the least and I'm sparing nobody in this matter. My eyes are too wounded. At Court and in town alike I'm offered nothing but spectacles which stir my bile. When I see men living as they do I fall into a black mood and deep anger ... I can't stand it any longer. It enrages me. I propose to lash out at mankind in general.'
[3] Namely the lie jocose, the lie officious, or designed to help, and the lie pernicious, or designed to harm; the first two being sometimes venial, the last one always a mortal sin.

the man of fashion, for damning his cherished sonnet (which took Oronte only a quarter of an hour to write), and that even when summoned before the Court marshals to settle their quarrel he will not give in. Philinte reports his reply to that august body with the driest of relish.

> 'Je le tiens galant homme en toutes les manières,
> Homme de qualité, de mérite et de coeur,
> Tout ce qu'il vous plaira, mais fort méchant autheur.
> Je loüeray, si l'on veut, son train et sa dépense,
> Son adresse à cheval, aux armes, à la danse,
> Mais, pour loüer ses vers, je suis son serviteur . . .'[1]

And Alceste turns to Oronte:

> 'Monsieur, je suis fasché d'estre si difficile,
> Et, pour l'amour de vous, je voudrais de bon coeur
> Avoir trouve tantost vostre sonnet meilleur.'[2]

And after the formal embrace, ordered by the court, he stalks out. It is quite obvious that he will never win the adorable Célimène, even after his three rivals, having discovered her to be a two-faced little baggage, leave him alone in the field. We know in short, even thus early, that this periwigged Quixote is going to lose every battle, and even thus early we are aware that the spectacle will not always be amusing. Molière turns his austere, impossible crank into a figure of such compelling pathos that Alceste captures our sympathy, and even a sort of affection, from the beginning.

And Célimène . . .

She is gay and golden and frivolous and just twenty years old. If *Le Misantrope* were a play of today she would naturally have been at one time or another the mistress of all four of her suitors, Alceste, Oronte, and the two marquis-fops Acaste and Clitandre; possibly of Philinte as well. But this was not the convention of 1666. The part was written by Molière for

---

[1] 'I esteem him a man of gallantry in every way, a man of quality, of merit, and of heart – everything you please, but a thoroughly wicked author. If you wish, I'll praise his style of living, his munificence, his skill in horsemanship, arms, and dancing. But when it comes to praising his verse . . . I'm his humble servant.'

[2] 'Sir, it grieves me to be so difficult. For love of you I wish with all my heart I could have found your sonnet just now a better one.'

Armande, and through five acts there is no possibility of assuming, though Célimène is described in the list of characters as *amante d'Alceste*, and Alceste and Oronte each figure as *amant de Célimène*, that the operative word could be taken in its modern sense. Among her other gifts Célimène has a mischievous zest for making fun of her acquaintances behind their backs, doing no great harm, and in a verbal duel, for example with the spiteful prude Arsinoé, she can use a dainty tongue most effectively. Her feeling for Alceste is difficult to define, even to herself. Eliante says as much to Philinte:

Comment pouvoir juger s'il est vray qu'elle l'aime?
Son coeur de ce qu'il sent n'est pas bien seur luy-même.[1]

Whatever she feels it is certainly not love as Alceste knows it. The gratification of an *élégante* at the enslaving of a bear of merit; fascination and thrills, mixed with trepidation, at the purring of the monster, liable to merge into a growl at any moment; a kind of half-disdainful affection for a victim so hopelessly stricken – this would seem to sum up Célimène's feeling not unfairly, and at their first encounter in the play (Act II, Sc. 1) we are allowed to guess that in rare moments of lucidity Alceste is well aware that this is all he will ever get from her. '*Morbleu! faut-il que je vous aime!*' The celebrated line is usually declaimed or boomed in a burst of uncontrollable fury and desperation. Murmured by the deep voice of an artist like Jacques Copeau, half in pity for his poor weak fool of a heart, half in a kind of sardonic wonder at its antics, these seven words were revelatory as a lightning-flash.

Célimène's bear, newly wounded, is soon to roar in formidable wise. Having been invited by the odious Arsinoé at the end of Act III to scan a letter of Célimène's addressed to Oronte, Alceste rushes off with it and confronts the astonished Célimène early in Act IV in a state of frenzy. 'What is all this about?' she asks wide-eyed, with half-opened fan. She then learns that the anger of Heaven, nay Hell itself has produced no viler thing than she.

[1] How can one judge if it is true that she loves him? Her own heart is not very sure of what it feels.

> . . . le sort, les démons, et le Ciel en courroux
> N'ont jamais rien produit de si méchant que vous!

Which seems a trifle excessive. The letter to Oronte is blameless enough, and the charming creature is surely at liberty to write to whom she chooses. However, the fury of her bear frightens her. She tries hastily to lie her way out, fails, turns finally defiant, admits esteem for Oronte, and tells Alceste he can go if he likes; whereupon Alceste surrenders at once with a great cry.

> Ciel! rien de plus cruel peut-il estre inventé?
> Et jamais coeur fut-il de la sorte traité? . . .[1]

Twenty lines of pain, and the steady drip of heart's blood heard in every line. He knows too well he cannot break his chain. The sombre magnificence of the verse is untranslatable.

> Ah! que vous sçavez bien icy contre moy-meme,
> Perfide, vous servir de ma foiblesse extréme,
> Et ménager pour vous l'excés prodigieux
> De ce fatal amour né de vos traistres yeux!
> Défendez-vous au moins d'un crime qui m'accable,
> Et cessez d'affecter d'estre envers moy coupable;
> Rendez-moy, s'il se peut, ce billet innocent,
> A vous prester les mains ma tendresse consent;
> Efforcez – vous icy de paroistre fidelle,
> Et je m'efforceray, moy, de vous croire telle.[2]

Célimène is relieved; even, perhaps, touched. 'You're quite crazy with your outbursts of jealousy,' she says severely. 'You don't deserve to be loved by anybody.' And she reminds him that he has received *de mes sentimens l'obligeante asseurance*, which in modern terms implies that at some time or other she has allowed him to assume that he has a good chance of winning

[1] Heavens, could any greater cruelty be invented? Was ever heart treated like this before?

[2] Ah, my perfidious one, how well you know to employ my utter weakness against me, to exploit the monstrous excess of this love, this fatal love, born of your false eyes! At least clear yourself of a crime which staggers me. Pretend no more to be guilty towards me. Prove to me, if you possibly can, that this letter is harmless – my tenderness is ready to give you every help. Force yourself here and now to seem faithful to me, and I will force myself to believe you so.

her. Which assurance, retorts Alceste bitterly, may be merely fine words meaning nothing at all.

> Vous me trompez sans doute avec des mots si doux.

Then Alceste says passionately that he could wish her to lose beauty, charm, rank, fortune – everything on earth, so that he could know the joy of holding her by his devouring love alone. 'An odd way of wishing me well!' she says, laughing merrily, and the entry of a footman interrrupts and ends the tension.

It is in the next – fifth and last – act, that the dénouement arrives, so far as *Le Misantrope* can be said to have one. Like Alceste, Oronte is impatient for an answer. The time has come, they agree, for Célimène to choose between them once and for all. At this moment the two youthful marquesses arrive, tittering with triumphant malice. Each flourishes a letter written by Célimène to the other. The letter to Clitandre, which Acaste proceeds to read aloud with appropriate smirks, shrugs and comments, reveals a Célimène as careless with pen as with tongue. She is complaining of the tiresome character of certain of her male acquaintance, among them Acaste (in the other letter it is Clitandre), Oronte, and 'the man in green ribbons'. And Alceste listens grimly to his love's prattle to an enemy behind his back:

> As for the man in green ribbons, he amuses me sometimes with his brusque ways and his sulky bad temper, but there are a hundred moments when he seems to me the biggest bore in the world . . .

When Oronte and the fops have retired, with frigid dignity and cuttingly polite farewells, Alceste begins with an effort to speak. Célimène interrupts him. Yes, yes, she says, he has the right to say anything to her he likes, he has the right to hate her. Alceste's answering grimace may be meant for a smile.

> Hé! le puis-je, traistresse?
> Puis-je ainsi triompher de toute ma tendresse?
> Et, quoy qu'avec ardeur je veüille vous haïr,
> Trouvay-je un coeur en moy tout prest à m'obeïr?[1]

---

[1] 'Ha! – but can I, my faithless one? Can I triumph over all my tenderness like that? However ardently I might long to hate you, would I find in me a heart to obey?'

He can still forgive her, he says, if she will accept his final terms. He is resolved to fly all human society and take refuge for the rest of his days in the desert – which in seventeenth-century Parisian society usually meant a country estate anywhere outside a fifty-mile radius of the capital – and she must share his exile. Célimène looks up, startled and shocked. He is surely not expecting her to retire from the world at her age? Oh yes, he is. If she makes him the only reparation possible, what can the world matter to her?

It matters of course a great deal. Who can blame a delicious butterfly for turning pale under her rouge? She is only twenty, she pitifully reminds her ogre; perfectly willing now to marry him, but –

> La solitude effraye une ame de vingt ans;
> Je ne sens point la mienne assez grande, assez forte,
> Pour me résoudre à prendre un dessein de la sorte . . .[1]

So Alceste turns on her for the last time, grinding his teeth. 'At this moment my heart detests you! Since you can't find your all in me, as I find my all in you, I reject you altogether!' And Célimène sails out of the play, cheeks aflame, head held high, red heels clicking, fan flicked sharply to its fullest extent.

In his grim despair Alceste turns to Éliante, there present with Philinte, apologising for not being able to offer her his heart, as in a previous crisis he had half intended. The equable Éliante smilingly assures him he need not worry. Her choice, if he happens to feel that way, is Philinte, who accepts and thanks her kindly. The little scene is deliciously reposeful after recent storms and stresses. The ranting and the fever are over, pulses beat calm and low, passion in the air has turned to a minuet-tune. So Alceste stumps off at last to his desert. His goal, Maurice Donnay ventures pleasantly to conjecture, is possibly the Jansenist haven of Port-Royal-des-Champs, round which a colony of well-bred refugees from Vanity Fair clustered in quasi-Calvinist seclusion. But one feels Molière would supply a more mundane refuge, some moated grange in the bleak

[1] 'A soul of twenty is terrified by solitude. I don't feel my own great or strong enough to take a resolution of that sort.'

Cevennes. As Alceste quits the stage and the curtain is about to descend Philinte turns to Éliante:

> Allons, Madame, allons employer toute chose
> Pour rompre le dessein que son coeur se propose.[1]

Thus the noble comedy of *Le Misantrope* ends, in the air. They may or may not succeed with Alceste. As for Célimène, it is fairly evident that she, if not her female friends, will have forgotten the whole business within six weeks, with the help of a new circle of adorers. From a couple of hours of utter absorption, of pure enchantment, pity, and, it may be time to recall, recurring amusement in dialogue and situation, the spectator awakes with the further impression, intended or otherwise, that Alceste has got off pretty lightly. Six months of marriage with a Célimène could have driven such a man to something quite violently desperate. Very properly, no succeeding French dramatist of quality has dared lay hands on such a triumph of transcending art as *Le Misantrope*. One nevertheless may regret secretly that among the works of Jean Giraudoux (who else?) there is no comedy of three acts in prose entitled *Alceste Marié*, or *Célimène au Pays des Ours*.

CHAPTER TWO

'I was alone the other night at the Comédie-Française' – the broodings of Alfred de Musset in his box may not be exclusively an exhalation of the gushful 1840's.

> J'étais seul, l'autre soir, au Théâtre-Français,
> Ou presque seul; l'auteur n'avait pas grand succès,
> Ce n'était que Molière . . .[2]

While the masters Dumas and Scribe and their camp-followers were packing the boulevard theatres, the company

---

[1] 'Come, Madame – let's do all we can to defeat this scheme he has at heart.'

[2] 'The other night I was alone at the Comédie-Française, or nearly alone. The author was not having a great success; it was only Molière . . .'

of the 'Maison de Molière' was playing *Le Misantrope* to an almost empty house. And what a play, the poet reflects.

Quel grand et vrai savoir des choses de ce monde!
Quel mâle gâité, si triste and si profonde
Que lorsqu'on vient d'en rire, on devrait en pleurer![1]

If *Le Misantrope* had become caviare by De Musset's time, and long before, it was certainly more than a *succès d'estime* at the outset, as La Grange's registers attest. Twenty-one consecutive performances speak not unhighly of the good taste of the Parisian public of the 1660's. There still lingers a story that owing to the disastrous reception of this masterpiece Molière was obliged to add a brand-new farce to the bill after the fourth night, but this is quite untrue. The farce in question, entitled *Le Médecin Malgré Luy* ('The Doctor Despite Himself'), had been given half a dozen times before Molière tacked it on to *Le Misantrope*.

It is a treasure of buffoonery in its own right, written for relaxation and having quite plainly diverted its creator as much as anybody. Based on four fugitive farces of Molière's provincial days – *Le Fagotier* (The 'Woodcutter'). *Le Fagoteux* (ditto), *Le Médecin Par Force*, and *Le Médecin Volant*, all four deriving from a popular medieval fabliau called *Le Vilain Mire* ('The Peasant Doctor') – this high-spirited rollick in three acts and eleven scences was produced at the Palais-Royal on August 6th, 1666, and rocked the town. Though Molière's health was at the moment much improved, the full-length onslaught on the dignity of the Faculty of Medicine he has now produced is a truly wicked one. It likewise displays his first exploitation of rural argot.

Once again we have a wayward daughter, Lucinde, rebelling against the matrimonial plans of her father, Géronte; determined to marry young Léandre and shamming sick. Géronte's butler, Valère, is despatched with the rustic Lucas in search of a doctor. On the way they inquire of a village housewife, Martine,

---

[1] 'What deep, true knowledge of the things of this world! What virile gaiety – so melancholy, so profound, that when one has just laughed at it one should weep as well!'

97

who is tired of being beaten regularly – 'like a gong', in the excellent phrase of Mr Noel Coward – by her drunken wood-cutter-husband Sganarelle, and is scheming revenge. 'Doctor?' says Martine, suddenly inspired. 'Whoy, there he be!' She points to an adjoining dell where Sganarelle is piling faggots. 'Over there,' says vengeful Martine in effect, 'and a queer old devil, too.' It seems that Dr Sganarelle is a confirmed eccentric, a great man but a trifle cracked ('Aren't they all?' agrees Valère), who loves chopping wood and will admit to being a medical phoenix only after receipt of a sound thrashing. 'That's his way, see?'

Thence we are swiftly plunged into a riot of fun. Duly thrashed and scenting advantage, Sganarelle finds himself a medical gown and a pointed hat and proceeds to attend his fair patient, spouting burlesque Latin and pseudo-medical patter (how acquired, like his educated speech, we are not told, nor does it matter), and airing the views on his newly-acquired science one might expect. Challenged at length by Léandre, Lucinde's aspirant, he cheerfully admits total illiteracy, explaining that he was practically forced into the profession and adding that it is, in terms of modern folk-speech, 'money for old rope'.

> A cobbler making shoes can't spoil a bit of leather without having to pay for it, but in this line you can spoil a man and it costs you nothing . . . What is really good about it is that there's so much honesty among the dead, and the greatest discretion in the world. You never hear of one of them complaining about the doctor who killed him.

Dr Sganarelle soars to true Gallic form when smitten suddenly by the charms of a comely stout nurse in Géronte's household, Jacqueline by name.

SGAN: Who's that large woman over there?
GÉRONTE: That is the wet-nurse of a small child of mine.
SGAN: Phew! A pretty bit of furniture, too! Nurse! Charming nurse! My medicine is the most humble slave of your nursery. Would I were the lucky little brat who sips the milk of your good graces! (Lays a hand on her bosom.) All my remedies, all my knowledge, all my skill is at your service.

Here the surly Lucas, standing by, intervenes gruffly.

LUCAS: Asking your paärdon, Meäster Doctor sir, you leäve
moy wife aloän, if you please.
SGAN: What! Is this your wife?
LUCAS: Ay.

Foiled by the watchful Lucas, though he manages to snatch
a couple of accidental embraces, Dr Sganarelle returns to the
attack at the first opportunity, a few scenes later.

SGAN: Here's the lovely nurse! Nurse of my heart, I am ravished
by this meeting! The sight of you, nurse, is the rhubarb,
the cassia, and the senna to purge all melancholy from my
soul.
JACQUELINE: Whoy, Meäster Doctor, that be arl too foine for
Oi. Oi doän't onderstand naun of all that there Latin
o'yourn.
SGAN: Fall ill, nurse, I beg of you! Fall ill for love of me! I'll
have all the pleasure in the world in curing you.
JACQUELINE: My sarvice to you. Oi doän't need no curing.

He expresses deep sympathy with her in having such a
suspicious churl of a husband, who will not even let her speak
to him. She says with a sigh that that is only a small sample of
Lucas's goings-on.

SGAN: Is it possible! Is there a man with a soul so low as to
treat a person like you in that way? Ah, lovely nurse!
I know somebody not far from here who'd be made happy
simply by being able to kiss the tiny tips of your bosom-
buds. Why must such a comely creature fall into the
hands of a regular animal, a brute, a dolt, a fool, a –
Forgive me, nurse, for speaking like this about your
husband.
JACQUELINE: Whoy, sir, he desarves all them neämes, Oi'm
sure.

Having assisted Léandre, disguised as his apothecary, to
elope with Lucinde, Dr Sganarelle evokes Géronte's vengeance, is handed over to the law, and is saved only by Léandre's
reappearance with the announcement that he, Léandre, has
just inherited a rich uncle's fortune. And the farce ends with a
final shot for the Faculty:

SGANARELLE (to Léandre): Very well. I forgive you all these drubbings in consideration of the dignity you've raised me to. But prepare yourself henceforth to treat a man of my consequence with great respect. Remember that the wrath of a doctor is more to be feared than you'd believe.

Undoubtedly Molière enjoyed every moment of this preposterous, irresistible vaudeville, on which all authorities agree that never has the fount of imaginative buffoonery spouted with more primal verve. The Faculty of Medicine could now nurse a fresh and ingenious insult; the spectacle of a drunken, ignorant lout of a peasant demonstrating to the vulgar that given a black gown and a pointed hat, anybody can do it.

Several lines from *Le Médecin Malgré Luy* have passed into everyday speech, such as Martine's offended cry when somebody tries to rescue her from Sganarelle's ever-ready stick – 'But suppose I want him to beat me?' The reply of Dr Sganarelle on being informed that the heart is usually on the left side – '*Nous avons changé tout cela*' – might be called the efficient leader-writer's Cliché No. 1. And as in the case of W. S. Gilbert, our native Molière, such drolleries have a curious fascination for after-dinner bores, in whose mouths their gold turns straightway into lead.

CHAPTER THREE

After almost simultaneously producing a couple of works of the calibre of *Le Misantrope* and *Le Médecin Malgré Luy* any modern playwright would leave his agent to dispose of the film-rights and retire with his laurels to the Riviera for a well-earned yachting holiday. There was no rest for Molière. Within a few weeks of the production of the latter piece the King had a new order for him. A series of fêtes at St Germain-en-Laye, to begin in December 1666 and to last three months, were the newest royal project. Something light and amusing was required of Molière, and he sat down to his writing-table again. The result, entitled *Mélicerte*, devised to come half-way in an elaborate ballet by Benserade, may be summed up in a shrugging line of Boileau's on a later piece:

Je ne reconnois plus l'auteur du Misantrope . . .

As before, Molière had been warned at the last moment. A note at the end of Act II, Sc. 7 of *Mélicerte* in the printed edition of 1682 speaks for itself:

This comedy was not finished; only these two acts were ready when the King asked for them. His Majesty having deemed them sufficient for the festival in which the piece was played, the Sieur de Molière went no futher.

But he managed to provide the verses for the ensuing *Pastorale Comique*, and an artistic jewel was on the way. As for *Mélicerte*, a comedy in verse concerning the passion of two noble shepherdesses, Eroxène and Daphné, for a very young shepherd named Myrtil, it is a surrender, probably reluctant, to the fashionable taste for *bergerie* then raging. It would have no significance in Molière's achievement but for the fact that Myrtil was played by a twelve-year-old actor, Michel Baron, a boy of excessive good looks and cleverness and, offstage, as spoiled and petulant a little *cabotin* as ever threw a temperament. He came from a troop of child-actors directed by a Mlle Raisin, and joined Molière's company for the production of *Mélicerte* by an order extracted by Molière from the King. If unpleasant rumours, duly recorded in *La Fameuse Comédienne*, were soon going the rounds of Paris, it must be said that Molière's behaviour and Armande's jealousy gave them a good handle. Young Baron was lodged forthwith in Molière's apartments in the Place du Palais-Royal, coached by the master in person, and indulged like a favourite son. Incensed to begin with at finding the boy given the lead in *Mélicerte*, herself being cast for one of the two shepherdesses, Armande one day boxed Baron's ears at the theatre, whereupon he flounced out in a huff and rejoined Mlle Raisin, with the King's permission. It may well be that Molière's interest in *le petit Baron* was purely paternal. Such, it need hardly be remarked, was not the construction placed by his enemies on a seeming infatuation.

He ignored the gossip and, with renewed worries over *Le Tartufe*, and the old racking cough returning, turned out *Le Sicilien, ou L'Amour Peintre*, one act and eighteen scenes in prose and verse, as his final contribution to the St Germain festivities. It was played there on December 2nd, 1666, and delighted Paris shortly afterwards.

Le Sicilien is the lightest of thistledown and completely fascinating in gaiety and grace. A French gentleman, Adraste, falling in love with a beautiful Greek slave, Isidore, the property of a grotesquely-jealous Sicilian, Don Pedro, presents a letter of apology and recommendation from an artist-acquaintance of the Don's who was engaged to paint Isidore's portrait, takes his place, and elopes with her. That is all. The dialogue, in rhythmic prose, is interspersed with incidental music, songs, and ballet, and the entertainment ends with a dance of Moors of both sexes and – at St Germain – of the highest quality, the King being among the men and Princess Henriette of England, Charles I's daughter and Monsieur's wife, with Mlle de la Vallière among the women. Not the least of the gaieties involved is the audacity with which the dashing Adraste makes love to the fair Isidore under the nose of her tyrant. Having begun by explaining to Don Pedro that to kiss a lady on introduction is the polite usage of France, he sets about posing her with deft touches.

ISIDORE: Am I all right like this?
ADRASTE: Yes. A little more upright, please. A little more this way, the body turned thus. The head a little higher, to show the beauty of the neck. This (he gestures towards her bosom) just a trifle more exposed. Good. That's right. Just a little more, the least bit . . .
D. PEDRO (to Isidore): You're giving a lot of trouble over this. Don't you know how to hold yourself?
ISIDORE: It's all new to me, and it's this gentleman's business to pose me the way he wants.

Towards the end a lady named Climène seeks Don Pedro, thickly veiled and claiming to be in terror of the jealousy of Adraste, her ever-loving husband; and Don Pedro soothes her and joins their hands with his blessing, and they depart. It is of course not Climène, actually Adraste's sister, but Isidore. The climax is led up to in the airiest way. Breathing fire on discovery of the trick, armed to the teeth and roaring for justice, Don Pedro bangs on the door of a merry senator whose mind is on the masquerade; being also, at least as played nowadays, slightly in his cups. They are at cross-purposes from beginning to end.

D. PEDRO: A dog of a Frenchman has played me a trick.
SENATOR: You never saw anything so fine in your life.
D. PEDRO: He has run off with a girl I had just freed.
SENATOR: It's a lot of people dressed like Moors. They dance quite admirably.
D. PEDRO: You'll see if it's the kind of injury one can take lying down.
SENATOR: Marvellous costumes. They've all been specially made for the occasion.

'Damn the fool and his masquerade!' barks Don Pedro at last. 'Devil take the bore and his troubles!' hiccups the senator; and the fiddles strike up, the Moors dance in, and the frolic comes to an end. Conceived by a man carrying such a load as Molière, Le Sicilien is as compelling an illustration of the schizophrenia of the artist as some of the hilarities Dickens produced in the thick of his domestic imbroglio. Played today, it remains fresh as an April morning.

In this summer of 1667 Molière's troubles were increasing. Apart from his cough, which had become so virulent – it was even rumoured in Paris that he was dying – that his doctors put him on a milk-diet, and his heart, still bleeding vainly for the cruel Armande, he suffered a new setback with *Le Tartufe*.[1] Attaching undue weight, it is presumed, to some non-committal words of the King just before setting out for Army GHQ in Flanders, he boldly produced his new version, re-titled *L'Imposteur*, at the Palais-Royal on August 5th. The script had undergone much revision. The hypocrite concerned

[1] The derivation of 'Tartufe' is unknown, except that it conveys oily cunning and may be connected with the old French *truffer*, to deceive. Molière may have taken it from a contemporary print by Laignier called *La Tartuffe*, representing the female of the species (Note by Monval).

had changed his name, already in use as a missile, to 'Panulphe', and the puritanical black serge breeches and doublet with the wide-brimmed hat and narrow white collar, *petit collet*, affected by lay Jansenists, in which he had made his appearance in the Versailles production, were exchanged for the dress of an ordinary man of the world, sword included. It did him no good whatever. Within twenty-four hours of a successful début an edict of the Parlement of Paris ordered *L'Imposteur* off the stage.

The King was away to the north in Lille, recently occupied by Marshal Turenne. Since the accession of Carlos II the war with Spain, Austria, and England had taken a fresh turn, and Louis, with two consummate masters of military science like Turenne and Vauban at his elbow, had thoroughly reorganized the French offensive. During his absence the administration of the capital fell to the Parlement of Paris, and the First President of this august tribunal, Guillaume de Lamoignon, a leading member of the Company of the Blessed Sacrament, held strong views on *Le Tartufe*.

Having been politely flattened by Lamoignon, whose last word on the matter has sufficiently been recorded, and having vainly enlisted the services of Madame, the frivolous and fascinating Henriette of England, one of his warmest adherents, Molière sat down to compose a desperate petition or *placet* to the King, and sent La Grange and La Thorillière galloping with it forthwith to Lille. The *placet* was duly printed with the final text. It is actually the second of its kind. In 1664, Molière had ventured to remind the King of his approval, with that of Cardinal Chigi and 'the greater part of our prelates', and of his revisions. His tone now is bitter.

> Sir, my new comedy seems incapable of benefiting by Your Majesty's kindness. I have in vain produced it again under the title of 'The Impostor', and dressed the chief character as a man of the world with a small hat, long hair, a large collar, a sword, and lace all over him . . . I do not doubt Sir, that the kind of people attacked in my comedy have been able to pull many strings in Your Majesty's entourage . . . It is not the interests of Almighty God which move them, as may be seen in the kind of plays they tolerate without the least protest. Such plays merely

attack piety and religion, for which they give not a straw. My own attacks them in person, and this they cannot endure.

He again sets forth the purity of his intention and his defence of true religion in the teeth of the persecutors.

It seems obvious, Sir, that I must give up writing comedies if the Tartufes have all the advantage; they will assume the right to persecute me more than ever and to find offence in the most innocent productions of my pen.

May your kindness, Sir, deign to afford me protection against their venomous rage, and may I be able, on Your Majesty's return from this glorious campaign, to assist You to relax from the fatigues of conquest, to offer You harmless amusement after Your noble labours, and to inspire laughter in a Monarch who has made all Europe tremble.

Impressive enough, but the Royal eyebrows may have gone up in amusement at the cry of martyrdom. Louis was perfectly aware that the backing for *Le Tartufe* was powerful and vociferous. Boileau records that since 1664 Molière had conducted a brisk advance-publicity campaign, reading his amended play, in whole or part, in the smartest Parisian drawing-rooms, including those of intelligent leaders of fashion like Ninon de L'Enclos and Mme de Sablé, at a series of patrician dinner-tables, and at the houses of the upper bourgeoisie and Academicians like Boissart and Habert de Montmort. Most of the Court and every person of taste in Paris knew the plot of *Le Tartufe*, and could often recite a line or two; being banned made it naturally the *dernier cri*. Performances at the châteaux of influential admirers like Monsieur and Condé had in addition brought Molière more solid tokens of sympathy than applause.

Rising from the conference-table at GHQ, the King received Molière's envoys benignly, scanned their chief's petition, dismissed them with a promise to re-examine the whole situation on his return to Paris, and, perhaps still smiling, resumed more important business. Meanwhile Molière had nothing to expect from President de Lamoignon, in whose presence, again according to Boileau, who accompanied him, he had been too agitated to do anything but blush and stammer.

The edict of Parlement was now reinforced by a *mandement* or charge of Hardouin de Péréfixe, Archbishop of Paris, forbidding the faithful to be present at any representation or recital of *L'Imposteur*, public or private, in whole or in part, under pain of excommunication; a kind of interdict which, as Anatole France was to discover at Buenos Ayres during that lecture-tour of 1909 so divertingly reported by Jean-Jacques Brousson, his ex-secretary, is apt to be no laughing-matter. So Molière gave in, closed his theatre, and retired for the next seven weeks to his leafy hermitage at Auteuil, weary, ill, and more depressed than ever. It is at this period that most authorities place the discussion with Chapelle, if it actually took place, of his domestic misfortunes. On September 25th, he returned to Paris and revived *Le Misantrope* for a short run. The King has now returned, giving no sign. On November 6th, Molière's company was summoned to Versailles. There may be resentful significance in his choice of a programme which included nothing of his own, the main piece being Corneille's *Attila*, with a couple of comedies by minor hands, *La Veuve à La Mode* and *L'Accouchée, ou l'Embarras de Godet*.

He had long since flung himself into fresh work, the artist's unfailing anodyne. On January 13th, 1668, a new verse-comedy in three acts and ten scenes entitled *Amphitryon* was presented at the Palais-Royal.

Molière had remembered his schooldays and gone to Plautus for his theme. It is not a pretty story. Rolling the usual lecherous eye from Olympus, Jupiter perceives that the beautiful and virtuous Alcmena, wife of Amphytrion, King of Thebes, is an ideal object for his next seduction. Alcmena being deeply in love with her husband, Jupiter is aware that such previous tricks as the shower of gold for Danaë and the swan for Leda will plainly be of no avail, Taking advantage of Amphytrion's absence on the battlefield, the Ruler of the Gods assumes his shape, descends on Alcmena with Mercury, his pimp, and is welcomed as he should be. A little later Amphytrion himself returns, discovers the swindle, rages, raves, and is warned by a roll of celestial thunder to desist. Alcmena being now pregnant with the twins Hercules and Iphicles,

Jupiter assures Amphytrion from a cloud that he, Amphytrion, has been greatly honoured, and the comedy ends with the reflection of Amphytrion's valet Sosie that discreet silence all round is best for all.

> Sur telles affaires toûjours
> Le meilleur est de ne rien dire.

A number of playwrights have been tempted by this theme. One only, so far, has been inspired to distil its crudeness into beauty. Re-reading Giraudoux' *Amphytrion* 38 after Molière's is like diving into a crystal pool after enduring many hours in an overheated nightclub. For Giraudoux the victory, after three acts of epigrammatic and exquisite fencing, is Alcmena's. Defeated by feminine art, a witty tongue, and passionate conjugal love, Jupiter shows that a racketty old debauchee can be a gentleman. Bowing to Alcmena's refusal to collaborate with him officially in forging a Hercules, he accepts her friendship (a new experience), hands her back to Amphytrion with the stoic grace of a *grand seigneur* who has lost the game, and takes his leave, dismissing all the persons of the comedy as dusk falls on the nuptial chamber and the stars come out.

> . . . Disperse, then, gods and supernumaries, to our zeniths or our caverns. And you, spectators there below, retire in silence, affecting the most complete indifference. For one last time let Alcmena and her husband appear in a ring of light, in which my arm will figure again only as a signpost showing the way of happiness. And on this pair – on whom adultery has never breathed and never shall, to whom the savour of the forbidden kiss will never be known – fall again, high curtains of the Night, enclosing this nest of fidelity with your velvet!

Beautifully written likewise is Molière's less delicate treatment. For the first time he has discarded the alexandrine in favour of flexible free verse, in the manner of La Fontaine at his best. The prologue between Mercury on a cloud and Night driving her chariot strikes the note of elegant cynicism from the start.

MERCURE

Tout-beau, charmante Nuit; daignez vous arrester.
Il est certain secours que de vous on desire,

107

> Et j'ay deux mots à vous dire
> De la part de Jupiter.

LA NUIT

> Ah! ah! c'est vous, Seigneur Mercure!
> Qui vous eust deviné là, dans cette posture![1]

What the celestial pimp requires of Night is a long stretch of darkness to assist a forthcoming *douce avanture*. His Olympian master, smitten with the loveliness of Alcmena, proposes to take advantage of the honeymoon.

> L'hymen ne les a joints que depuis quelques jours,
> Et la jeune chaleur de leurs tendres amours
> A fait que Jupiter à ce bel artifice
> S'est avisé d'avoir recours . . .[2]

And thus it happens. Alcmena is duly deceived. It seems that her eminent seducer yearns to be loved for himself alone; as the lover, not the husband whose shape he has stolen. 'The lover and the husband,' says the innocent Alcmena fondly, dismissing metaphysics, 'are equally precious to me.' Next day the true Amphitryon returns from the front, to learn from his bride that he occupied the marital chamber the night before. Astounded cross-questioning reaches its peak when Alcmena reminds him that 'after supper we went to bed'.

AMPHITRYON: Together?
ALCMENA: Most certainly! Why ask?
AMPHITRYON: Ah! This is the cruellest blow of all!

She cannot understand his sudden blind and jealous fury, and he cannot explain it to her. 'I don't know – but that was *not I*. It makes me so desperate that I'm capable of anything . . .'

At the first Court representation of *Amphitryon* at the

---

[1] Merc: Gently, charming Night! Be so good as to pull up. There is a certain assistance we require from you. I've a word or two to say to you in Jupiter's behalf.

  Night: Aha! It's you, my lord Mercury! Who would have guessed you were here in this guise!

[2] Marriage has mated them only for a few days, and the youthful heat of their tender love has decided Jupiter to avail himself of this delightful artifice.

Tuileries, a few days after the public début, a resplendent audience must have had some difficulty in the Royal presence in avoiding each other's eyes. The gentle and beautiful De la Vallière was not there. She had broken with the King, and illness was already turning her thoughts, not for the first time, towards the Carmelite house in the Rue St Jacques where she was to spend the rest of her life; the columned door by which she entered is, or was till quite recently, still there, down an entry near the convent chapel. Her successor, Athénais de Mortemarte, Marquise de Montespan, was a different character; sharp-tongued, domineering, unscrupulous, infidel, an addict in due course to black magic. Her husband accepted his fate more resignedly than Amphitryon in the play, and was undoubtedly envied by half the Beau Monde. Had he been present that night, nevertheless, he could hardly have avoided hearing a suppressed titter or two as Jupiter booms a farewell from his cloud to Amphitryon just before the final curtain.

> Un partage avec Jupiter
> N'a rien du tout qui des-honnore;
> Et sans doute il ne peut estre que glorieux
> De se voir le rival du souverain des Dieux.[1]

Coincidental or deliberate? And had Molière cast a sly side-glance in the prologue at two noble procuresses who, as all the smart world knew, had steered Mme de Montespan successfully into the King's arms? 'A pretty occupation!' exclaims Night laughingly when asked to collaborate with Mercury in sport of this kind.

> Et l'on donne un nom fort honneste
> Au service qu'il veut de moy![2]

The contemporary name for ladies performing the joint services of the Princess of Baden and Mme de Montausier, wife of the most puritan peer in France, was *dariolette*, a much

---

[1] 'Sharing with Jupiter has nothing dishonourable in it whatsoever. Undoubtedly there can be nothing but pride in finding oneself the rival of the Sovereign of the Gods.'

[2] 'And there's a very nice name for the kind of service he (Jupiter) expects of me!'

prettier word than the modern *maquerelle*. The theory that Molière seized the opportunity of linking Jupiter, Alcmena, and Amphitryon very deftly with Louis XIV, Mme de Montespan, and her husband is the historian Michelet's, and the parallel is certainly engaging; but all question of the time-factor apart, the corollary that Louis XIV himself must have at least approved this unquestionably wrongs a monarch who could never have stooped to a thought so vulgar. Like our own Macaulay, the eminent Michelet was ever a slave to the picturesque. Everybody knew that Mme de Montespan, with her two guardian angels, had followed the King to Flanders, among other Court ladies, and taken part with the long-suffering Queen in the triumphal entry of Turenne's troops into Arras. Molière probably learned plenty more when La Grange and La Thorillière returned from GHQ after presenting the petition for *Le Tartufe*. Spending a fair amount of time at Court, we may recollect, he knew all the gossip that was going. Topical, high-spirited, amusing, a totally charming work of art, totally immoral, *Amphitryon* was in any case a huge success. It leaves a slightly bitter after-taste. In the most mellifluous fashion an ideal marriage has been wrecked by the trickery of an insatiable old goat, and the victims bidden to congratulate themselves. In the time of Plautus a chaste Roman matron could presumably do this on the stage without raising a laugh. Some time later the infiltration of exotic rites from the Orient and the cultus of the Emperor were to make the goings-on of Olympus look as comic as they seemed to the Paris of Louis XIV. It might be reasonably noted in Louis' defence that his passion for the Montespan broke up no happy domesticity. He was not her first lover nor her last, and M. de Montespan was doubtless used to it.

A mood of bitterness, dark and pessimistic, is perceptible in Molière's next forthcoming work, another Royal command. In February 1668, an offensive under Condé took the Franche-Comté with brilliant ease, and the subsequent treaty of Aix-la-Chapelle left France more powerful and respected in Europe than ever. To celebrate this, to gratify Mme de Montespan, and to annoy the enemies of France, Louis XIV ordered a sumptuous fête at Versailles and a new comedy from Molière. On July 18th, 1668, accordingly, was presented *George Dandin, ou le Mary Confondu*; three acts and seven scenes in prose, with a wealth of choreographic and musical trimmings, dropped for the Palais-Royal production on November 9th. The Versailles setting was oddly gorgeous for such sombre merriment. The open-air theatre erected on the site of the present Bassin de Saturne, hung with magnificent tapestries and lit by thirty-six crystal chandeliers, burning six wax candles apiece, seated twelve hundred spectators, who included the whole Royal family, six ambassadors, and the entire Court.

The theme of *George Dandin* is social; what today would be called ideological, and even 'class-war'. A rich peasant is stupid enough to marry into the *petite noblesse*. Patronized and despised by his parents-in-law, fooled and humiliated by his young wife and a lover of her rank, he ends by throwing himself into the river, or at least implying that resolution at the end. With virulent relish Molière embroiders the imbecility and conceit of the rustic nobility of his time, the butt of all the Court. The De Sotenvilles – one might deduce these particular *sots* from their title to be Norman[1] – are typical cocks on their local dunghill. To them Dandin's first suspicions of Angélique's carryings-on suggest something monstrous, a thought unspeakable; not on George Dandin's account but the family's, the blazon of the De Sotenvilles on the male side being as immaculate as that of the De la Prudoteries on the female.

Dandin, poor, wealthy, bewildered, melancholy, pathetic lout, is by no means blameless. He married Angélique de Sotenville against her will, by arrangement with her parents, and in one of their quarrels she reminds him of this with vindictive satisfaction.

> Did you ask my consent before we were married? Was I even asked if I liked you? No. You only consulted my father and mother – it's they, properly speaking, who married you, and you're perfectly right to complain to them whenever anybody may do you a wrong. So far as we're concerned, I never having

[1] There is a village near Dieppe called Sottenville, and another on the nearby coast called Sottenville-sur-Mer.

asked you to marry me, and you having taken me without consulting my wishes, I claim to be free from any obligation to obey you like a slave.

She is young, as she says. Life has a lot of harmless fun to offer, and she proposes to take as much of it as she can, to mingle in society and receive a few agreeable compliments. To this end she is encouraging an admirer, the young Vicomte Clitandre. Having slipped back late one night from a *tête-à-tête* with Clitandre to find herself caught out, she handles the situation with all the pretty aplomb, perhaps, employed by an Armande in similar circumstances.

It's quite true I've done wrong, I admit it again, you're perfectly right to be angry with me. I slipped out while you were asleep, and it was to meet the person you mention. But this is the sort of thing you ought to forgive in somebody my age . . .

Pure girlishness, an innocent romp, *des emportemens de jeune personne*, and Angélique is terribly, terribly sorry. If George will only overlook it and please, please not tell her parents:

I'll be the best wife in the world to you ever afterwards, and I'll show you so much affection, so much, you'll be absolutely satisfied.

To which Dandin growls '*Crocodile!*', and he is right. More tricks will be played. She loathes her bondage, and him. Did it ever occur to Molière during the writing of the piece that since Angélique's enforced marriage to Dandin is in the Church's eyes no marriage at all, she could reasonably apply for an annulment? If the thought obtruded itself he must have promptly dismissed an issue which would have defeated his sombre intention. Angélique is to be freed, it seems, only by assisting to drive the unfortunate Dandin to desperation.

One may lawfully ask oneself whether Dandin's punishment for giving way to an impulse of snobbery is not needlessly savage. Three times he is grossly humiliated; once by being forced to ask Clitandre's pardon for suspecting him, again by being beaten by Angélique while she is pretending to chastise Clitandre – an incident putting a great strain, one might observe, on credulity and goodwill – and the third time by being compelled to apologize to his wife for finding her gallant in his house at night. As he stands outside parleying with Angélique the De Sotenvilles appear and take charge.

M. DE SOTENVILLE: We'll handle it. (to Dandin) Now then, down on your knees.
DANDIN: On my knees?
M. DE SOTENVILLE: On your knees, and hurry up.
DANDIN (kneels): Oh, my God! What must I say?
M. DE SOTENVILLE: 'Madame, I beg you to forgive me . . .'
DANDIN: Madame, I beg you to forgive me . . .
M. DE SOTENVILLE: 'For my crazy behaviour . . .'
DANDIN: For my crazy behaviour (under his breath) in marrying you . . .
M. DE SOTENVILLE: 'And I promise to behave better in the future.'
DANDIN: And I promise (etc., etc)

They leave him then, and on his suicidal brooding the curtain falls. The painfulness of his abjection sent seventeenth-century Parisian audiences into hysterics, apparently. It would have done the same anywhere else, domestic trouble being a stock farce-motive of the period. If *George Dandin* seems a brutal play today, in a century actually crueller, it is perhaps because for the majority marriage has ceased to be of any importance as a human relationship; Angélique nowadays would simply pack a bag after the first domestic upheaval and join Clitandre, pending her divorce, at Antibes. It was only when two human beings were normally bound to each other by sacramental vows, valid even after a judicial separation, that their clashes made farce-material. Since the mid-fifteenth century, indeed, a comic-satiric textbook on the subject had been available to all in *Les Quinze Joyes de Mariage*, by Antoine de la Sale. Not without significance is the fact that George Dandin has apparently never given Angélique a beating. Might it be that Molière, who knew a good deal about feminine psychology, forbade Dandin this old and proven rustic recipe for ensuring conjugal love, with a reluctant sigh? In the past he may even have tried it himself, during some furious domestic *scène à faire*, and without the least effect, on Armande.

Towards the end of 1668 an immense satisfaction came to alleviate his gloom. Wearied by intermittent pleas and reproachful looks, and by the urgings of powerful backers, Louis XIV gave way at last over *Le Tartufe* and decided, Jove-like, to ignore the still-operative bans of Parlement and Archbishop alike. On February 9th, 1669, this satiric verse-comedy in five acts and seven scenes was produced with the King's permission at the Palais-Royal.

CHAPTER FOUR

The curtain rises on the parlour of a gentleman's house in Paris. Except for Orgon, its head, the whole family is present – Elmire, his wife, Madame Pernelle, his mother, Cléante, his brother-in-law, Damis and Mariane, his son and daughter, and two maidservants, Dorine and Flipote. The atmosphere is strained and irritable. Tempers are short, tongues are sharp. A malignant invisible presence overhangs the scene. Though the greasy villain Tartufe will not make his entry till the second scene of Act III, we know all about him long beforehand. Or do we?

Perhaps because Molière had to cobble and re-cobble this play so much, a certain amount of Tartufe's 'this-ness' remains obscure, and the ink since expended on filling in the blanks achieves very little. Certainly Tartufe is not a cleric. Nothing else is absolutely clear. Having come to life in 1664 in the garb of a lay Jansenist, he possibly still belongs to this sect. He may equally possibly have some connection with the Company of the Blessed Sacrament, which partly existed to combat the Jansenist heresy. The Duc de Ventadour's foundation had some achievements to its credit; its charitable work in hospitals, prisons, and the galleys, and among the sick poor, was immense, and it had likewise been able to prevail on Louis XIV to ban duelling, which murderous pastime was thinning out the French nobility. On the other hand the Company had revived the 'discipline of the Secret' of the Catacombs age, for which reason, among others, Rome had sedulously withheld official sanction, and it was becoming in one of its aspects a kind of spiritual Gestapo. In 1660, pamphlets of clerical provenance attacking the Company as a secret society conspiring against Church and State gave the French hierarchy the opportunity it was waiting for. François de Harlay, Archbishop of Rouen, called to the Minister, Mazarin, for action, and the ensuing ban by the Parlement of Paris on all societies unauthorized by royal letters-patent dealt the Company of the Blessèd Sacrament a mortal blow. It managed nevertheless to survive six years more, and in 1664 it was still sufficiently influential in high places, as already noted, to decide Louis XIV against licensing *Le Tartufe*. Molière would hardly have forgiven this. Though the Company itself can have harboured few or no Tartufes, its discipline being more than military, the hostility it had long since aroused in so many quarters would make it an obvious reprisal-target for Tartufe's creator after the ban of 1664. As for a typically nineteenth-century theory that Tartufe represents the Society of Jesus, Racine himself remarked that the Jesuits' impression was the exact contrary; and in fact why a generous creature like Molière, owing the Society so much, should take sides with its foes of Port-Royal would be difficult to comprehend, the more so because of his Royal employer's detestation of Jansenism at all times. His spokesman Alceste's protest in *Le Misantrope* against being accused of the authorship of *un livre abominable* – it was an anti-Jesuit broadside – is not without significance in this connection.

Internal evidence is slight but not negligible. Orgon in the play may be heard speaking at least once with a definite Jansenist twang acquired from Tartufe:

> Il m'enseigne à n'avoir affection pour rien,
> De toutes amitiez il détache mon ame . . .[1]

Few spectators in the better seats could fail to recognize the accents of Port-Royal here. All else apart, there was little reason for a man of the theatre to cherish any affection for a sect which – *teste* Pascal, and even more Nicole, who described

[1] 'He teaches me to have no affection for anything, and weans my soul from friendships of every kind.'

dramatic poets as 'public poisoners' – considered his whole profession an abomination of Satan. On the whole it seems not unreasonable to conclude that Tartufe more or less represents Jansenism as the Spintexts and Saygraces and other Restoration stage-predecessors of the deathless Stiggins represent its English Puritan equivalent.

Returning to Orgon's parlour, we learn that this brave, upright, dictatorial, stupid, sincerely religious man, till lately fighting for his King against the Fronde, is the dupe and plaything of an odious hypocrite, once lean, now fat, whom he has taken under his roof as his spiritual director, and who now dominates him entirely. Glowering young Damis is more than ready for what is called the showdown, but the time is not yet ripe. From the free-tongued maidservant Dorine, talking to Orgon's brother-in-law Cléante, we get a sufficient précis of the situation. Orgon has gone crazy over this person, she says.

> Enfin il en est fou; c'est son tout, son héros;
> Il l'admire à tous coups, le cite à tout propos;
> Ses moindres actions luy semblent des miracles,
> Et tous les mots qu'il dit sont pour luy des oracles.[1]

As for Tartufe:

> Luy, qui connoist sa dupe et qui veut en joüir,
> Par cent dehors fardez a l'art de l'éblouïr;
> Son cagotisme en tire à toute heure des sommes,
> Et prend droict de gloser sur tous tant que nous sommes ...[2]

In a word, she says, Tartufe now rules the house, lecturing, scolding, and tossing away rouge-pots, face-patches, and ribbons, while Orgon stands by admiring. All this Orgon amply confirms on his return home, having no ears for news of any of the household but one. '*Et Tartufe?*' – the recurring refrain has admirable and immediate psychological significance.

[1] 'Well, he's mad about him; the man's his hero and his all, he admires everything he does and quotes him every other minute; his slightest act seems to Master Orgon a miracle, every word he speaks is an oracle.'

[2] 'Knowing his dupe, and wanting to make the most of him, he has a way of dazzling him with a hundred show-off tricks; his hypocrisy makes something out of this all day long, and he makes bold to criticize everything we do.'

The pious Orgon is in fact, until his eyes are rudely opened in Act IV, an abysmal fool.

Orgon's credulity might be styled abnormal. His suspicions are not awakened by the most blatant tricks. 'Ah!' he says to Cléante, 'if you'd only seen him in church!' And he describes Tartufe at his public devotions, attracting all eyes by the vehemence of his sighs, his eye-rollings and prostrations, his abased humility and ostentatious charity. Any intelligent child of ten would smell imposture at a hundred yards. Not so Orgon. His great desire now is to marry his daughter Mariane to his detestable guest, who at last makes his appearance in the third act, throwing a characteristic order to a servant offstage.

'Laurent! serrez ma haire avec my discipline!'[1]

Characteristic of Tartufe, perhaps; not, as La Bruyère and later critics pluming themselves on some knowledge of psychology have argued, characteristic of a finished hypocrite. Says La Bruyère, etching his own portrait of the type in *Les Caractères*:

> Onuphre never says: 'My hair-shirt and my scourge.' If he did, he would appear to be what he is, a hypocrite, whereas he desires to appear what he is not, namely a devout person.

Further, adds La Bruyère, your master-hypocrite does not, like Tartufe, make frontal attacks on the virtue of married women, still less does he worm himself into a fortune if this necessitates the ousting of the legal heir. His whole technique, in fact, is subtler, more oblique, more delicate than Tartufe's, for which Léon Bloy in the 1880's found a characteristically apoplectic phrase – 'the repercussions in the brain of a clown (Molière) of the pietistic belly-rumblings of an ignoble century'.[2] To neither critic, seemingly, did it occur that the fine shades of Onophre, as of Barbey d'Aurevilly's *diaboliques*, would be utterly wasted on the stage. Even so, perhaps, there are degrees of greasepaint. It might be added that in the long congratulatory *Lettre sur l'Imposteur* following the 1682 text a singular phrase is applied to Tartufe: *il feroit presque pitié*. As

[1] Laurent! Lock up my hair-shirt with my scourge!
[2] *Belluaires et Porchers*, XI.

created by the plump, babyfaced Du Croisy, Tartufe was a semi-comic villain. Can it be that Molière had some subtlety in mind which never got across the footlights?

The full extent of Orgon's hypnosis is revealed soon after Tartufe's appearance on the scene. Young Damis, who longs to crush him like a slug, overhears Tartufe making advances to Elmire, his benefactor's attractive wife and Damis' step-mother –

> J'aurai toûjours pour vous, ô suave merveille,
> Une devotion à nulle autre pareille;
> Vostre honneur avec moy ne court point de hasard,
> Et n'a nulle disgrace à craindre de ma part . . .[1]

– and at once informs his father, in Tartufe's presence. A quaint scene ensues. Tartufe kneels and abases himself in vague and general terms, in an orgy of luxurious humility. Orgon refuses to listen to the traducer of a saint, raves, roars for a stick, drives Damis out for good, and in reparation makes Tartufe, his prospective son-in-law, sole heir to his property and fortune. It is not until Act IV that the fantastic dupe's eyes are finally opened. Another attack by Tartufe on Elmire's virtue is in progress and a trap has been set for him. He assures her she need have no foolish scruples. Such matters can always be discreetly arranged with Heaven.

> Le Ciel défend, de vray, certains contentemens,
> Mais on trouve avec luy des accommodemens . . .
> De ces secrets, Madame, on sçaura vous instruire;
> Vous n'avez seulement qu'à vous laisser conduire.[2]

'Guidance' – a perfect Tartuffish line, skilfully developed. 'A rascal is speaking', explains a bracketed note in the printed text of 1682, with unnecessary officiousness. 'Escobar in terms of the theatre!' Sainte-Beuve will cry two centuries later; but as Sainte-Beuve like most people derives his impressions of the

---

[1] 'Sweet marvel! I shall always have a devotion for you beyond compare. With me your honour runs no risk; it has no disgrace to fear where I am concerned . . .'

[2] 'Certainly, Heaven forbids us certain delights, but one can come to terms with it . . . You shall learn all about these secrets, Madame. You've nothing to do but let yourself be guided.'

ethics of Escobar y Mendoza from Pascal's travesty in the *Provinciales*, the citation is more picturesque than accurate. In any case the sleek rascal concerned is at last over-reaching himself, being unaware that Orgon is in the room, concealed by arrangement with his wife under a table. Just before Tartufe steals out, at Elmire's suggestion, to make sure that her husband is not in the adjacent gallery, Orgon hears the truth about himself. 'Why worry about him?' asks Tartufe with a grin. 'He can always be led by the nose. I've got him to the point where he could see everything and not believe it!' However, to humour her he glides out. On his return a terrible Orgon confronts him and orders him out of the house.

Orgon has suddenly turned into a man of action and intelligence. But the cunning devil with the rosy plump face goes out smiling, having a couple of trumps up his sleeve. Not merely has Orgon transferred all his property to him ('This house is mine,' he points out before going), but he has actually entrusted Tartufe with a casket containing dangerous papers placed in Orgon's care by a friend accused of offences against the State. Behold, therefore, the return of Tartufe, accompanied by Monsieur Loyal, an official of the High Court of Justice, with orders to eject Orgon and his family forthwith; eventually, being a man of feeling, Monsieur Loyal will allow them till next day in consideration of the keys being handed over and ten bailiffs being lodged in the house for the night, *sans scandale et sans bruit*.

On the heels of this disaster arrives young Valère, Mariane's aspirant, with news that Orgon has just been denounced by Tartufe to the King in the matter of the casket papers. Before long Tartufe returns again with an *exempt* or police-officer to arrest Orgon for treason. 'Carry out your orders,' he snarls to this functionary. 'Very good, sir,' says the officer. 'Be so kind as to accompany me to prison immediately.' The villain cannot believe his ears.

TARTUFE: Who, sir? Me?
OFFICER: Yes, you.
TARTUFE: Prison? What for?
OFFICER: It's not my business to give you a reason.

And he turns to the dumbfounded Orgon:

> Remettez-vous, Monsieur, d'une alarme si chaude,
> Nous vivous sous un prince ennemy de la fraude,
> Un prince dont les yeux ce font jour dans les coeurs,
> Et que ne peut tromper tout l'art des imposteurs . . .[1]

So all ends happily. Tartufe is haled off to expiate behind bars, Orgon is promised a pardon from the King for his indiscretion, Damis is back in the fold, Valère wins his Mariane, and the curtain falls on a family perhaps less dazed by tricksy fate than the audience. 'Now I breathe again!' exclaims old Madame Pernelle. So do we all.

'I would never have allowed it on the stage,' said Napoleon Bonaparte one day, speaking of Louis XIV and *Le Tartufe*. Though no great practitioner in either religion or art, Napoleon was sufficiently a Latin to be aware that *pietas* in all its aspects is the cement of the civilized State. It is precisely *pietas* in its primal meaning which comes off badly in Molière's play.

A key-passage added during the final revision, on the advice of the great Condé, was intended to mollify the devout once for all by making a clear distinction between true religion and the kind exploited by a Tartufe. Sixty lines in Act I, Sc. 5, were accordingly put into the mouth of Cléante, Orgon's brother-in-law, for this purpose. He is, so to speak, Molière's spokesman, addressing the world at large. Beginning with an excellent diatribe against religious charlatans, the *dévots de place*

> Qui sçavent adjuster leur zèle avec leurs vices,[2]

Cléante turns out to have nothing to produce in contrast after all but the Code of the Joneses. 'Look,' says Cléante, 'at Ariston, look at Périandre, Oronte, Alcidamas and Clitandre!'

> Ce ne sont point du tout fanfarons de vertu,
> On ne voit point en eux ce faste insuportable,
> Et leur devotion est humaine et traitable . . .[3]

---

[1] 'Take heart again, sir, after this severe alarm. We live under a prince who is the enemy of fraud – a prince whose eyes see clearly into all hearts and whom all the skill of imposters cannot deceive . . .'

[2] 'Who know how to adjust their vices to their zeal.'

[3] 'These are no exhibitionists of virtue; you see none of that intolerable display in their actions; their devotion is human and tractable.'

Above all, no zeal! – Talleyrand's cry is heard a century in advance.

> Et ne veulent point prendre avec un zele extréme
> Les interests du Ciel plus qu'il ne veut luy-même.[1]

The fundamental weakness of *Le Tartufe* is patent. Loudly as its author claims to have stated the case for true religion he does nothing of the sort, being temperamentally incapable of so doing. The balance of the play is wrong. The fight is rigged. The *dévots* of the piece are poor limp mediocre specimens. Neither Orgon, his old mother, his wife, nor his brother-in-law manifests any kind of spiritual *élan*, or even intelligence, though the *Introduction à la Vie Dévote* of Monsieur de Genève, composed precisely for the *homme moyen sensuel*, was a best seller of the period. Tartufe himself is an impressive blackguard enough, and there are hypocrites of varying degree in every age. But the Tartufes certainly did not swarm in contemporary France as they seem to under the eye of Cléante, who might be reviewing the march-past of a couple of Army Corps.

Molière's actual models for Tartufe, according to contemporary gossip, were the Abbé Roquette, familiar to every lover of the letters of Mme de Sévigné, and the Abbé de Pons, both notorious; a certain Sieur de Charpy was also in the running. Like every great artist Molière probably took a few lineaments from one and the other and supplied the rest himself. The vigour of the brush-strokes limning Tartufe and the lack of conviction about his other outlines may be accounted for, no doubt, by his own epicurean temperament. Like his master Rabelais he was allergic to discipline of any sort, and spiritual discipline above all, and it may be noted that authorities who place *Le Tartufe* on the level of *Le Misantrope* are almost invariably of Molière's way of thinking.

Yet even in craftsmanship *Le Tartufe* is well behind its predecessor. All that revision-work did the play no good. If there is a good dramatic case for leaving Tartufe's entry till the third act, while the darkness piles up, as it were, all round

[1] 'And (they) have no desire to pursue the interests of Heaven with an extremity of zeal it does not itself require.'

him, it may be that the lovers' quarrel, Dorine assisting, on the pattern of *Dépit Amoureux* which takes up half of Act II, the abruptness of Orgon's gift of his fortune to Tartufe, and the missing reason for Damis' early vendetta all point to haste, or weariness, or boredom. The sudden twist of the dénouement, with its fanfare for the King's clemency, is surprising but not incredible. It is difficult to think of any other happy ending equally plausible. A Tartufe in real life could have had audience of Louis XIV in the circumstances, and would be severely dealt with for falsely accusing an honest soldier of treason. Even Orgon's fantastic legacy is possible, though no contemporary court of appeal would have upheld it. The flaw of *Le Tartufe* is that so much of the orchestration is off-key. Himself spiritually tone-deaf, the master should perhaps have had some authority at his elbow to advise him in this field of experience. An exponent of elegant letters like M. de Genève would have been ideal for the purpose. But Geneva's bishop, St François de Sales, died in 1622, and Molière apparently had not come across his works.

Le Tartufe ran for forty-four consecutive performances, making what show-business today calls a smash-hit.

Book V

By the mid-1660's a new cloud of disturbing dimensions was rising steadily on Molière's horizon. It took the shape of a lean, dark Italian face with glittering eyes, a face expert in grimaces as his own and as capable of lightning changes; the face of the extraordinary Giovanni Battista Lulli of Florence, who had begun his career in France as scullery-boy to the Duchesse de Montpensier and by 1653, at the age of fourteen, was Master of the Royal Music.

In 1668, to which year we return, the subtle Florentine now naturalized as Jean-Baptiste Lully was well on the way to challenging Molière for the Royal favour. Avaricious, ruthless in ambition, vindictive, treacherous, with irresistible comic gifts and a zest for slave-driving, he could, when he chose, switch on a voluble charm. As an acrobat-clown of quite mirific lunacy no professional of the fairs could compete with him, and as a musical genius he ranks with the Samurai. He imposed vivacious new rhythms on the ballet and the beautiful and difficult French horn, *cor de chasse*, among other instrumental novelties, on the orchestra. Much of his music, ever agreeable to a civilized ear, is as vital today (e.g. *Bois Épais*, the nocturne in *Le Triomphe de l'Amour*, and the march in *Thésée*) as when it was written, and he is the acknowledged father of French opera. Lully was likewise to achieve the most musicianly of ends, hitting himself on the big toe while conducting a *Te Deum* with a long baton, setting up a fatal abscess, and on a penitent dying-bed composing his last song, *Bisogna morire, peccatore*.

Whatever his detestable qualities he was a man of outstanding eminence, and one suspects La Fontaine's cry of hate and terror after trying to work with him at the Opera –

>   Sa femme, des enfants, et tout le genre humain,
>   Petits et grands, dans leurs prières
>   Disent le soir et le matin;
>   'Seigneur, par Vos bontés pour nous si singulières,
>   Délivrez-nous du Florentin!'[1]

– to be chiefly the squawk of laziness chastised and smarting.

Lully's dark features, grimacing in joviality or rage, must have seemed to Molière before long to overhang the Court like the grin of the Cheshire Cat. Their orbits had first coincided in 1664, when Lully as Court composer supplied the incidental and ballet-music for *Le Mariage Forcé*, first of a series of collaborations. Sizing up his man, Molière plainly decided for the velvet glove, the Florentine being as irascible as a hornet and a painstaking enemy. That Molière played from the beginning on Lully's vanity is discernible in the preface to *L'Amour Médecin* – '*les airs and les symphonies de l'incomparable monsieur Lully*' – and their long *entente*. At those Auteuil supper-parties the Florentine's response to his host's call ('Make us laugh, Baptiste') never failed, it seems, except with the supercilious Boileau, whose lines to Seignelay on a *bouffon odieux*, coupled with a *coquin ténébreux*, raising cheap laughs at table can apply to no one else. In December 1670, finally, Molière lent Lully, who was always in debt, 11,000 livres. It was not till 1672 that the inevitable break fell due.

Lully had nothing to do with the master's next forthcoming piece, *L'Avare* ('The Miser'), five acts in prose, which took the Palais-Royal stage on September 9th, 1668; two months after *George Dandin*, though Molière must have been engaged on it much longer. Once more hard-pressed for a new show, he had again gone to Plautus, whose *Aulularia* supplies the basis of the plot.

If any miser can be amusing, old Harpagon of *L'Avare* should be, especially when, flying in the teeth of Plautus, he covets the penniless young Mariane and decides to marry her. The attempt to combine the same two reciprocally-destructive obsessions in one personality was made likewise by Dickens.

---

[1] 'His wife, his children, and the entire human race, great and small, pray night and day: "Lord, of Your singular goodness towards us deliver us from the Florentine!" ' (*Le Florentin*).

Perhaps old Gride, of *Nicholas Nickleby*, whose reflexes are exhibited with surprising frankness for the period, is a trifle more credible in amorous guise than Harpagon? But Harpagon, the sensitive may find themselves concluding, after a fifty-seventh survey, is not credible, let alone pleasing, in this guise at all.

How far *L'Avare* is really a comic piece – *miser* is a very pregnant Latin word – might be a question for debate. Harpagon runs his household as a maniac-skinflint would, and his son and daughter, Cléante and Élise, are in a perpetual state of despair and rebellion. Ardent to marry the poor and beautiful girl of his choice, Cléante has no money. An obliging broker, Maître Simon, finds him a moneylender at 25 per cent, with stringent conditions. When they meet Cléante finds that the bloodsucker is his own father, and a bitter scene breaks out between them.

HARP: So it's you who are trying to ruin yourself by such damnable loans!

CLÉANTE: So it's you who are trying to enrich yourself by such damnable usury!

HARP: Tell me, aren't you ashamed to fall into such debaucheries, and get yourself involved in such frightful expense, and make such a shameful waste of the money your forebears have got together for you with such sweat?

CLÉANTE: Don't you blush to dishonour your position by the kind of business you go in for, to sacrifice honour and reputation to an insatiable urge to pile up coin, and to go one better, in the matter of interest, on the most infamous tricks invented by the most notorious usurers?

HARP: Out of my sight, rascal, out of my sight!

CLÉANTE: Who is the greater criminal, d'you think – the man who buys money he needs or the man who steals money he doesn't?

A succeeding clash between them over Mariane, on whom, unknown to Cléante, Harpagon has fixed his senile fancy, ends almost in blows.

HARP: I forbid you to see me again.

CLÉANTE: That's all right.

HARP: I cast you off.
CLÉANTE: Cast away.
HARP: I disown you.
CLÉANTE: By all means.
HARP: I disinherit you.
CLÉANTE: Anything you like.
HARP: And I give you my curse.
CLÉANTE: I don't want your gifts.

Not thus did decent sons, even under extreme provocation, answer their fathers back under the Old Régime, and one can hardly quarrel with Rousseau's comment to d'Alembert that a comedy which makes a Cléante attractive is hardly a school of good morals; on which, as all the world knows, Jean-Jacques was, in the intervals of dropping his illegitimate offspring into hospices, a recognized authority. If such scenes are not funny, there is a sufficiency of legitimate laughter in *L'Avare*, supplied by Harpagon himself in his varying moods of mania, by Harpagon's comic servants, and notably by Frosine, the professional matchmaker hired by Harpagon to handle *l'affaire Mariane*. Frosine's demonstration that Mariane's lack of a dowry is equivalent to a handsome annual income should be familiar to every candidate for a B.Sc (Econ.) with aspirations to a university chair. Eating very little and very plainly, being unaccustomed to expensive dresses, jewellery and furniture, and having an aversion from games of chance quite providential, and uncommon among women ('I know one not far from here who has lost twenty thousand this year at *trente-et-quarante*'), the penniless Mariane represents a saving to Harpagon of 9,000 livres a year. 'Add a thousand crowns saved on her food', says Frosine, 'and there we are – a clear twelve thousand a year. Am I right?' But Harpagon, alas, has not read any contemporary Mill or Tawney, and dismisses this thesis with a snort.

The piece has its full quota of such humours, faultlessly inset and deft 'theatre', for example the scene – stolen from a Commedia farce – of Mariane's formal visit, during which Cléante suddenly removes a fine diamond ring from Harpagon's finger, hands it to the girl to admire, and, while the old man executes a sort of apoplectic dance in the background, insists that it is a present from his father. But the climax of *L'Avare* is Molière at his most wayward. With the irruption of a mysterious, wealthy 'Seigneur Anselme' on the last scene but one we know all too well that the *deus ex machina* has arrived to clear up everything in five minutes, as indeed he does. Mariane is his long-lost daughter, Élise's lover Valère, who has been masquerading throughout the piece as Harpagon's butler, is his long-lost son, and he himself can hardly believe it.

> ANSELME: O Heaven! how great is thy power, how manifest the working of miracles by thyself alone! Kiss me, my children, and mingle your joint transports with your father's!
> VALÈRE: You are our father?
> MARIANE: It is you my mother mourned so long?
> ANSELME: Yes, my daughter, yes, my son. I am Dom Thomas d'Alburcy, whom Heaven saved from the waves with all the fortune I possessed, and who, having believed you both dead for sixteen years (etc., etc.).

And the curtain falls at length on Harpagon hurrying out to nurse his precious casket of gold.

With all its incidental hilarities *L'Avare* depresses, as any clinical study must. Even when played (how memorably) by the late Charles Dullin, Harpagon is a monster obsessed by the ugliest of vices, totally devoid of human dignity and feeling. Contemporary box-office returns seem to show that he made the contemporary Parisian public as vaguely uneasy as he makes others, since *L'Avare* managed to achieve no more than twenty performances over three months. Being for some reason more highly esteemed by British pedagogy than any other comedy of Molière's, it has assisted for generations in the formative process of young England, and few end-of-term displays are complete without an excerpt. Many of the thoughtful have asked themselves how far Master Jean Poquelin, who was due to die, at 76, in the year after its production, and in reduced circumstances, may have contributed to Harpagon's portrait. Surely, one may surmise, very little? A close-fisted type, perhaps, and antipathetic always, more or less, towards his eldest son. But after all he launched Jean-Baptiste into the world with the best education purchasable in France.

On September 17th, 1669, the Royal Comedians left Paris by command to attend the Court at Chambord on the Loire. At this fairest of Renaissance châteaux another of those ornate festivities which Louis XIV so regularly ordered, not merely for his pleasure but for their publicity-value in the eyes of a jealous Europe, was on the schedule. For once Molière had been given reasonable time. On October 6th, he presented the Court with *Monsieur de Pourceaugnac*, a three-act farcical comedy in prose, with interludes, ballets and incidental music by Jean-Baptiste Lully, who likewise played a part in it. Brilliantly vital, unflaggingly inventive, not a little ruthless, the new piece is as riotous a sequence of laughs as any *farceur* of genius brooding over the dust and ashes of success could possibly devise.

Undeniably most of the fun of *Monsieur de Pourceaugnac*, in which a harmless rustic gentleman is exploited by metropolitan roguery, is quite villainously heartless. Round about this period Louis XIV, like Charles II in England, was engaged in a purge of the provincial nobility, numbers of whom, fair game for Court wits in any case, sported titles and coats unregistered by the Royal heralds. There is nothing amiss with M. de Pourceaugnac's pedigree, however. The ignominies he has to endure through three acts are due simply to his arrival in Paris by arrangement to marry Julie, daughter of the wealthy bourgeois Oronte and a girl of disquieting tenacity. Through the ingenuity of Éraste, Julie's own choice, assisted by two skilled professionals of intrigue, the Neapolitan Sbrigani and a lady of dubious character named Nérine, a pair of swindlers as bland and precious as their lineal descendants in *Der Rosenkavalier*, the poor gentleman is fooled, humiliated, terrorized, and finally routed bag and baggage. M. de Pourceaugnac (*pourceau*, a hog) comes from Limoges in the Limousin. The

128

natives of this province were and had been for centuries stock butts for metropolitan humour – e.g., the Limousin scholar in Rabelais – as the most Boeotian of clods, said to live on turnips and ranking as clowns one degree above the yokels of Auvergne. Their gentry and *noblesse* were especially risible. Squire Jerry Blackacre, Wycherley's 'true raw Squire' of *The Plain Dealer*, the nearest equivalent to M. de Pourceaugnac on the contemporary English stage, is a thing of tissue-paper in comparison.

Between Sbrigani, a very near relative of the rascally Brighella, his fellow-Neapolitan of the Commedia, and the fair Nérine there is a graceful opening exchange. Nérine is introducing her fellow-crook to Julie and Éraste.

> Madame, here's a real ace. Your affair could not be in better hands. He's the hero of the century for his exploits – a gentleman who has dared the galleys twenty times or more to serve his friends, and has brought the most difficult operations to success at the risk of his arms and shoulders (i.e. of floggings and brandings). As you see him now he's an exile from his country on account of I don't know how many honourable enterprises generously undertaken.

The dark, smiling Sbrigani bows elegantly and returns the bouquet.

> I'm really confused by all the compliments you honour me with. I should in justice pay you a few on some of the marvels of your own career – above all for the glorious and honourable way you swiped twelve thousand crowns at cards from the young foreign gentleman they introduced you to, and again when you so charmingly faked that contract which ruined a whole family, and again when your lofty soul enabled you to deny the deposit they'd made with you, and once more when you so generously offered that testimony which hanged a couple of people who didn't deserve it.

To which Nérine in modest confusion replies 'Mere trifles, sir – really not worth mentioning. Your praises make me blush.' All four get down forthwith to business, and a pretty business it turns out to be. Attaching himself in pure altruism to M. de Pourceaugnac as he gets off the coach from Limoges, a trifle dazed and dizzied by the bustle of Paris, Sbrigani is very soon able with Éraste's co-operation to have him examined by a couple of doctors as a mentally-afflicted relative. The ensuing consultation, a little masterpiece of grave tomfoolery stuffed with Latin tags and citations from Galen and Hippocrates, and issuing in a diagnosis of that same *mélancholie hypocondriaque* for which Dr Mauvilain was supposed to be treating Molière at the same time – the whole scene reads as if the saturnine Mauvilain had just left his patient reaching for his pen and choking with laughter – ends in the chase of a frantic M. de Pourceaugnac by a whole covey of doctors and apothecaries brandishing enormous syringes and clysters. In the Chambord production they were led by a fantastic spring-heeled 'Dr Chiachiarroni', grimacing like a madman, whose gambols reached a peak, apparently, with a tremendous flying leap, Nijinsky-wise, into a harpsichord, smashing it to matchwood. With mixed feelings Molière must have surveyed a King and Court limp with laughter at the antics of the Florentine, now increasingly his supplanter in the royal favour.

Fortunately he had no need to depend for laughs on Lully's clowning. The play was full of them. With devilish or Neapolitan ingenuity Sbrigani continues to earn his money; now, in the guise of a Flemish merchant, warning Oronte in confidence that M. de Pourceaugnac is an all-but-bankrupt pursuing this marriage solely to pay off a horde of creditors, now warning the astounded Pourceaugnac, equally in confidence, that his intended bride is – well, let us be quite fair, says Sbrigani.

> To say that the young lady leads 'a gay life' would be a trifle too much. Suppose we try to put it in more agreeable terms. The word 'light' won't do either. To describe her as 'a finished coquette' seems what we need. In fact I use it here and now to describe to you quite honestly what she's like.

'Are they trying to make a dupe of me?' asks the poor dazed gentleman from Limoges, but he has little time to brood over this possibility. The next ordeal on the schedule is already upon him. It is the advent of two strange young women, natives of Picardy and Languedoc respectively, each attacking him in incomprehensible jargon as her fugitive husband and the father of her half-dozen children. A couple of singing lawyers warn him that polygamy is a matter for the gallows, and on Sbrigani's advice he gets away in feminine disguise, only to fall in later with a couple of brawny Swiss on their way to the Grève to see a certain 'Monsiu de Porcegnac' figure in a very pretty little hanging, *un petit pendement pien choly*. In the meantime they proceed to make improper advances to the seeming beauty. While the unfortunate gentleman is still fighting them off the police arrive and arrest him. Having finally released himself at the price of much gold, M. de Pourceaugnac is able to catch the next coach back to Limoges. The ever-kindly Sbrigani sees him off. 'You're the only honest man I've come across in this accursed town', says M. de Pourceaugnac huskily, wringing his benefactor's hand, and the farce ends with Julie betrothed to Éraste and a final ballet-masquerade.

In print alone *Monsieur de Pourceaugnac* is irresistibly comic, if one can suppress one's better feelings. In its original form – the interludes and ballets were dropped for the Palais-Royal presentation on November 15th – with Lully's music, and the Florentine himself gambolling like an inspired lunatic, it must have had the impact of a continuous stream of Chinese crackers. On October 20th the moody author was back in Paris with his load of disillusion and his continual cough. One may picture him brooding in the wings, dark and preoccupied, while a packed house roars itself hoarse and the sweating actors come and go. Might it be, as has occurred to more observers than one, that at this period he was deriving a little grim pleasure from exploiting himself for public entertainment? In *George Dandin* he had aroused laughter at the fate of a husband deceived and betrayed; in *Monsieur de Pourceaugnac* he utilizes hypochondria (there is sufficient testimony to the depth of his own depressions at this time) to mock at the Faculty of Medicine once more. Did the enormous success of such jests afford him the satisfaction of a kind of cynical Prometheus egging on the vultures tearing at his liver? The touch of near-sadism in his latest comedy certainly invites the thought.

Monsieur de Pourceaugnac did not seem a brutal play to seventeenth-century Paris. In a more pernickety age Michelet was to find it 'horrible', and Faguet to dismiss it as 'a spectacle for lackeys'. Dispassionately considered it is, of course, as ethically indefensible as a Punch-and-Judy show. A decent, kindly man is maltreated by rogues who today would find themselves very properly doing a 'stretch'. On the other hand one may reflect that the gentleman from the Limousin would have been infinitely worse off had he married Julie, a girl of slightly shuddersome charm. One could not go so far as to describe her as a Brinvilliers or a Voisin *in posse*, though arsenic was as procurable in Limoges as anywhere else. There are more ways of killing a cat than choking her with cream. Whatever M. de Pourceaugnac endured, it seems clear that he at least escaped the slow poison of inevitable cuckoldry.

Before the year was out another Royal requisition ordered Molière into harness again. But now a considerable ray of light had pierced his gloom. Madeleine Béjart and Chapelle and other intimates had been at work. The still-adored Armande had been prevailed on to consider living with him again. It is perhaps time to recall that even a fashionable actor-manager has a private life of sorts.

CHAPTER THREE

He was a rich man in the 1660's, even as successful actor-managers went, and go.

Grimarest fixes his annual income tentatively at 30,000 livres, a cosy figure for the period, something like £10,000 a year in modern money. It was made up of four, and at times five, shares in the Palais-Royal theatre, his royal pension, and solid money-gifts following frequent performances at the houses of Royalty and the nobility, not to mention contributions by his publisher. Moreover Madeleine Béjart in the old days had invested in his behalf very shrewdly. Though Molière entertained on a lavish scale and was notoriously generous, alike to charities, to hard-up fellow-actors, and to old Master

Jean Poquelin, whom he assisted in his penurious last days, he had at least no financial worries, even when Armande in the early days of marriage was making the money fly; as she apparently did with some insouciance. It is on record that at least once she failed to account for some 200 livres of a repaid 1,000-livre loan to somebody or other by her husband. As he was careless enough over money matters this may not be a unique instance.

To prepare for her return to him, which entailed his leaving the Béjarts, in close proximity with whom – and Catherine de Brie – he had been living for the last four or five years when he was not at Auteuil, he found a house in the exclusive Rue de Richelieu which contemporary estate-agents doubtless described as 'this eminently desirable bijou mansion'. No. 40 now marks the site. It belonged to one René Baudelet, apparently a financier, and was one of a street of similar houses tenanted by the wealthy, each with servants' quarters, stables and other outbuildings on an appropriate scale. The spacious ground floor, mezzanine, and first floor, fourteen rooms in all, were for occupation by Molière and his wife. If there was a nursery for five-year-old Esprit-Madeleine there is no mention of it. The child may have been boarded out with her nurse, suitably to the custom of the period, at Auteuil, where she is glimpsed once or twice round about this time cheering her father's solitude.

A certain opulence in the furnishing and appointments of the house in the Rue de Richelieu is discernible from the envious diatribe of Le Boulanger de Chalussay:

> Ces meubles précieux sous de si beaux lambris,
> Ces lustres éclatants, ces cabinets de prix,
> Ces miroirs, ces tableaux, cette tapisserie
> Qui, seule, épuise l'art de la Savonnerie . . . [1]

An inventory discovered by Soulié in the nineteenth-century more or less confirmed this. The domestic arrangements of a later magnate of the theatre like the great Belasco of New York

[1] 'This costly furniture, under such handsome panelling, these dazzling chandeliers, these expensive cabinets, these mirrors, pictures, this tapestry, in itself exhausting all the art of the Savonnerie . . .'

could show something more impressive, perhaps, in the shape of rococo-Gothic chambers full of chimes and incense and tall stained-glass windows, with a throne-room for audiences distantly recalling the Vatican. Content to leave drama to the stage, Molière expressed himself merely in terms of Flemish tapestries, Savonnerie and Turkey carpets, a liberal sufficiency of silver plate and linen, a service of sixty-eight pieces with numerous vases and mantel-ornaments of fine Dutch porcelain, and a selection of paintings unidentified; chiefly, no doubt, Italian, with perhaps a Claude and a Poussin or two, and, undoubtedly, at least one of the flattering portraits by his friend Mignard.

A significant item is the extensive *batterie de cuisine*. What kind of a table Molière kept is nowhere on record, but the supper-fare outlined by the man-about-town Dorante, entertaining the marquise Dorimène at Monsieur Jourdain's expense in *Le Bourgeois Gentilhomme*, may be taken as evidence that an habitual gourmet held the pen. 'This, Madame,' begins Dorante, indicating a luxurious table laid for three, and adopting the best manner of the Wine and Food Society, 'is not a very distinguished effort. No doubt you'll detect a few lapses and solecisms in it. If Damis had ordered it you'd see what true elegance and erudition can do.' He proceeds to outline the kind of symphony the master Damis would have composed for her, combining such themes as *pain de rive*, which is a roll of delicate golden crustiness baked to perfection at the edge of the oven; a velvety wine, at once well-bred and assertive; a fine neck of mutton with parsley garnishing; a river-trout melting on the palate like almond paste; a brace of well-hung partridges of 'surprising bouquet', and, to complete a masterpiece, a concentrated bouillon ushering in a young, plump, tender turkey, flanked by squabs and crowned with white onions and chicory. 'For myself,' adds the impudent Dorante with a sigh, 'I admit my ignorance, and as Monsieur Jourdain here has justly observed, Madame, I wish this repast were more worthy to be offered you.'

Molière's guests in the Place du Palais-Royal and at Auteuil alike may therefore have raised their glasses not infrequently to his old cook, a character named Renée Vannier, known for some reason as 'La Forest'. Though her successors there and in the Rue de Richelieu were each called 'La Forest' likewise, it seems to be the original Renée Vannier on whom, according to a well-known story of Boileau's which has inspired more than one Salon canvas of the past, the master would occasionally test new work by going into the kitchen to read the comic scenes to her and making corrections accordingly. He took her with him to the theatre now and again, as La Grange's registers attest.

Two other domestics are named as serving the Molière household – a chambermaid named Catherine Lemoyne, possibly acting as lady's-maid in addition, and a footman-valet hailing from Provence, and in the fashion of the day named 'Provençal' accordingly. We learn from Grimarest that this man was a semi-moron, more than once kicked over backwards by his testy employer while trying to force a shoe on the wrong foot. For it seems that Molière could be highly temperamental at home.

> He demanded more service than any man in the world. He had to be dressed like a *grand seigneur*, and he would never have deigned to arrange the folds of his cravat. The exactitude of his requirements made him difficult to please, and nobody could satisfy him, however attentive. A window opened or closed one moment before his order threw him into convulsions – he was petty on such occasions – and if anyone misplaced one of his books it was enough to put him off work for a fortnight.

What dressing like a *grand seigneur* implied for a fashionable seventeenth-century actor – the vision of a celebrated Edwardian survival, last of his species, rises inevitably before the mind's eye, monocled and top-hatted, taking the summertime air of the Piccadilly of the 1920's more immaculately garbed in the correct morning costume of a vanished age than any duke, hardly less of a museum-piece than a dodo – was something sufficiently complicated. The ruffled cambric shirt and wristbands, the choice of the day's velvet suit, the arrangement of the elaborate Mechlin cravat and the lace *canons*, falling so decoratively from knee to mid-calf, the matching tints of silk stockings, shoe-rosettes, and, in winter, a muff, the hang of the broad embroidered sword-band, and above all the exact poising of a three-decker peruke with its forepeak and its double shower of curls, needing regular combing and perfuming – to adjust all these matters properly required unremitting attention and a skilful valet. Testiness over his toilet was therefore excusable in Molière. Removing a book from a library table is a graver matter, as every writer will recognize, and a far more agonizing experience than anything calculated to drive others of the Muses' favourites into tantrums.

Molière's library is nowhere described. More ornate, no doubt, than La Fontaine's, which is, it would similarly display the contemporary bibliophile's addiction to adorning his shelves with classical busts of terracotta or plaster. Those of Horace, Terence, and Plautus would most fittingly crown Molière's, since he was deeply read in all three. Perhaps a bust of Lucretius could join them. In moods of pessimist nihilism Lucretius must have been the ideal companion. The bookshelves one can legitimately furnish with editions of the Latin poets and playwrights, prizes from Clermont and later volumes ornately bound in mellow calf with, perhaps, a neat gilt monogram, together with presentation-copies of their works from Boileau, La Fontaine, Racine, Cyrano, and other friends or ex-friends. One or two scientific works by his old tutor Gassendi might be added; certainly Montaigne's essays and a set of *Pantagruel*, highly likely a few books on the Commedia dell' Arte, some of them gifts from Tiberio Fiorillo. Even so early there was a spate of these, in Italian and French. The *Della Scena* of Locatelli (Rome, 1622) containing 103 scenarios, would be a godsend to any playwright in an emergency. Perhaps a set of the novels of Mlle de Scudéry might be added. They were all food for amusement.

With such sedatives at hand, if no work was impending, Molière could cool down and recover from nervous hysteria incurred elsewhere in the home. It is only just to recall again that any outbreaks of temperament illustrated by Grimarest were compensated by an unfailing generosity of heart. Even so it may be surmised that the blame for any crises in the Molière *ménage* was not invariably Armande's. Nor, perhaps were all such crises merely extensions, in Molière's case, of that stage-existence which for many of the theatre's children becomes the real one. The artist who makes his living by continually counterfeiting violent emotions in public is perfectly capable of feeling real pain at home. To the contributory factors in Molière's fundamental melancholy – betrayed and unrequited love, hypochondria due to ill-health and unending labour, the disillusion of success, the satiety of the epicurean – may certainly be added the loss of Armande's first child, the infant Louis, in 1664. To one of his friends, the sceptic philosopher La Mothe Le Vayer, who lost a son about this time, he sent a consolatory sonnet, urging him to give full play to his grief, which throws some light on his own state.

> Aux larmes, Le Vayer, laisse tes yeux ouverts,
> Ton deuil est raisonnable encor qu'il soit extrême,
> Et lorsque pour toujours on perd ce que tu perds,
> La sagesse, crois-moi, peut pleurer elle-même . . . [1]

If this is not great poetry, and not to be compared with a similar theme of Malherbe's ('*Et rose elle a vécu ce que vivent les roses . . .*'), it surely affords a glimpse of a wound unhealed by time?

> On sait bien que les pleurs ne ramèneront pas
> Ce cher fils que t'enlève un imprévu trépas,
> Mais la perte par là n'en est pas moins cruelle.[2]

These lines will re-echo in the grief of the bereaved king in *Psiché*, a production of the near future. Though it is admittedly difficult, when contemplating any genius of the theatre, to discern where the acting starts and stops, where the symbolic green-baize carpet of drama and the Wilton of domesticity begin and end, it can hardly be said of Molière that he offered the spectacle of his private emotions to any but a tiny circle of

[1] 'Give your eyes full scope for tears, Le Vayer; your grief is reasonable, however extreme; when one loses for ever what you have lost, believe me, wisdom itself may weep . . .'

[2] 'We well know tears will not bring back the dear son rapt from you by an unexpected death; but his loss is none the less cruel for that.'

intimates. He had had a few other losses during these last fifteen years in Paris. His old comrade and fellow-trouper Joseph Béjart died in 1659, his brother Jean Poquelin in 1660, his sister Madeleine Boudet in 1665, the fascinating Marquise du Parc in 1668, Molière's father in 1669. It is likely that all these bereavements together did not affect him as much as the loss of his son and Armande's.

His little circle of intimates remained – with the exception of Racine, with whom he had no further dealings after 1665 – his mainstay: Boileau, La Fontaine, Mignard, Dr Rohault, and Chapelle, the oldest friend of all, with who he had only one brush worth mentioning in forty years. This was in 1661, when Molière, pressed for time and entrusting the undependable Chapelle with the Caritidès scene in *Les Fascheux*, had at the last moment to rewrite it, despite which Chapelle went round for a time boasting in all the taverns of Paris that the best thing in *Les Fascheux* was his own. The ensuing clash was vigorous but not fissile.

The handsome house in the Rue de Richelieu will shortly, therefore, be the background of a repaired marriage, Armande returning to her husband at the end of 1671. She seems to have created a little trouble over Catherine de Brie, now finally deposed. Any adventures of her own during the years of separation must have been conducted discreetly enough to escape the roving eye of her enemy of *La Fameuse Comédienne*. What chances the restored *ménage* had of permanency can scarcely be judged, since at the end of 1671 Molière will have just over twelve months to live.

CHAPTER FOUR

Yielding to irresistible temptation, one may strive to catch the overtones of a conversation-piece possibly taking place at the Louvre, or Versailles, or Fontainebleau, one evening in the spring of 1670. It would begin, one imagines, more or less thus:

'You sent for me, Sir.'

'I did, Molière. I want something for the autumn.'

'Yes, Sir.'

'Something on the grand scale this time, Molière. Everything in it. Heroic comedy, ballet, singing, dancing, machines, masques, mythology, astrology – you know the sort of thing. I have spoken to Lully. I propose taking part in a ballet or two myself.'

'Yes, Sir.'

'Say as Neptune, or Apollo, or something of the sort.'

'Very good, Sir.'

'I take it you have no idea at the moment, Moliere?'

'Not at the moment, Sir.'

'Good. I have the idea for you, as it happens.'

Whether or not such a conversation ever took place, its essence may be easily discerned in Molière's preface to the printed result.[1] Louis XIV himself indicated the theme of *Les Amans Magnifiques* ('The Splendid Lovers'), which was produced at the royal château of St Germain-en-Laye on September 7th, 1670. Except that the King changed his mind about appearing as Neptune and Apollo, it was the most regally sumptuous of shows. What changed the royal mind, after mature reflection and apparently at the last moment, was a hint conveyed by Louis' admired Racine in *Britannicus* a few months previously. The lines concerned refer to Nero's addiction to making a public exhibition of himself at the Games,

> A disputer des prix indignes de ses mains,
> A se donner luy-même en spectacle aux Romains . . . [2]

Louis XIV took the hint, says Boileau, and danced in the ballet no more.[3] Contemporary Parisian gazettes confirm this.

[1] 'The King, who prefers the extraordinary in everything he undertakes, proposed to afford the Court an entertainment composed of everything the theatre can provide. To embrace this vast conception, combining so many divers items, his Majesty chose as a subject the rivalry of two princes who', etc. etc.

[2] Competing for prizes unworthy of his hands, offering himself as a spectacle to the Romans . . .

[3] *Lettre à M. de Monchesnay, sur la Comédie.* La Grange nevertheless forbore to strike out the verses for the King's entry ('pour le ROY, repre-

It has always been the fashion to dismiss *Les Amans Magnifiques*, five acts and six interludes in prose and verse, as a wearisome taskpiece, the least Molièresque of all Molière's works. Boldly tackled, this stately pantomime has more hidden charms to disclose than one.

These do not derive from the spoutings of Iphocrate and Timocles, the two rival princes (and bores) seeking the hand of the Princess Eriphile, or from six long, grandiose interludes, into which are crammed practically everything mythological and decorative except the sea-serpent, or even from the quips of the comic Court astrologer Anaxarque, who provides what amusement there is. The principal charm of *Les Amans Magnifiques*, if one may make bold so to suggest, for apparently the first time in three hundred years, lies in the speech and bearing of the gallant Sostrate, who secretly loves and is loved by Princess Eriphile, rescues her from a wild boar, and ultimately carries her off under the noses of the two offended visiting royalties. For Sostrate is a poor general in the Thessalian Army, and a more eloquent brass-hat never left Staff College.

Generals are not for the most part, as history testifies, skilled in love, being given to short barks and long, scowling silences. What Napoleon's wives and mistresses said behind his back is fairly well known. Listen however to General Sostrate, to whom Princess Eriphile has just regretfully announced that only rank and destiny prevent her from yielding to her heart.

> Ah, Madame! This is too much for an unfortunate man! I was not prepared to die with so much glory, and I cease, at this moment, to blame my destiny. If it caused me to be born in a rank far lower than that of my desire, it caused me likewise to be born happy enough to inspire pity in the heart of a great princess . . . Yes, Madame. Ever since I have dared to love you – and it is you, Madame, who deign to allow me this bold word – ever since, I say, I have dared to love you, I have condemned the pridefulness of my desires and created myself the kind of destiny I should look for. My death, Madame, will have nothing in it to

sentant NEPTUNE'), when he printed the play for the first time in 1682. It may be that Louis danced at the opening performance in order not to disappoint the Court.

surprise me, since I am prepared for it. But your kindness crowns it with an honour for which my love would never have bade me hope. I go to my death, after this, the happiest and most glorious of all mankind!

All he asks of her is to remember him occasionally. 'Go, Sostrate,' says the Princess in agitation. 'To ask me to remember you is to care very little for my peace of mind.' But the stars and the wild boars of Thessaly intervene for the happiest of endings. Accepting the ruling of the gods and blessing, in Act V, her daughter's future as *Madame la Générale* – it must have occurred to every spectator that General Sostrate might find himself gazetted Marshal, GOC, before very long – the Dowager-Princess Aristione, Eriphile's mother, disposes of the slightly unprincely resentment of Sostrate's superb and discomfited rivals with truly Edwardian poise. 'We will overlook these unfortunate remarks,' she says in effect, 'since they are occasioned by feelings deeming themselves hurt. This contretemps will not in the least prevent our enjoying the Pythian Games now to follow. Let us hasten to conclude a marvellous day with this elaborate spectacle' – '*Allons-y de ce pas, et couronnons par ce pompeux spectacle cette merveilleuse journée.*' Thus announced, in the very accents of a Grand Dame of the Primrose League dismissing a scuffle between a couple of MPs at her garden-party, the sixth ballet-interlude ends the piece.

Together with such incidental diversions *Les Amans Magnifiques* contains a little scene (Act II, Sc. 2) in which every palate of sensibility may discern a distinct foretaste of Marivaux. A whimsical courtier named Clitidas, played by Molière, informs the Princess Eriphile, played by Armande, that his friend Sostrate, played by La Grange, is deeply in love, implying fairly obviously that she is the object. She affects regal astonishment and indignation. 'How dare he have the audacity!' 'Oh, but Sostrate is not in love with you, Ma'am,' says the wicked Clitidas hastily, shocked despite himself. 'He respects your Royal Highness far too much for that! It is one of your maids of honour – young Arsinoë.' As Eriphile pales and winces under this blow Clitidas relents and tells her the truth.

It is herself with whom Sostrate is in love, but desperately. On which she turns on him.

ERIPHILE: You insolent fellow! You come here and make me betray my feelings? Go away, leave me! You dare to dabble in reading souls, to try to penetrate the secrets of a princess's heart? Out of my sight, don't let me see you ever again! . . . Clitidas!

CLIT: Ma'am?

ERIPHILE: Come here. I forgive you.

CLIT: You are too kind, Ma'am.

ERIPHILE: On condition, and mark my words, that you never open your mouth to one single person in the world, at the peril of your life.

CLIT: That suffices.

ERIPHILE: So Sostrate has told you he loves me?

Certainly the essence of *marivaudage*, and a by-product of Molière's fancy which he never repeated, and left to a successor to develop into a system. One more of the incidental charms of *Les Amans Magnifiques* has not, perhaps, been sufficiently noted and admired – the free rendering of Horace's ode to Lydia which Molière slips into the third interlude, to be sung by a shepherd to his shepherdess following a dance of fauns and dryads:

> Quand je plaisois à tes yeux,
> J'estois content de ma vie,
> Et ne voyois roy ni dieux
> Dont le sort me fit envie . . . [1]

Simpler and more elegant than Herrick's, or even Mr Gladstone's, or that of possibly 75 per cent of the ten thousand other translators of an untranslatable ode, this version may – who knows? – have been resurrected from one of Molière's exercise-books at Clermont. But alas, such graces, Sostrate's included, failed to make *Les Amans Magnifiques* a box-office success. In 1688, fifteen years after Molière's death, La Grange put it on again, shorn of its 'machines' and sumptuosities. It ran for only nine performances.

[1] Compare Herrick's attempt:
> While Lydia, I was lov'd of thee,
> Nor any was preferr'd 'fore me,
> To hug thy whitest neck, than I:
> The Persian King liv'd not more happily . . .

At the beginning of the autumn of 1670 the King's Comedians received another summons to Chambord, where the King was on a hunting holiday. Once again his Majesty required new entertainment, having this time stipulated beforehand to Molière that it should include 'some sort of Turkish buffoonery'.

The reason for this order, which blossomed into superb farcical comedy, is itself entertaining. Some months previously an envoy of the Grand Turk, Mohammed IV, had arrived in Paris to discuss the Cretan question. Candia had recently been taken by the Turks from the Venetians, a number of whose French allies, some of them men of rank, had been killed or captured, and the French Ambassador had been recalled from Constantinople. The envoy Soliman Pasha was, in the phrase of modern diplomacy, given the full treatment. Having been allowed to wait four weeks for an audience at Versailles, he was received at length amid a formidable parade of troops and ushered with his escort into a gallery where the King of France sat superb on a high dais, wearing a hat and a suit of clothes blazing with – according to Court rumour – fourteen million francs' worth of diamonds. Monsieur, similarly bedizened, sat beside him. To the mortification of every courtier, and of Louis himself, the show failed to make any impression on the Oriental mind except that Soliman Pasha, incensed at the hauteur with which Louis accepted the Sultan's letter of greeting, withdrew in a huff and soon afterwards returned to Constantinople. There exists a painting of the episode, showing the Pasha and his twenty attendant Turks before a dazzling Sun King; all plainly garbed, mediocrely turbaned, and wrapped in imperturbable calm. They had seen displays of precious stones before, and far larger ones.

Though the matter rankled at the time, Louis decided to treat it as a joke. Hence the order to Molière. The result was *Le Bourgeois Gentilhomme*, five acts in prose, incidental and ballet-music by Lully. Staged, after its success at Chambord, at the Palais-Royal on November 3rd, 1670, it captured the town.

It is certainly one of Molière's six masterpieces. There are pedants who complain that a satiric social comedy which turns midway into uproarious farce is not good art. To combat this other pedants have evolved the theory that Molière is thereby establishing his moral. Snobbery and vanity will swallow anything; therefore a fool like Monsieur Jourdain can plausibly be persuaded, within the canons, that the Grand Turk's visiting son and heir desires to marry his daughter Lucile and to create him, Jourdain, a *mammamouchi* of the Sublime Porte beforehand. It might be on the other hand that Molière has no message of the sort, and is simply enjoying himself. The Turkish *motif* is introduced with the gayest insouciance. Says the valet Covielle suddenly to his master Cléonte, Lucile's lover: 'There was a masquerade a little time ago which would go splendidly here. I'm thinking of it for a game I'd like to play on this imbecile of ours. The whole idea smells a bit of the theatre (*tout cela sent un peu sa comédie*),' adds Covielle frankly, 'but with him anything goes.' What could be fairer? The aim of comedy is to amuse.

This it certainly does. It was, it still is, superb entertainment from beginning to end. At Chambord the *turquoiserie* of the climax was very carefully produced and rehearsed under the eye of a notable Oriental traveller, the Chevalier d'Arrieux. The presiding mufti was Jean-Baptiste Lully, wearing an enormous turban decorated with lighted candles and at the top of his form, though unable in this costume to repeat his famous harpsichord trick. Molière himself played M. Jourdain, prostrating himself, receiving the ceremonial bastonnade, grotesquely whirling in a dervish-dance, chanting 'Hou la ba, ba la chou, ba la ba, ba la da', and finally tumbling in a heap. The King held his royal sides, according to report. The marquis tribe could not complain that in his new piece Molière was making them look fools again. Dorante, their representative in *Le Bourgeois Gentilhomme*, is merely an elegant sharper.

Social ambition is no crime, but it is undeniably amusing. From the time of Petronius down to World War I the parvenu-aspirant to gentility has almost everywhere been a classic source of guffaws. Before the recent British social revolution began taking shape, from 1919 onwards, *Punch* existed largely on two jokes, the quaint solecisms of the proletariat and the antics of the vulgarian social climber, especially in the hunting-field. The rich Parisian ex-draper M. Jourdain gets off much better at Molière's hand, one may note, than his predecessor in ambition, George Dandin, having at home a Madame Jourdain of the sturdiest Sancho Panza breed to deride and scold. M. Jourdain himself is far from unlikeable. We share Molière's sardonic affection for this stout zany, helpless as a child in the hands of his tailor, his music, dancing, and fencing masters, his philosopher-tutor, and above all his sponsor Dorante, who plays his own game so effectively while pretending to steer an eager neophyte into the Beau Monde. It must be admitted that M. Jourdain invites all this, being a snob almost to the point of mania. His delight at hearing Covielle remark casually that his, M. Jourdain's father was 'a very honest gentleman' is ecstatic.

M. JOURDAIN: You knew him well?
COV: Certainly.
M. JOURDAIN: And you knew him to be a gentleman?
COV: Undoubtedly.
M. JOURDAIN: Well, I don't know what sort of world this is.
COV: Why?
M. JOURDAIN: There are a lot of fools about who enjoy telling me he was a tradesman.
COV: What, him? It's an absolute libel! He never was. It just happened that he was very obliging and very helpful, and as he knew a lot about cloth he went round everywhere choosing it and having it sent home, and letting his friends have some of it for money.
M. JOURDAIN: I'm delighted to know you.

Noble families have been founded ere now on the drapery-trade. Though not so noble or powerful, as Debrett's pages confirm, as those founded on pimping or loot, they demonstrate that M. Jourdain's qualms over his origins are perhaps excessive. Even in the France of the 1670's he could have found himself a title of sorts without much difficulty, Louis XIV's purge of the nobility notwithstanding. But an arrived and accepted M. Jourdain would be far less funny than a M. Jourdain striving and fooled.

He is richly fooled throughout the comedy and doubtless deserves to be, most of all when he begins making passes, in the technical phrase, at Dorante's flame, the fair Dorimène, a lady of quality with whose languid amusement goes undoubtedly a certain lack of scruple. How far she is unaware that Dorante owes the Bourgeois eighteen thousand francs already and is exploiting him on her account without mercy is debatable. However, ethics are hardly an issue in a farce of these dimensions. The sequence in which Cléonte, arrayed as the heir to the Grand Turk and attended by his interpreter Covielle and three pages, all in Turkish disguise, arrives to make his prospective father-in-law a dignitary of the Sublime Porte is pantomime of an irresistible kind from the beginning.

CLÉONTE:	*Ambousahim oqui boraf, Jordina, salamalequi.*
COVIELLE:	That means: 'Monsieur Jourdain, may your heart throughout the year be a flowering rose-tree.'
M. JOURDAIN:	I am His Turkish Highness' most humble servant.
COVIELLE:	*Carigar camboto oustin moraf.*
CLÉONTE:	*Oustin voc catamalequi basum base alla moran.*
COVIELLE:	He says 'May Heaven give you the strength of lions and the prudence of serpents.'
M. JOURDAIN:	His Turkish Highness honours me too much. I wish him every kind of prosperity.
COVIELLE:	*Ossa binamen sadoc babally oracaf ouram.*
CLÉONTE:	*Bel-men.*
COVIELLE:	He says you must accompany him at once to prepare yourself for the ceremony, so that he may view your daughter and conclude the marriage.
M. JOURDAIN:	All that in two words?
COVIELLE:	Yes. The Turkish language is like that.

It was a good joke, and it died hard. Two centuries later Kinglake's bored dragoman in *Eothen* will translate a long animated flow of Turkish rhetoric by 'The Pasha compliments the English'. The triumph of the ruthless Ataturk put an end, alas, to compliments and costume alike. It seems that pashas in the horn-rims and business-suits of 1959 are not very flowery.

Behind all the fantasy of *Le Bourgeois Gentilhomme* looms the monumental figure of Madame Jourdain, incarnation of the French bourgeoisie, in whose cry of 'God forbid!' when her husband announces that Lucile must marry a marquis is all that horror at getting out of step which traditionally rules her caste.[1] She says as much herself, picturing how the neighbours will view a future visit from her daughter in a coach-and-four. '"Look", they'll say, "d'you see that Madame la Marquise who puts on such airs? She's the daughter of Monsieur Jourdain. She was only too glad to play the madam with us when she was a little girl. Both her grandfathers were drapers by the Porte Saint-Innocent. They made a lot of money, but maybe they're paying for that now in the next world. You don't get as rich as all that by being honest folk!"' However, if Madame Jourdain fears the neighbours she fears nobody else on earth. Neither the cynical Dorante nor the supercilious Dorimène, let alone Monsieur Jourdain, is any match for her, and in the end Lucile gets her Cléonte, gentleman or no gentleman, as her mother had promised. A tremendous woman, to whom those opulent official busts of 'Marianne', the Republic One and Indivisible, might well be a slightly-idealized national tribute. Owing as much to the ripostes of Madame Jourdain as to the cowlike gambols of her husband, *Le Bourgeois Gentilhomme* ran for twenty-four consecutive and enthusiastically-applauded performances at the Palais-Royal and has been constantly revived ever since, never failing to yield some of the pleasure it undoubtedly gave its author. For as the tender dialogue-portrait of Armande in Act III alone may testify, the blackest cloud was lifting. The worst of the pain was already gone. She was thinking of coming back.

CHAPTER FIVE

By the end of 1670 he had a delightful new part ready for her. She was to play the *ingénue* heroine of a piece any leading lady of twenty-eight would welcome with squeals. Working against time once more, Molière was able only to furnish the plot and

[1] The Madame Jourdain of the opening run was one of Molière's small-part actors, André Hubert, who apparently made the one and only hit of his life in this part.

write the prologue, Act I, and the opening scenes of Acts II and III of *Psiché*, an heroic tragicomedy-ballet; five acts in free verse, music by Lully, interludes by Quinault, produced at the Tuileries on January 17, 1671. But he had fallen back for support on a master. The rest of the play bears the hall-mark of the crusty and superb Corneille, with whom, since his treatment of the art of tragedy in *La Critique*, Molière had been on barely nodding terms, despite his production of some of Corneille's dramas. Having himself supplied some verse of quality for *Psiché*, Molière could have engaged no collaborator more gifted, old age notwithstanding.

Between them, with Lully's music, they produced a fantasy in porcelain, a *colifichet* for a collector of Dresden. Louis XIV's order had carried a stipulation. In the lumber-rooms of one of the royal palaces was an elaborate stage-set only once used, representing the underworld of Pluto. Prefiguring Mr Crummles with his pump and tubs, the King required a piece utilizing this. Turning for help to La Fontaine, Molière found his theme. In the fifth book of *The Golden Ass* of Lucius Apuleius of Madaura, that ever fragrant second-century novel, is a story about the loves of Cupid and Psyche told by an old woman in a thieves' den in Thessaly. La Fontaine had lately turned it into a poem. It proved the very thing for his friend.

The *clou* of what its first English translator, Master Richard Adlington of University College, calls this 'pleasaunt and delectable tale'[1] is the exquisite, disobedient Psyche's discovery by lamplight that the newly-wed young husband by her side, whose features she has been forbidden to view during his nocturnal visits, is the god of love himself, asleep with bow and arrows beside him. As she clasps him yet more ardently, 'broyling with the love of Cupid', a drop of hot lamp-oil falls on his naked shoulder – '*O rash and bolde lampe! how darest thou bee so bolde as to burne the god of all fire?*' – and Cupid wakes and flies away, seemingly for ever. Perfect poetry, mime, or ballet-material as this sequence provides, Molière took the easier way. His Psyche merely plies Cupid with daylight questionings

---

[1] *The XI Bookes of the Golden Asse, conteininge the Metamorphosie of Lucius Apuleius.* London, 1566.

('*Laissez-moy mon secret!*') till he vanishes, together with the enchanted palace and garden created for her.

With a few other deviations from Apuleius and La Fontaine, Molière preserves the African Platonic's main theme. The marriage of Cupid and Psyche, a King's beautiful daughter, is a *mésalliance* driving Venus his lady mother into a passion of fury. Not content with robbing her, Venus, of the worship of mankind, who have all gone Psyche-mad, the creature has now entrapped her only son, whose orders were to avenge Venus by causing Psyche to fall in love with the lowest ruffian on earth. From a subsequent interview between Venus and Psyche it would seem, however, that the anguish of a mother has yielded to some extent to the venom of the affronted leading lady:

> Orgueilleuse Psiché, vous m'osez donc attendre,
> Aprés m'avoir sur terre enlevé mes honneurs,
>> Aprés que vos traits suborneurs
> Ont receu les encens qu'aux miens seuls on doit rendre?
>> J'ay veu mes temples desertez,
> J'ay veu tous les mortels, séduits par vos beautéz,
> Vous offrir des respects jusqu'alors inconnus . . . [1]

Poor little innocent Psyche is nevertheless spared all the punishments devised for her by Venus in Apuleius' story except the final one. Her despatch on a mission to Proserpine in the underworld brings in the left-over scenic set which was to some extent, and most happily, the 'onlie begetter' of the piece. As the background to the fourth interlude it was sufficiently impressive, judging from the printed play. In the midst of a sea of stormy fire, surrounded by blazing ruins, rises the palace of Pluto, King of Hades, from which issues a ballet of the Furies, dancing for joy at the rage they have implanted in the heart of the goddess of love. While they are so occupied Psyche passes in Charon's barge on her return to the upper air, swooning on the way. But in the play, as in Apuleius, Venus relents at last and all ends well.

[1] 'So you dare to linger, proud Psyche, after robbing me of my honours on earth – after your provocative charms have received the incense due to mine along? I have seen my temples deserted, and all mankind, seduced by your beauty, offering you tributes hitherto unknown! . . .'

Jupiter vous fait grace, et ma colère cesse.
Vivez, Vénus l'ordonne; aimez, elle y consent.

PSICHÉ, *a L'Amour*
Je vous revois enfin, cher objet de ma flâme!

L'AMOUR, *a Psiché*
Je vous possède enfin, delices de mon ame! [1]

And Jupiter blesses them, raising Psyché to the rank of a divinity, and the inevitable ballet-sequence ends the play. It proved an enormous success with Court and public alike, running at the Palais-Royal for thirty-two consecutive performances. At the penurious end of a long and splendid career Pierre Corneille of Rouen was still inimitable at heroic rhythms; a trifle longwinded now and again, perhaps, but nobly musical always, a master of high poetry, and still capable of writing a love-scene with anybody. Thus Cupid, tenderly warning Psyche during their brief early honeymoon that his jealousy is omnivorous:

PSICHÉ
Des tendresses du sang peut-on estre jaloux?

L'AMOUR
Je le suis, ma Psiché, de toute la nature:
Les rayons du soleil vous baisent trop souvent,
Vos cheveux souffrent trop les caresses du vent,
Dés qu'il les flate, j'en murmure;
L'air mesme que vous respirez
Avec trop de plaisir passe par vostre bouche . . . [2]

Is that not charming? The aged poet himself was in love again, in his courtly way, this time with Armande-Psyche. But his sighs had little chance. The Cupid of the piece was

[1] Venus: Jupiter pardons you and my anger is over. Live, then, at Venus' order. Love each other; she consents.
  Psyche: (to Cupid) So I see you again at last, dear object of my passion!
  Cupid: (to Psyche) At last I possess you, delight of my soul!

[2] Psyche: But can one be jealous of family affection?
  Cupid: Psyche mine, I am jealous of all Nature. The sun's rays kiss you too often. Your hair too freely suffers the wind's caress — directly he strokes it I complain. Even the air you breathe passes with too much pleasure into your mouth . . .

le petit Baron, now a matinée-idol and a professional Lothario of seventeen, back at Molière's theatre for this engagement. By all accounts a perfect pair of stage lovers, he and Armande are alleged in *La Fameuse Comédienne* to have made up their former differences and spent most of their time offstage during the run of the piece, loosely and picturesquely speaking, in each other's arms. Whether this is true or not remains indiscoverable. Things could certainly have happened thus between two ineffable specimens of the coquette and the coxcomb *de chez Thalie,* and nothing in such an arrangement would surprise their world then or now. Pointing out that Armande was only eleven years older than her leading man, one of her champions in a more pragmatical age has argued from the *Nozze di Figaro* ('The Rosinas have passed their thirties before they begin love-duets with the Cherubinos' – the starcrossed Marschallin of *Der Rosenkavalier* could have been cited more effectively) that their collaboration must have been entirely blameless. Such laws do not necessarily apply to Bohemia, as everybody knows. After Armande's return to marital life it seems that Baron, who was to remain some time with his benefactor's troop, was often in and out of the house in the Rue de Richelieu. That he left the King's Comedians for the Hôtel de Bourgogne during the crisis following Molière's death, when Armande took over, may indicate not so much the end of an 'affair' as the fact that the dashing youth's eye was ever on the main chance. It is quite possible, however, that *La Fameuse Comédienne* occasionally told the truth.

A six months' gap occurs between the Court production of *Psiché* and the first public performance in July 1671. It was found that the heavy 'machines' and elaborate scenery of this charming fairytale called for backstage alterations at the Palais-Royal. On these the company decided, against the wish of Molière, who wanted to follow up the Tuileries success immediately. When the contractors' work was finished in April *Psiché* was still not in shape for production. As something had to be found meanwhile, Molière sat down and dashed off *Les Fourberies de Scapin* ('Scapin's Rascalities'), a prose farce in three acts on the Italian model; bursting with verve, totally irresponsible, unblushingly plagiarist, and based chiefly on the *Phormio* of Terence, with a whole scene, including a celebrated 'gag-line', filched without acknowledgment from Cyrano de Bergerac. Its central character is a Molièresque version of the Commedia valet Scapino (*scappare*, to flee), created by that same Nicolò Barbieri, actor and playwright, who years before had provided the intrigue of *L'Estourdy*. Arranged by the magical reed-pen of Callot, Scapino appears to be twin-brother to the sinister playboy Brighella, but this is merely because Barbieri affected the costume of the Neapolitan proletariat of the period. It was not till the early eighteenth century that Scapino took to domestic livery.

The scene of *Les Fourberies* is Naples, with Scapin, the valet-crook to end all valet-crooks, exploiting those concerned with a vitality and a virtuosity which becomes a trifle exhausting. The formula is familiar. Two mean angry old men, Géronte and Argante, are opposing their sons' and daughters' marriages. Abetted by Silvestre, a fellow-valet, Scapin defeats them with a boisterous sequence of ruses, cheats, subterfuges, saucy tricks and actual mayhem. The scene belonging to Cyrano is lifted bodily from *Le Pédant Joué*, a farce in which the pedant – actually the eminent Granger, Rector of the Collège de Beauvais, against whom Cyrano had a grudge – is persuaded by the rascal Corbinelli that his, Granger's, son has just been kidnapped aboard a Turkish galley in the Seine and carried off to slavery. The same story, substituting Géronte's son Léandre, serves Scapin to extort a ransom of five hundred crowns from Léandre's tight-fisted parent. At every third sentence the bewildered Géronte breaks in with the same cry, 'But what the devil was he doing in this galley?' – '*Que diable alloit-il faire dans cette galère?*' It had been Cyrano's great line, and the Granger of his farce had, as the profession would say nowadays, put it across with a bang. Thanks to Molière's unscrupulosity it has become perhaps the smoothest-worn cliché in the French language.

As *Les Fourberies* rattles along at the breathless pace of a harlequinade, Scapin's principal butt, Géronte, suffers more indignities; that of being induced to hide in a sack to escape an imaginary assassin and being soundly beaten in the process must have drawn the biggest laugh. But the piece, admittedly a trifle too long, grieved the judicious Boileau to the soul.

> Dans ce sac ridicule où Scapin s'enveloppe
> Je ne reconnois plus l'auteur du Misantrope.[1]

Posterity has agreed for the most part with Boileau, though more than one tight-lipped critic of later centuries has awarded Molière a reluctant high mark for *verve gigantesque* and even *bouffonerie épique*. In its treatment of parental old age it is not the most edifying of object-lessons for the young, even today.

In the matter of artistic larceny Molière had of course no more conscience than any other of the masters down the ages. 'I take it where I find it,' he himself declared, being franker on this question than Shaw, whose shyness in admitting the theft of *Pygmalion* from Smollett was at such striking variance with his customary poise.[2] And the theft from Cyrano was well timed. That formidable character had been dead sixteen years. Had *Les Fourberies* been produced in his lifetime, as Rostand contrives it, he would undoubtedly have been moved to an utterance slightly less noble than the one given him in the last act of *Cyrano de Bergerac*:

> C'est justice, et j'approuve du seuil de mon tombeau:
> Molière a du génie et Christian était beau.[3]

With a matamore like the real Cyrano still stalking the streets of Paris and liable to whip out a highly-skilled blade on the least provocation Molière would, one feels, have laid no hand on *Le Pédant Joué* at all. He was not a man of wrath, and one may pause a moment to reflect that he may frequently have been glad of his royal protection. Noblemen of the period deeming themselves insulted by scribblers, actors, and suchlike trash normally hired thugs to teach the offender a lesson. Thus suffered for a satiric song, and despite patronage in high

---

[1] 'In this ridiculous sack in which Scapin envelops himself (he incidentally does not) I no more recognize the author of *Le Misantrope*.'

[2] *Vide Peregrine Pickle*. Chap. LXXXVII.

[3] 'It (the theft) is justice, and from the threshold of my tomb I approve it; Molière has genius and Christian (Cyrano's late successful rival in love) was handsome.'

quarters, the poet Marc-Antoine de Saint-Amant, severely thrashed on the Pont-Neuf by hirelings of the Prince de Condé; nor was Saint-Amant by any means the only seventeenth-century literary gentleman to pay thus for a passing whimsy. There is no record of Molière's being offered violence by any irate nobleman except the Duc de la Feuillade. The story, which went round Paris at the time, is preserved, as from an eye-witness, in a memoir of 1725. Apparently La Feuillade, a dull and truculent grandee about the Court, who had been lavishly employing the phrase 'Tarte à la crème' from L'Escole des Femmes to convey contempt for the piece, and may have believed it to be his own invention, was enraged to find Molière using it again as the slogan of the chicken-brained marquis in La Critique. Encountering Molière at Court shortly afterwards, the Duke knocked off his wig and seized him by the ears as he bowed low, scrubbing the actor's face against his diamond buttons till the blood flowed and crying 'Tarte à la crème, Molière! Tarte à la crème!' The King is said to have sent for La Feuillade afterwards and rebuked him severely. The story became current gossip and afforded the implacable Donneau de Visé a bland reflection. 'I fancy "Élomire" will never don his wig henceforth without remembering that it is not a good thing to make fun of dukes. They are less insensitive than comic marquises.'

Produced at the Palais-Royal on May 24th, 1671, Les Fourberies de Scapin, though not the popular hit it would seem inevitably to be, filled the bill sufficiently with other pieces till July 24th, when Psiché at last took its place, and as already recorded ran, enthusiastically received, for thirty-two successive performances.

Molière's work for the year was not over. Twelve months previously the King's brother, Monsieur, had lost Madame, his vivacious and intelligent young English wife, Henriette Anne, preaching at whose funeral-Mass Bosseut uttered the cry which stirred even the cold heart of a Strachey, and seems to re-echo under the arches of St Denis still.

O nuir désastreuse! O nuit effroyable, oú retentit tout-à-coup comme un éclat de tonnere, cette étonnante nouvelle: 'MADAME

se meurt, MADAME est morte!' Qui de nous ne se sentit frappé
à ce coup, comme si quelque tragique accident avoit désolé
sa famille?[1]

A year later Monsieur married the Bavarian Princess Palatine
and celebrations were ordered at St Germain-en-Laye. Again
Louis XIV supplied Molière with his theme. The spectacle, to be
called *Le Ballet des Ballets*, was to include the cream of all the Court
dance-shows over the past ten years or so, with a new comedy for
a link. On December 2nd, accordingly, a piece in prose and verse
embracing a pastoral now lost, entitled *La Comtesse d'Escarbagnas*, was presented at St Germain. For the Palais-Royal production in the following July it was stripped of spectacular and
choreographical trimmings and condensed into a single act of
eight scenes. As such it was subsequently printed by La Grange.

This lightest and sketchiest of satires is aimed at provincial
absurdity and at the social circles of Angoulême, for some
reason, in particular. Once more the Limousin is to amuse the
capital, and with *Les Précieuses Ridicules* and, to some extent,
Monsieur de Pourceaugnac, for what each has to offer, this sketch
is, one may observe, the only fruit of fourteen years' experience
of the French provinces. The Comtesse d'Escarbagnas with
her airs and graces is the reigning *grande dame* of Angoulême,
highly conscious of her rank, her angular charms, her taste,
and her acquaintance with Paris, and exacting due homage from
two grotesque aspirants to her hand, Councillor Tibaudier,
the local intellectual, and Monsieur Harpin, the receiver of
taxes. To further his own ends a young Vicomte, Cléante by
name, in love with her ward, Julie, their families being at
enmity, pretends to be one more suitor to the Comtesse. The
piece ends artlessly enough. As the house-party is seating itself
to view a show presented by a travelling company, a letter
is brought to Cléante. It informs him that the family feud is
over and that he is free to marry his Julie. 'Egad, Madam,'
he says to the Comtesse, 'here's our own comedy finished,
at any rate.' The scene proceeds:

[1] 'O disastrous night! O fearful night, in which all at once this astound-
ing news resounded like a thunderclap: "Madame is dying, Madame is
dead!" Which of us did not feel stricken by this blow as if some tragic
accident had shattered his own family?'

JULIE:	Cléante! What happiness! Could our love have wished anything better?
COMTESSE:	What? What does all this mean?
CLÉANTE:	It means, Madame, that I am marrying Julie, and if you'll take my advice and make the comedy complete, you'll marry Monsieur Tibaudier, and give Mademoiselle Andrée (her maid) to his footman, who'll make him a valet.
COMTESSE:	What! How dare you treat a person of my quality in this fashion?
CLÉANTE:	No offence, Madame. Comedies require this sort of thing.
COMTESSE:	Very well. Monsieur Tibaudier, I'll marry you, just to infuriate everybody.
M. TIBAUD:	This is a very great honour for me, Madame.
CLÉANTE:	And while we're all being infuriated, Madame, pray be so kind as to let us see the rest of the show.

Which, at St Germain-en-Laye, served to introduce the ballets forming the main entertainment. That Molière's *Wanderjähre* produced nothing better than this squib is a grievous loss, not to France alone. In an age when self-expression in every social sphere had not been flattened out into a uniform drabness, as by a steam-roller, and every province of France had its own dialect, costumes and customs, with 'characters' and grotesques in infinite variety, small-town society anywhere was an aquarium of fantastic shapes for a metropolitan observer. It seems strange also that having heard (as he must more than once have heard) the drums and the fifes, the jests and songs and oaths of Turenne's infantry on their way to the front, Molière felt no curiosity about the men whom a century later Godard d'Aucour was to display in his *Académie Militaire* more amusingly than a Kipling. Acute and humorous observer as he was, Molière is not very well served by the legend which makes him a kind of walking dictaphone registering every nuance of the passing show. In the provinces the mechanism seems not to have been working to any extent.

Most disappointingly, then, *La Comtesse d'Escarbagnas* barely scratches the surface of the provincial comedy-scene. The Countess's simperings and affectations and imperiousness, the doltishness of her servants, Councillor Tibaudier's essays at highflown verse, the uncouth jealousy of Monsieur Harpin of the Inland Revenue – it is thin stuff, amounting to no more than a revue-sketch, and not a particularly amusing one apart from some of the Councillor's poetic efforts:

> Vous devriez a vostre tour,
> Vous contentant d'estre comtesse,
> Vous dépouiller, en ma faveur, d'une peau de tigresse,
> Qui couvre vos appas la nuit comme le jour.[1]

In Molière's defence it could be reasonably argued that if he knew little more of small-town life than any other seventeenth-century Parisian it was hardly his fault. During his years of touring the provinces he may never once have crossed the threshold of a Tibaudier or a Harpin, let alone a d'Escarbagnas. For such as he it was far easier to be a guest at some lordly château outside the town. Then as now small-town society in France, as elsewhere, was rigidly enclosed, aloof, and perennially suspicious of strangers, and strolling players ranked with tramps and gypsies. Along the main street mothers would undoubtedly drive their daughters shrilly away from unshuttered windows as the Bohemian cavalcade went by ('Oh, lassie, beware of them actors!' begins a satiric chant which may occasionally be heard at London theatre-parties today). The small town moreover was not yet on the literary map. There is practically nothing about it in seventeenth-century French literature. The great Corneille, who lived in Rouen most of his life, was no more aware, artistically speaking, of local society than was La Fontaine of the *salons* of his native Château-Thierry. Hence to scold Molière, as has been done, for getting so little out of the high-life of Angoulême, a town he may have selected, like the Limoges of *Monsieur de Pourceaugnac*, in remembrance of a shower of rotten apples during his tragedian days, may be unjust. If he were ever in the town at all he would most likely have seen nothing of it but the façade. To penetrate into the arcana of the provincial bourgeoisie and *petite noblesse* was, roughly speaking, the work

---

[1] 'Content with being a countess, you should in turn divest yourself, in my favour, of the tigress' skin which covers your charms by night as by day.'

of a lifetime. One may note nevertheless that however fleeting Molière's glimpse of the humours of Angoulême, it was comic enough for the Parisians. Produced, without music or ballets, at the Palais-Royal on July 8th, 1672, *La Comtesse d'Escarbagnas* achieved a success described as *très vif*. It was quite possibly something out of the bottom drawer.

Book VI

1672 opened gloomily.

On February 17th, Madeleine Béjart died, after a three months' illness, in the family house in the Place du Palais-Royal (old Madame Béjart had died in 1670). It was a rambling medieval caravanserai known as the Singe Vert; apparently two large houses knocked into one, and occupied by at least four of the eleven Béjarts and, for some years, *sub regno* Catherine de Brie, by Molière, whose apartments were separate, with an entrance in the Rue St Thomas-du-Louvre. Here Madeleine had been occupying – very modestly, considering her comfortable financial position – a bedroom and a kitchen-anteroom on the fourth floor, ever since the end of her affair with M. de Modène.

If we have lost sight of Madeleine Béjart for a few years, the Palais-Royal public had not. La Grange's registers are instructive. Few ex-leading ladies and co-directors in the history of the stage can have descended to a succession of minor parts with more cheerful zest than Molière's old comrade, who retired at last, in her fifty-second year, at the end of the run of *Monsieur de Pourceaugnac*, in which she played Nérine, the Neapolitan adventuress. Most of her other Palais-Royal roles – Climène in *La Critique*, herself in *L'Impromptu*, an Egyptian fortune-teller in *Le Mariage Forcé*, Philis in *La Princesse d'Élide* – had given her nothing very striking to do, but as the maidservant Dorine in *Le Tartufe* Molière had handed her a fine long racy part which included the actual unmasking of the villain, and her Frosine in *L'Avare* could take advantage of a wealth of good lines likewise. Madeleine had now removed rouge and hog-fat for the last time.

> I see that makaris amang the lave
> Playis here their padyanis, syne gois to grave:

Sparit is nocht their facultie;
Timor mortis conturbat me.

The bony finger was beckoning to Madeleine Béjart, and she responded as such a woman would. At the beginning of her illness, in that orderly fasion which had been her habit all her life, the elderly comedienne summoned her lawyers and a priest from St Germain-l'Auxerrois, her parish church, wound up her temporal affairs, and made her preparations for the end. Her very devout will was dictated on January 9th and corrected and revised, with a codicil or two, on February 14th, on which date her signature is almost illegible. The poor are suitably remembered in it. Stage players of this period, as always, responded generously to every call of charity. During the time when the troop was at Lyons there is a record of a grant of 18 *livres tournois* to an old widow *recommandée par la demoiselle Béjarre, comédienne*. Madeleine's will establishes a pension in perpetuity of five sous apiece daily for five poor persons, in honour of the Five Wounds, to be distributed by the *curé* of St Paul. For her own good estate she founded two weekly Masses of requiem at St Germain-l'Auxerrois. She left no debts and very little jewellery – two diamond rings, four of other stones, a necklace of seventy baroque pearls of 'medium size'. The bulk of her 26,000-livre fortune went, after various family bequests, not to her elder sister Geneviève but to Armande and her heirs. Endless argument has failed to decide the relationship thus confirmed.

So Madeleine Béjart received the last Sacraments and died in peace, shriven and houselled. Her old fellow-trouper and lover was not at her bedside. Since February 9th the company had been playing before the King at St Germain-en-Laye. On receiving the news of her death Molière was immediately granted leave. As the burial-certificate attests, he was present at the requiem at St Germain-l'Auxerrois and accompanied the body to the Hervé vault under St Paul's church near the Bastille. The long slow mournful journey across Paris has inspired much reconstructive prose, along obvious lines. '*O ma jeunesse, c'est vous qu'on enterre!*' – it may well be that Marcel's cry at Mimi's graveside in *La Vie de Bohème* represents the sum of Molière's heavy brooding that February day. St Paul's church, where Rabelais is said to have been buried – his grave was actually in the adjoining cemetery, long since built over – vanished in the tornado of the Revolution, and with it the Hervé vault and the stone which Madeleine placed over her mother, with its affectionate epitaph recording a daughter's gratitude for '*son amitié et des soins qu'elle a eus d'elle*'. Molière certainly retained some of Madeleine's affection likewise; Armande a great deal. Here an unsolved mystery protrudes itself again. If Madeleine knew Armande to be her daughter and Molière's, would she have assisted so warmly, as it is generally agreed that she did, towards the restoration of an incestuous *ménage* – a reconciliation so thorough that before she died she undoubtedly learned from Armande that another child of Molière's was on the way? If there is any solution at all, it was buried with Madeleine's confessor.

Reporting her death in his gazette, one Robinet, a rhyming Parisian gossip-writer, awarded her no more than her due:

> Ayant paru bonne chrétienne
> Autant que bonne comédienne,
> Et rempli, ce dit-on, des mieux
> Ce rôle des plus sérieux.[1]

At the time of Madeleine's death Molière had a new play in rehearsal; a five-act satiric comedy in alexandrines on which he had been at work, off and on, for at least four years; a play written for once to please himself. Why *Les Femmes Sçavantes*, produced after a Court performance at the Palais-Royal on March 11th, 1672, achieved the high esteem of the literate and only nineteen public performances is not difficult to understand. Its theme, the higher education of women, is a topic the general public does not greatly care about, even when an anti-feminist turns it into fun. Although *Les Femmes Sçavantes* is a sequel to *Les Précieuses Ridicules*, it lacks the Fourth Form humour of that piece; the comic airs and graces of the high-

---

[1] 'Having shown herself as good a Christian as she was an actress, and having, they say, played this most important of roles in the best way possible.'

brow ladies, the jolly fooling of them by a couple of footmen dressed up, the final thwacks and yells. *Les Femmes Sçavantes* is less hilarious and far more 'literary'. A discussion on poetry ending in a brawl between two rival poets takes up much of the third act. Demos is no more amused by the squabbles of Parnassus than by scientific bluestockings. As Voltaire remarked, Molière in this piece is attacking an absurdity 'calculated to amuse neither the public nor the Court, to whom this particular absurdity was equally unfamiliar'. And excellent as is most of the verse, he overdoes the lash. The satire is acid and unjust. Plainly the work of a sick and embittered man, *Les Femmes Sçavantes* was almost entirely composed, one may reflect, before Armande's return.

Once again, as in *Le Tartufe* and *L'Avare*, we see an upper middle-class Parisian household disrupted by the eccentricity of its head. Philaminte, wife of the wealthy bourgeois Chrisale, is a militant feminist intellectual who reads Plato and Descartes, plans a philosophical circle, dabbles in astronomy, bullies her easygoing husband, preaches cultural equality for women, and lets her household go hang. This Mrs Jellyby of the intelligentsia was a type as yet almost exclusive to the French upper bourgeoisie, though a few years hence Fontenelle's exposition of the principles of astronomy to a fascinated marquise would become a bedside-book for women of *ton*. Philaminte has two daughters, Armande and Henriette; Armande being an intellectual like her Mamma, with a near-Lesbian disgust for marriage in addition, and Henriette – played at the Palais-Royal by Molière's Armande – one of those charming sensible little misses in whom Molière delights. There is a third spring of comedy in the household; the maiden aunt Bélise, Chrisale's sister, whose mania is that every man who sets eyes on her falls instantly and madly in love. Against a formidable trio of petticoats Chrisale eventually puts up a successful fight, with the assistance of his brother Ariste. His cry after Philaminte has burst into a raving fury with the maidservant Martine for mishandling her verbs in peasant fashion is plainly Molière's as well:

Qu'importe qu'elle manque aux loix de Vaugelas

Pourveu qu'à la cuisine elle ne manque pas? . . .
Je vis de bonne soupe, et non de beau langage![1]

Thence Chrisale takes a wider sweep. What need has any
decent woman to study the stars and fuss with philosophical
clubs? Her business is to bring up children and run her home
properly, as our forefathers decreed. The modern woman, says
Chrisale, the old Tory, proceeding to a familiar refrain:

Les femmes d'à present sont bien loin ce ces moeurs,
Elles veulent écrire et devenir autheurs,
Nulle science n'est pour elles trop profonde,
Et céans beaucoup plus qi'en aucun lieu du monde. . . .
Et, dans ce vain sçavoir qu'on va chercher si loin,
On ne sçait comme va mon pot, dont j'ay besoin.[2]

Young Clitandre agrees. Clitandre has been temporarily
dazzled by Armande and has paid court to her. Rejected by this
dainty prig because the carnal implications of matrimony and
the *appétit grossier* make her shiver, he has turned to her younger
sister, the tender Henriette, whose ambitions extend simply to
un mary, des enfans, un ménage. Henriette accepts him, they are
truly in love, and Clitandre's attitude towards females of the
Philaminte-Armande school and those who bolster their
pretensions can be summed up thenceforth in two lines.

Et c'est mon sentiment qu'en faits comme en propos
La science est sujette à faire de grands sots.[3]

But Clitandre is not going to be allowed to dispose of his
life so easily. The loftiest highbrow may be subject to vulgar
jealousy. Having lost him to a girl she patronizes and despises,
her sister Armande wants her young man back, and to get him
back she will stick at nothing – even at a final offer, when it is

[1] 'What's it matter if she breaks the laws of Vaugelas (the grammarian)
so long as she doesn't break any in the kitchen? . . . I live on good soup,
not fine language!'
[2] 'Women today are very far from these traditions. They all want to
write and to turn author. No knowledge is too deep for them, in this house
more than anywhere. And while they're hunting for useless learning so far
away, nobody knows how my pot is boiling – which is something I need.'
[3] 'And my feeling is that in words and deeds alike learning is liable to
give birth to considerable fools.'

163

too late, of surrender to every ignominy the wedded state may imply. In the meantime she abets her mother in arranging the marrying-off of Henriette to the pedant Trissotin, for whom she has a sovereign contempt, employing in the process a few little feminine tricks surprising in an intellectual. Armande is in fact a complicated unhappy creature of a strangely modern species. Dress her in the hideous clothes of the 1880–90's, give her a bicycle, and she might be the New Woman and an Ibsen type. Hearing her cry for

Cette union des coeurs où les corps n'entrent pas,

could not one also glimpse a balloon-sleeved sisterhood surging from a later period, terrible as an army with banners inscribed 'Votes for Women'? Armande stands out from the crowd of Molière's women characters in enigmatic and almost sinister relief. She is a puppet with a secret life, like Petrouchka. We want to know what happens to her, in a pre-barbituric age, after the final curtain. She will certainly not go back in the box with the others.

Good comedy is supplied by Aunt Bélise, from whom Congreve stole a little for Lady Plyant of *The Double Dealer*, in a scene with Clitandre, whom Bélise believes to have, like every other man in sight, designs on her; to his extreme annoyance ('Devil take the fool!'). The love-making of Clitandre and Henriette is notable for wasting no time on the sudden quarrels and reconciliations so frequent among Molière's young lovers. The charming, modest Henriette is a girl with a firm French grip on reality.

Je sçay le peu de bien que vous avez, Clitandre,
Et je vous ay toujours souhaité pour épous . . .[1]

Henriette has gone discreetly into the matter of Clitandre's finances, like a sensible *jeune fille à marier*. One foresees she will make a devoted housewife, bring up half a dozen or more children in the best possible way, and probably (seeing the kind of family she comes from) open no secular book other than

[1] 'I know how little money you have, Clitandre, and I've always wanted to marry you . . .'

Le Cuisinier François from the day of her marriage. But the most arresting novelty of *Les Femmes Sçavantes* is the acrimony with which Molière pillories Philaminte's intellectual pet and son-in-law elect, the pedant-poet Trissotin. The original name given by Molière to this grotesque personage, who comes almost to fisticuffs with his brother-poet Vadius ('Greek! He knows *Greek*, my dear!') in Act III, was 'Tricotin', altered after the first few performances, since by that time the many-headed had no excuse for not recognizing Molière's principal target.[1] The cognoscenti had of course done so immediately; as well they might, seeing that Molière uses some of the Abbé Cotin's actual verses to scourge him with.

A recent quarrel between the Abbé and his fellow-rhymester Ménage, both severe critics of Molière in public and private, had diverted all the literary drawing-rooms, and the opportunity was too good to miss. Stripped of topicality, their clash still makes a diverting interlude. From an exchange of gravely judicious compliments – the pastorals of Vadius, affirms Trissotin, excel anything by Virgil or Theocritus, to which Vadius replies that Trissotin's odes leave Horace miles behind – the two literary gentlemen proceed by way of reciprocated criticism to abuse. Finally:

TRISSOTIN
    Allez, petit grimaut, barbouilleur de paper!
VADIUS
    Allez, rimeur de bale, opprobe du mestier!
TRISSOTIN
    Allez, fripier d'écrits, impudent plagiare!
VADIUS
    Allez, cuistre![2]

And they rush away to expose each other at Barbin's celebrated bookshop in the Palais, the contemporary Authors' Club and rendezvous of literary Paris. Undoubtedly Molière

[1] 'Tricotin' signifying 'thrice a Cotin'; 'Trissotin' signifying 'thrice a fool'.

[2] Triss: Get out, you peevish little paper-spoiler!
  Vad: Get out, you twopenny rhymester, shame of your trade!
  Triss: Out, you cheapjack scribbler, you impudent plagiary!
  Vad: Out, pedant!

knew the inky world almost as intimately as the stage. Undoubtedly, also, the Abbé Cotin and his friend Ménage had asked for trouble, having denounced Molière to the Rambouillet set for caricaturing Monsieur de Montausier – who, as noted already, was delighted – in *Le Misantrope*. But Molière's counter-attack is so savage as to suggest that he was suffering from his chest-complaint, and perhaps from Armande, more than usual when he composed the Trissotin-Vadius sequence. For Trissotin turns out to be a vulgar fortune-hunter and poltroon, a kind of literary Tartufe. Midway through a family conference called by Philaminte, with a notary in attendance, to draw up his marriage-contract with Henriette, a couple of letters are handed to Chrisale, who has been stubbornly but ineffectively opposing the match. Chrisale is thunderstruck to learn from these that he has just lost an expensive lawsuit and his entire fortune. This device Molière has used before. It is of course the last-moment inspiration of Chrisale's brother Ariste, and its effect is immediate. Poor Chrisale collapses with a cry of despair. His wife disdains such weakness.

CHRISALE: Heavens! To lose all my fortune like this, at one
              stroke!
PHILAMINTE: What a shameful reaction! Fie, it's nothing! For
              the truly wise man there's no such thing as a fatal
              reverse. He may lose everything, but he retains
              himself. Let's finish this business, and get rid of
              your despair. (She nods towards Trissotin.) He's
              got enough for himself and for us as well.

The estimable Trissotin is already reaching for his hat.

TRISSOTIN: No, Madam. Pray go no further. I perceive
              everyone here is against this marriage. It's no
              plan of mine to coerce people.

And he trips out a moment later. 'A mercenary creature', observes Philaminte stoically as the door closes. 'How very little philosophy in such conduct!' The tension is relieved by an immediate offer from Clitandre to place his modest fortune at the service of a ruined father-in-law elect. Ariste then smilingly reveals his hand, and the final curtain falls amid the proper congratulations and blessings. It was grossly unfair of

166

Molière to handle the Abbé Cotin, a bad poet but a perfectly honest man, in this fashion. Ménage as Vadius gets off, on the other hand, with being made merely to look a pedant and a fool. He too was immediately recognized, and arranged his poise accordingly. 'Are you going to allow that impertinent fellow Molière to treat you like this?' Mme de Rambouillet asked him during the early run of *Les Femmes Sçavantes*. 'Madam,' replied Ménage, 'I have seen the piece. It is beautiful in every way. One can find in it nothing for complaint or criticism.' To an experienced ear the voice is just a trifle too sonorous, perhaps, a thought too mellow.

'After this firework-display of pride and bitterness,' murmurs Cyrano's friend Le Bret, taking his arm in Rostand's play, 'tell me quite simply – she doesn't love you.' Thus might Boileau or Chapelle have murmured in Molière's ear after scanning the manuscript of *Les Femmes Sçavantes*, which exhales a misogyny, a gynophobia, almost a hatred of women, not uncommon among men most enslaved by them and sick of their chains. Boileau himself wrote an acid satire – the Tenth – against the entire sex. Molière's thesis, so far as it is clearly revealed in this play, is that since women do sufficient damage in the world anyway, they should be kept away from books; a woman of parts is simply a monster. There were a number of these in France already – for example, Mme Dacier, the Greek scholar, the equivalent of our Mrs Elizabeth Carter, Mme de Maintenon, the enchanting Mme de Sévigné and the less enchanting but indefatigable Mlle de Sçudéry, Mme de Sablé, and Mme de Rambouillet, to name only a few. In the next century there would be a perfect plague of bluestockings, '*femmes-docteurs*' in Clitandre's contemptuous phrase, in France as elsewhere. It should be noted that Clitandre, speaking for his creator, has no objection to all-round intelligence, *clartés de tout*, in a woman. His aversion is *la passion choquante de se rendre sçavante afin d'être sçavante*, learning for learning's sake, as manifested in Armande, a maladjusted introvert on whom her despised senses avenge themselves all too thoroughly. There is a sudden pathos in Armande's cry to her mother as Clitandre embraces Henriette just before the last curtain.

'Then you're sacrificing me to their happiness?' To which Philaminte heartlessly replies 'Sacrifice? You've got the aids of philosophy, haven't you?' As indeed she has, poor dear.

Six months after the production of *Les Femmes Sçavantes* Molière's own Armande more than made up for any lingering disappointments due to its cool reception by presenting him with another son, born on September 15th and baptized Pierre Jean-Baptiste, the godfather being Boileau's brother Pierre and the godmother a daughter of the painter Mignard. Molière's delight was short-lived, alas. With the little white coffin he followed to the cemetery a fortnight later was buried yet another concentration of hopes and dreams. His illness was increasing, and his doctors could do nothing for him to speak of. In addition the inevitable clash with Lully had arrived. The Florentine had at last displaced him in the King's favour.

It was early in 1672 that Lully became aggressive. For some time he had been increasingly irritated by the success of a certain Abbé Perrin, a brother-musician who by a royal warrant of 1659 held the monopoly for establishing academies in the principal cities of France. The flourishing state of the chief of these, later called the *Académie Royale de Musique*, a converted *jeu de paume* in the Rue Mazarine, was intolerable. The Florentine was able to dispossess the Abbé at length in the March of 1672; not without some difficulty, we gather from Perrault's memoirs. For some time the King and Colbert, his minister, refused to consider what was a plain injustice, but on Lully's finally flying into a passion and threatening to return to his native Italy Louis could not, as he confessed to Colbert, hold out against such a master-purveyor of *divertissements*. So Lully got what he wanted. His warrant prohibited the performance anywhere in France of any vocal work entire, in any language, without the written permission of *le Sieur Lully*. But this was not enough. A few days later Lully extracted from the King another privilege, striking directly at his friend Molière. It prohibited the theatres of France from employing during a given performance more than six singers and a dozen instrumentalists, and these must not be in the employ of Lully.

Thus the greater part of Molière's repertoire was affected.

Molière retorted almost immediately by reviving *Le Mariage Forcé*, dropping Lully's score in favour of a new one ordered from Charpentier, one of the Florentine's many *bêtes-noires*. Lully had already scored off Charpentier, *maître de chapelle* to Monseigneur, by securing the music-monopoly for the three Chapels-Royal. Infuriated this time by Charpentier and Molière alike, he sought the King again and emerged with yet another privilege which virtually deprived Molière thenceforth of a considerable income, since it gave Lully the exclusive copyright not only of 'all airs purely of his own invention, and of such a quality that the least alteration or omission would make them lose their natural grace', but all the words to which his music had so far been set. By way of demonstrating what this meant in practice, Lully produced on November 16th, 1672, a piece by his man Quinault called *Les Fêtes de l'Amour et de Bacchus*, in which several of the musical numbers were taken back from Molière, with Molière's words.

For countenancing such highway-robbery Louis XIV has been charged with fickleness and ingratitude. Yet giving in to the ruthless Lully was perhaps inevitable. The Florentine was indispensable to the Court, now and for years ahead, whereas Molière, whose period of service was nearing its end, could well afford to rest on his laurels and his wealth. It may be too that Louis XIV was hypnotized despite himself by the monstrous nerve and rapacity of his musician. La Fontaine hardly exaggerates in *Le Florentin*, a tribute already quoted:

> C'est un paillard, c'est un mâtin
> Qui tout dévore,
> Happe tout, serre tout; il a triple gosier.
> Donnez-luy, fourrez-luy, le glout demande encore;
> Le Roy même auroit peine à le rassassier.[1]

Obviously Molière did not sit back acquiescent under all

[1] 'He's a libertine, an all-devouring, all-grabbing, all-hoarding mongrel with a triple throat. Give him anything, stuff him with it, the glutton demands more; the King himself would have trouble in appeasing him.'

this. What representations he made to the King are not known, but on November 11th he revived *Psiché* with Lully's original score, employing the same number of singers and dancers and an orchestra of the same dimensions as before. It would seem that Louis waived Lully's patent without demur. The concession doubtless had its tonic effect, and Molière turned with lighter spirits to the comedy he was now finishing. While he brings to an end an onslaught on an infallible Faculty, powerless to cure him, compared with which all his previous attacks are merely a game of kiss-in-the-ring, it may be convenient to pause a moment and glance at his clinical dossier over the past few years.

CHAPTER TWO

Since Maurice Raynaud's careful piece of research in the 1860's, *Les Médecins au Temps de Molière*, not a few medical authorities have re-examined this illustrious case, without throwing much fresh light on it. It is impossible, apparently, to get a final diagnosis. Consumption, an aneurism, or pneumonia – what La Grange calls *une fluxion sur la poitrine*? The chief symptoms reported are a continual cough, oppression of the chest, recurring loss of voice, and stomach-trouble which required a milk-diet more than once. The hypochondria so significantly exploited in *Monsieur de Pourceaugnac* possibly began with the crisis of February 1666, when Molière was reported to be dying. Attacks on the doctors in five comedies, varying between rollicking high spirits and savage satire, begin with *Dom Juan* in 1665 and end with *Le Malade Imaginaire* in 1673. Only once, so far, has he had a relatively good word to say for the Faculty. It occurs in the preface to the final version of *Le Tartufe*:

> Medicine is a profitable art, revered by all as one of the most excellent things we have; yet there have been times when it has made itself odious, and it has often been made an art for poisoning men.

At the same time, flushed with his overnight triumph over *les Tartufes*, he addressed a *placet* to the King on behalf of a son of his personal physician, Mauvilain. It is printed before the play in the 1682 edition:

SIR,

A most honourable doctor, whose patient I have the honour to be, promises me – and is ready to confirm before notaries – thirty years' more life if I can obtain him a favour from Your Majesty. I have told him I am not asking that much, and would be satisfied if he swore not to kill me. The favour, Sir, is that of a canonry in Your chapel-royal of Vincennes, now vacant. Dare I, Sir, ask this extra grace of Your Majesty on the day of the resurrection of Tartufe, raised to life by Your kindness? This favour has reconciled me with the devout; the one I ask now will do the same for me with the doctors . . .

Optimism was quite unjustified in either case, but Dr Mauvilain's son duly got his canonry. And the attacks on the Faculty continued.

There are few more elaborately macabre jests in drama or literature than *Le Malade Imaginaire*, the last mockery of a dying man. Undoubtedly Molière's spirits were raised very high by Armande's return at the end of 1671 and the resumption of their marital relations. How long exhilaration lasted who can tell? The age-old saying, melancholy as the tinkle of an eighteenth-century musical-box, that every human mating is composed of *l'un qui baise et l'autre qui tend la joue* is far from being universally true; but where it happens to apply, the psychoses of *l'autre qui tend* may embrace anything from the lightest of boredom to something very serious indeed, as is well known. In the *Impromptu de Versailles* of 1663 there is an exchange between Molière and his recent bride which may convey a little more than jesting, Everyone on the stage, we may recall, is in a state of irritable tension; the King is expected at any moment, nobody knows his or her part, and Molière is at his wits' end. 'You should have written a show all for yourself!' snaps Armande at length. This dialogue ensues:

MOLIÈRE: Shut up, my dear, you're talking like a fool.
ARMANDE: Many thanks, dear husband! That's how things are! Marriage does something to people. You wouldn't have said that to me eighteen months ago!
MOLIÈRE: Will you kindly be quiet?

ARMANDE: It's odd how a short ceremony can deprive some people of their best qualities, and how different the same person can appear to a husband and a lover!

MOLIÈRE: Too much chatter!

ARMANDE: Good Lord! If I ever wrote a play I'd defend women against a lot of things they accuse us of, and I'd make husbands pretty sorry for the difference between their uncouth ways and a lover's politeness!

MOLIÈRE: Oh, forget it! This isn't the time to argue, we've got other things to do.

Armande had had a lot for which to thank her husband since then. Since 1664 he had created some brilliant roles for her — Célimène, Psyche, the Princess d'Élide, Princess Eriphile of *Les Amans Magnifiques*, most of his heroines, including opportunities of radiating virginal allure like her Lucile in *Le Bourgeois Gentilhomme* and her Henriette in *Les Femmes Sçavantes*, said to have been ravishing. The debt was by no means one-sided, of course. In whatever else she failed Molière, Armande at work was the most rewarding of partners, as contemporaries testify; the Printemps of the Guitry of her age. Like at least four more of the Béjarts she had the theatre in her blood. Her gifts embraced a *beauté du diable*, a technique ripened by experience from childhood, a skilfully-exploited charm, and a tart sense of humour enabling her to get the utmost out of a satiric line. Her speaking-voice was musical, she sang delightfully, and she was a graceful dancer. Having with all this the inestimable advantage of being fitted with part after part by a master of his craft, rigorously directed by him, frequently playing opposite him, Armande could hardly fail to triumph. She had her limitations. Tragedy was no more Armande's business than it was Molière's. She made up for this, apparently, on the occasions on which she played the lead in pieces by Corneille, Racine, and others, by sheer dazzle. The gazeteer Robinet, who saw her Cléofile in Racine's *Alexandre* just before the break, bursts into a hymn of praise to make any modern actress's press-agent heartsick:

O justes dieux! qu'elle a d'appas!
Et qui pourroit ne l'aimer pas?
Sans rien toucher de sa coiffure,

Ni de sa belle chevelure,
Sans rien toucher de ses habits,
Semés de perles, de rubis,
Et de toute la pierrerie
Dont l'Inde brillante est fleurie,
Rien n'est si beau ni si mignon! . . . [1]

In a word, concludes the hack in ecstasy, La Molière is the Cyprian Queen herself in miniature. Her rueful husband himself echoes some of this in *La Princesse d'Élide*, putting the praise of Armande into the mouth of Euryale. She is adorable at all times, says Euryale; she is young and lovely and cruel and haughty and enchanting, spurning a crowd of aspirants, *cette foule d'amans qui briguent sa conqueste* (Armande did nothing of the sort, if one-tenth of contemporary gossip was true), and seeming to walk like Diana in her splendour. Thus we may glimpse her sweeping to and fro in high tragedy under the candle-light of half a dozen chandeliers, dominant and glittering as a Byzantine empress. But she was no Rachel, Bernhardt, or Duse, and her husband was aware of it. Like a Guitry he had a perfect comedy-instrument to play on. Like his successor in virtuosity he made the most of it.

As for their off-stage relations on the eve of reconciliation, the Parisian gossip-columnists – the above-mentioned Robinet, who did his stint in verse, is a model, when quotable, for all later aspirants – reported in September 1671, at the height of the success of *Psiché*, that Armande had been taken ill and had left the cast. The indisposition, apparently fairly severe, lasted some weeks and may quite well have disposed of a lot of domestic griefs. But after the death of his second son in 1672 it is permissible, knowing of Molière what we do, to see him sitting for hours in his library wrapped in a dressing-gown, fingering some favourite book, a Horace or a Lucretius, staring into vacancy; more and more silent and moody, coughing ever more frequently and painfully, testier and more difficult with the servants, testier perhaps with Armande equally.

[1] 'Just gods, what charms she has! Who could help loving her? Without mentioning her coiffure and her beautiful hair, without mentioning her costumes, studded with pearls and rubies and all the jewels which flower in India, nothing could be lovelier or more adorable! . . .'

Towards the end of 1672, fortunately, the theatre was giving him plenty to do. His new farcical comedy in three acts and fourteen scenes had three musical and ballet interludes, the finale being a burlesque medical reception ceremony on the grand scale. Designed for the pre-Lent Carnival of 1673, it was, as the preface proclaims, an attempt 'to divert our august Monarch after his glorious fatigues and victorious exploits', namely the campaign of Holland in 1672, which ended in the bursting of the dykes by the Dutch and overtures for peace. *Le Malade Imaginaire* opens accordingly with a pastoral ballet in which his Majesty is offered a wealth of bouquets and fireworks by Flora, Pan, and a covey of shepherds and shepherdesses.

> Pour chanter de LOUIS l'intrepide courage,
> Il n'est point d'assez docte voix,
> Point de mots assez grands pour en tracer l'image . . . [1]

Incited by Flora's transports, the shepherd Tircis soars to classical heights.

> Des fabuleux exploits que la Grèce a chantez
> Par un brilliant amas de belles veritez
> Nus voyons la gloire effacée;
> Et tous ces fameux demy-dieux
> Que vante l'histoire passée
> Ne sont point a nostre pensée
> Ce que LOUIS est à nos yeux![2]

Almost on the eve of production, unfortunately, the Dutch rose again under a new Stadtholder, William of Orange, and took back the thirty-six towns of which Louis' troops had deprived 'these Calvinist cheese-mongers' the year before, and Molière had hurriedly to find a new prologue. A relatively brief lyrical exercise on the theme that love is invulnerable to medicine supplanted the *feu de joie*. Both prologues are printed in the 1682 edition, making a piquant contrast.

[1] 'To sing the intrepid courage of LOUIS no voice is sufficiently skilled, no words great enough to summon up its image . . .'
[2] 'We see the glory of the fabulous exploits celebrated in Greek song eclipsed by a brilliant array of splendid realities, and all the famous demigods lauded by history in the past are nothing in our minds compared with the sight of LOUIS!'

The musical score for the new comedy was supplied by Marc-Antoine Charpentier, not without having to be trimmed beforehand by Lully's orders. It seems that Molière should have given our old bottle-nosed acquaintance d'Assoucy the assignment. Such at least was d'Assoucy's fixed impression. After a wealth of grotesque misadventure in France and Italy he had found himself some months previously in the prisons of the Holy Office at Rome, owing partly to what the French police would nowadays call his 'special morals', partly to a recent outbreak of anti-clerical jocularity. From this durance the clemency of Pope Clement IX delivered him before long, several shrill appeals and a long rambling penitential screed called *Les Pensées de M. d'Assoucy dans le Saint-Office de Rome* having achieved their end. Subsequently encountering Charpentier in Rome, d'Assoucy scurried back to Paris to publicize a voluble grievance against Molière, who seems to have vaguely promised at some time or other to use him. D'Assoucy was by no means a negligible musician. He had provided the score for Corneille's tragedy *Andromède* and given recitals before Louis XIII at St Germain. To find himself, an acknowledged master of *beaux airs* and *doyen de tous les musiciens de France*, discarded at seventy by his friend and idol Molière for a Marc-Antoine Charpentier provoked him, therefore, to bitter resentment and inevitable rhyme:

> J'ay toujours été serviteur
> De l'incomparable Molière,
> Et son plus grand admirateur . . .
> Que voulez-vous? C'est un malheur,
> L'abondance fuit la misère,
> Et le petit et pauvre hère
> Ne quadre point a gros seigneur.[1]

A few other misfortunes, including short terms in the Bastille and the Châtelet, need not concern us here. It may well be that a reputation like his was a liability in a collaborator which

---

[1] 'I have always been the humble servant of the incomparable Molière, and his greatest admirer . . . However, what can you expect? It's bad luck. Opulence flees from misery, and there's no place for a poor unfortunate devil in the scheme of the lordly great.'

even a Molière could not accept. Charles Coypeau d'Assoucy died in 1674, a year after his illustrious friend, leaving a mass of mediocre burlesque verse, a manuscript-volume of music, *Airs de Monsieur Dassoucy*, of which only the catalogue-title survives, and those breathless harum-scarum memoirs. The all-but-concluding apologia from his Roman prison (he scribbled another in the Châtelet) has the vintage d'Assoucian quality of what might be called 'runcibility', whether d'Assoucy is discoursing gravely on piety and atheism, with sidelong swipes at Cyrano de Bergerac and other *gassendistes*, on music and the harmony of Nature, or on dreams, with special reference to his recent arrest. For he had dreamed it all, three nights beforehand. The same red-cloaked corporal of the Governor's police who a month previously had nabbed the page Pierrotin – another story – sprang on M. d'Assoucy, assisted by two *sbirri* in grey, as he was turning a street corner. He was handcuffed with the same green-and-white silk cord, bundled into the same official coach, taken before the Governor of Rome, remanded to the Holy Office, interrogated there by the same black-and-white habited Dominican on duty, and shoved into a cell, all precisely as in his dream. 'I ask you, dear reader, as I have asked many others, if this does not seem a most extraordinary experience'. There would have been plenty more to relate, no doubt, if he had not been compelled to close down so abruptly.

Here, dear reader, are some of the reflections with which I solaced my holy solitude, and now share with you. But I hear a stentorian voice and a jangling of keys. It is my gaoler arriving to bid me goodnight and extinguish my candle. I can write only one word more – the word '*Believe*'.

One feels Molière could have done something for the poor old mountebank.

CHAPTER THREE

The aroma of the sickroom is wafted over the footlights as the curtain rises on *Le Malade Imaginaire*. Dressing-gowned and muffled, seated at a table in his bedroom, the professional invalid Argan is checking the latest bill from his apothecary, Monsieur Fleurant. To the race of hypochondriacs for which Dr Cheyne wrote his classic treatise *The English Malady*, and which today, the statisticians aver, swallows more patent nostrums in a month than any other nation in twelve, Argan's recital of Fleurant's items should afford the pure delight of the gourmet. The mere thought of translation destroys their bloom.

> Un petit clystère insinuatif, préparatif, et remolliant, pour amollir, humecter, et rafraîchir les entrailles de Monsieur . . .
> Un julep hépatique, soporatif, et somnifère, composé pour faire dormir Monsieur . . .
> Une prise de petit lait clarifié et dulcoré, pour adoucir, lénifier, tempérer, et rafraîchir le sang de Monsieur . . .

Argan's own mouth waters, as we may well presume, though he is standing no overcharges from Monsieur Fleurant and enjoys cutting down his bills. Argan is yet another major exhibit in the Molièresque gallery of eccentrics, yet another victim of egotist mania turning his household upside down. He is in fact a case for the psychiatrist. Physically no invalid at all, he suffers from what is called a traumatic neurosis, the fear of death; according to Léon Daudet in *Le Rêve Éveillé* the dominant obsession of mankind, despite Freudian babble about sex. This fear, as M. Filerin, representing the Faculty, had pointed out long ago to the assembled doctors in *L'Amour Médecin*, being heaven's greatest gift to medicine, Argan is accordingly exploited by the redoubtable M. Purgon, his physician, and M. Fleurant, his apothecary, working hand in glove.

Someone else is exploiting the ridiculous Argan's mania with equal verve and brio – his second wife, Béline, who lives for the day when Argan will poison himself once for all with his filthy doses and leave her his considerable fortune; to hasten which end Béline spares no trick of encouragement, sympathy, flattery, anxiety, and honeyed cooing. Her two stepdaughters, Angélique and Louison, she naturally detests. A mere child like Louison can do her plans no harm, but Angélique is nubile and due to benefit considerably at Argan's death. The harpy's ambition is to have her put into a convent, where, by taking vows, she will be disinherited automatically by Canon and civil law alike. Simultaneously there is the routine Molièresque clash over the love-interest. Her father is determined to marry Angélique to Dr Dyafoirus' son Thomas, a medical booby of the choicest, or else pack her off to the convent aforesaid. Angélique is equally determined to marry nobody but her own choice, young Cléante. One other member of the family offsets Argan and acts as Molière's mouthpiece. This is Argan's *raisonneur*-brother Béralde, a kind of chorus to the play, in whose view the human machine, or what the medievals called the Microcosm, is a mystery and the vast majority of doctors presumptuous fools.

Thus the stage is set like a Spanish arena, with the Faculty of Medicine as the bull – a bull of the ferocious but stupid breed, or *pegajosos* – and Molière in person, when his picadors and banderilleros have done their work, delivering the final thrust with the impeccable style of a Belmonte. His Argan, with Armande playing Angélique, turned out by all accounts a display of comic bravura which astonished the most ardent of the *afición*. The last of the six great comedies will prove a re-sounding triumph for the comedian and the playwright alike. As a swan-song moreover it provided the perfect climax to an actor-manager's career. Irving in recent times quitted the world's stage almost as fittingly after a spectacular death in *Becket*. But Irving died in the provinces.

After six brief opening scenes *Le Malade Imaginaire* begins really to move with the appearance of Argan's wife, Béline. Up to this point Molière has been skilfully building up Argan's imbecility and tyranny in wordy conflicts with Angélique and the maidservant Toinette. Fussing round her exhausted invalid with pillows, caresses, and cries of sympathy, the harridan's ears are ravished by a piece of news she has long been waiting for. 'Dear heart,' sighs the grateful fool, 'in return for all your love I've decided to make my will.' A pleasing exchange ensues:

BÉLINE: Oh, my dear, don't let's talk about such things, I im-plore you! I can't bear the thought of it! The very word 'will' makes me shudder.
ARGAN: I asked you to speak to your lawyer about it.

BÉLINE: He's here. I've brought him with me.
ARGAN: Tell him to come in, my love.
BÉLINE: Oh, my dear! When one loves one's husband one can hardly bear to think of such things!

The notary, a grave Monsieur Bonnefoy, paces in forthwith. And while Béline hovers in the background, Monsieur Bonnefoy opens with the remark that he has discussed the affair with Madame. Unfortunately there is no means, under the *coutume* or common law of Paris involving husband and wife, of signing away Argan's fortune to Béline at his children's expense. Nevertheless, adds M. Bonnefoy smoothly, finger upraised, as Argan chokes, there are ways and means of gliding gently over the law, *des expédiens pour passer doucement par dessus la loy* – if there were not, where would the lawyers be? We perceive M. Bonnefoy to be a practitioner lacking in strict probity. His advice to Argan is to select some trusty friend of Béline's and to make him his heir in proper form, the bequest to be handed on by arrangement. Argan may also immediately contract a vast number of obligations with creditors acting for and in behalf of Béline, and in her name. He may finally present his wife, here and now, with a sufficiency of ready money or bills drawn to her account. At all this Béline breaks down and weeps, and after a touching domestic scene Argan transfers twenty thousand francs in cash and bills to her on the spot. The scene, extremely comic in itself, shows that Molière's acquisition of a diploma from the Law Schools of Orleans was not money spent in vain.

After a graceful musical interlude involving a lovesick Polichinelle out of the Italian Comedy serenading his mistress and embroiled with the police, the trumpets sound for the first round with the Faculty. The pompous Dr Dyafoirus enters on the scene with his son and heir Thomas, a weedy, solemn young gawk, newly qualified and stuffed with the rhetoric of the Schools. It is a call of ceremony. Having begun by mistaking his prospective bride for her stepmother, the younger Dyafoirus advances, one wary eye on his father, and producing a roll of manuscript like a conjuring-trick, offers it to Angélique with an awkward obeisance.

DYAFOIRUS: I have drawn up a thesis against the propagators of the circulation of the blood, which (with Monsieur Argan's permission), I presume to offer Mademoiselle in due homage as the firstfruits of my talent.

ANGÉLIQUE: It's quite useless to me, sir. I know nothing about these things.

TOINETTE: Go on, give it her. It's worth having for the picture anyway. It will do to decorate the room.

DYAFOIRUS: (to Angélique): And (once more with Monsieur Argan's permission), I invite you to be present on a future date at the dissection of a female cadaver, on which I am to deliver an allocution.

This pair of medical grotesques is diverting enough – the vexing thing about attending the great, remarks Dr Dyafoirus during the conversation, is that they insist on being cured – but they are not the star turns of the corrida, so to speak. The *toro de libras*, the great bull, Argan's demigod and tyrant, the terrible Dr Purgon himself, is due to be despatched later, with skilful handling, in a magnificent scene of frenzy, after Béralde has incited the quaking Argan to rebel against one of his prescriptions. Meanwhile young Cléante is pursuing his suit, and it is disconcerting to find that Molière can think of nothing better than the substitution-disguise trick already played by Clitandre in *L'Amour Médecin* and by Adraste in *Le Sicilien*. Cléante is to pose as Angélique's music-master and to make love to her under Argan's nose, as Adraste did to Isidore under Don Pedro's. So charmingly does he do it that the master is easily forgiven. But there are two grieving examples of whimsy to follow. We are asked to accept a quick-change act by the young maid Toinette, appearing and disappearing alternately as herself and as a ninety-year-old visiting specialist with a long white beard, and in the latter guise prescribing for Argan with complete success (to do him justice Argan notes a fleeting resemblance, but is quickly tut-tutted out of it by Béralde). Some time later we find Argan, by arrangement with Toinette, shamming dead for the purpose of discovering his family's true feelings towards him, and the machiavellian Béline accepting Toinette's announcement of his sudden demise without query. It does not even occur to this schemer to check it for accuracy by feeling her dear one's pulse. 'Your husband's dead,' sobs Toinette, and shows her the alleged corpse humped in its chair. 'Thank God for that!' grunts the harridan. 'That's the last of a big burden! What are you crying for?' The scene continues:

TOINETTE: I thought one ought to cry, Madame.
BÉLINE: Come, come, it's not worth the trouble. What sort of a loss is he? What on earth was the use of him? A nuisance of a man to everybody – dirty, disgusting, always with some enema or medicine in his belly, forever blowing his nose, or coughing, or spitting, a dull, bad-tempered bore, wearing everybody out the whole time and scolding the servants day and night!
TOINETTE: A nice funeral oration, I will say!
BÉLINE: Toinette, you must help me. (Etc., etc.)

Undeniably comic, especially when the corpse comes to life, but, like the other scene, a strain on goodwill. Two of the sort in one evening have the effect, amid the whirling gaiety and noise, of a bullet-wound; the real pain arrives later. Being unburdened with the prickly sensibilities of the twentieth century, the seventeenth apparently saw nothing incongruous in the mixture of such fair-ground fun in the same play with Béralde's long indictment of the medical profession, which is about as frivolous as a *Times* leader and more than once pregnant with Molière's despair. When a doctor talks to you about the secret of assisting Nature and prolonging life by his treatment of your ailing organs, says Béralde to Argan, that is merely the romance of medicine. 'When you come to test its truth by experience you find nothing of this whatsoever. It's like one of those splendid dreams which leave you on waking with nothing but the vexation of having believed them.' From any treatise on seventeenth-century medicine one may perceive that Béralde's judgment was fair enough. For one single doctor of the calibre of a Harvey, Dr Purgon's great bugbear, there seem to have been ten thousand empirics and charlatans. But when Béralde goes on to assert that for Argan a far better treatment than Purgon's rubbish would be a few good laughs derived from 'one of the comedies of Molière', Argan is stung to proper indignation. 'And a pretty impertinent fellow your Molière is, to make fun of honourable men like the doctors!'

BÉRALDE: It's not the doctors he makes fun of, it's the absurdities of medicine.

ARGAN: It's not his business to meddle in the practice of medicine. . . . Damme, if I were a doctor I'd pay him out for his insolence, if he were taken ill, by letting him die without treatment. No matter what he said or did I wouldn't order him the tiniest bleeding or the smallest enema. I'd say 'Go on! Kick the bucket! That'll teach you to make fun of the Faculty!'

A macabre piece of near-prophecy, as it turned out, and perhaps a fleeting premonition came to Molière as he ended the scene and turned to finish off Dr Purgon. Monsieur Fleurant, the apothecary, syringe in hand, interrupts Argan's talk with Béralde. He has an order for an enema from Dr Purgon. Béralde laughs it and Purgon to scorn, and Monsieur Fleurant flees in horror. A moment later the glowering Purgon himself looms in the doorway in his great black periwig like a thundercloud. So his orders have been spurned? Argan cowers under his flaming eye. Ha! Rebellion! So be it! Dr Purgon abandons him to his entrails, his bile, and his foeculent humours forthwith:

ARGAN: Oh, my God!

PURGON: And within four days I trust your state will be incurable.

ARGAN: Mercy!

PURGON: Turning to bradypepsia.

ARGAN: Master Purgon!

PURGON: From bradypepsia to dyspepsia.

ARGAN: Master Purgon!

PURGON: From dyspepsia to apepsia.

ARGAN: Master Purgon!

PURGON: From apepsia to lientery.

ARGAN: Master Purgon!

PURGON: From lientery to dysentery.

ARGAN: Master Purgon!

PURGON: From dysentery to dropsy.

ARGAN: Master Purgon!

PURGON: And from dropsy to the death to which your folly will have brought you. (*Exit.*)

But Argan recovers from the shock and all turns out well in the end. For Angélique's sake Cléante is on the verge of swearing to become a doctor, as Argan demands, when Béralde has a better idea. Why should not Argan himself qualify? Nothing is easier. With the medical gown and the medical biretta any jargon becomes scientific. Thence we are plunged straightway into the final ballet, the reception of Argan into the bosom of the Faculty of Medicine; a fantastic and hilarious Walpurgis-Night romp of surgeons, physicians, and apothecaries mopping and mowing amid the chanting of dog-Latin verse glorifying the Faculty and all its works, with the recurring refrain;

> Clisterium donare,
> Postea seignare,
> Ensuitta purgare,
> Reseignare, repurgare, et reclisterisare![1]

And Argan finally takes the triple oath, swearing never to swerve by a hairsbreadth from the laws and customs of the Brotherhood, should the patient burst meanwhile. '*Juro!*' intones Argan solemnly thrice, and when all have paid him ungainly reverence the whole Faculty breaks into a festal dance, as attendant apothecaries bang mortars merrily with pestles, ending with a final chorus of '*Vivat, vivat, vivat!*' The whole gambol had been devised at a supper-party given by Ninon de l'Enclos, Boileau supplying the medico-Latin.

CHAPTER FOUR

For the first time in Molière's career as director of the Royal Comedians there was no Court *première* of his new play. Under Lully's domination the King had neglected to order it. Presented at the Palais-Royal on February 10, 1673, *Le Malade Imaginaire* was an immediate and rapturous success, as may well be conjectured; but the slight from Louis was a grievous one for a sick and tired man, and Molière took it hard.

[1] 'To adminster clysters, then to bleed, then to purge; then to re-bleed, re-purge and re-clysterize!'

He was still brooding over it before the fourth performance on Friday, February 17th. On this day his fatigue and depression were sufficient to awaken concern in Armande and Baron, from whom Grimarest reports the poignant little scene. They asked him how he did. Molière answered with an effort. 'So long as my life was an equal mixture of pleasure and pain I could believe myself happy. But now I'm so burdened with troubles, with no hope of a single moment's remission or solace, that I can see it's time to pack up (*quitter la partie*). I can't fight any more against miseries and vexations which don't give me a moment's respite.' He paused a moment and added slowly, 'What a man has to suffer before he dies! I think I'm finished.'

It alarmed them both. They begged him to take a rest from the theatre that day. He shook his head. The *punto de honor* which his profession shares with the Cid Campeador and the Chevalier Bayard is a constant, and he had no choice. 'What else can I do?' Molière asked them, raising a haggard face. 'There are fifty poor devils depending on their day's work for a living – what will happen to them if I don't go on?' It was unanswerable, and they tried no further persuasion.

He roused from his despair at length, and Armande and Baron took him to the theatre and handed him over to his dresser, and he doggedly assumed the make-up and dressing-gown of his comic valetudinarian and went on, clowning at first with effort but gradually stimulated by laughter and applause to something very near his usual form. Whether Argan's lines concerning himself ('Go on! Kick the bucket! That'll teach you to mock! . . .') were charged or not with any premonitions this February afternoon, they produced the same roars. So, exhausted and sweating under his paint, the comedian came at last to the final extravaganza, and a rednosed President of the Faculty of Medicine put the first of the three ritual questions to him:

Juras gardare statuta
Per Facultatem praescripta,
Cum sensu et jugeamento?[1]

[1] 'Do you swear to observe all the statutes prescribed by the Faculty, with sense and judgment?'

'*Juro!*' answered Argan-Molière. As he pronounced the word he was seized with a convulsion and staggered. Covering this with a loud laugh, ghastly enough in the circumstances, he pulled himself together instantly and carried on. Those of the company and the nearest spectators who saw the incident noticed nothing unusual thenceforth. After the final curtain he changed and made his way to Baron's dressing-room – Armande would be busy – and sat down. 'What do you think of the show?' he said after a moment or two. The young man, who did not entirely lack a heart, was consternated to perceive that Molière was deathly white and shivering. His hands were icy and he complained of a chill to the bones. Handing him a muff, Baron at once summoned his coach and took him home to the Rue de Richelieu. Grimarest may continue:

> When he got into his bedroom Baron tried to make him take a little bouillon, of which La Molière always had some at hand, for nobody could take better care of herself than she did. 'Oh, no,' said Molière. 'My wife's bouillons are absolute poison to me. You know all the stuff she puts into them. Get me a bit of Parmesan instead.' La Forest brought some. He ate it with a piece of bread and was helped to bed. He had not been there a moment before he sent to ask his wife for a pillow stuffed with a drug (? herbs) which she had promised him to make him sleep. 'I'll gladly take anything, except internally,' he said. 'The medicines they make one take frighten me. I want nothing which might make me lose what remains to me of life.' A moment later he began to cough violently, and after spitting he demanded a light. 'Look, here's a change,' he said. Seeing the blood just coughed up, Baron gave a cry of alarm. 'Don't be frightened,' Molière said to him. 'You've seen me bring up more than that.' He added, 'Tell my wife to come upstairs.'

He then demanded a priest, urgently, repeating it more than twice or thrice. A few minutes later, despatched either by Baron, or the cook La Forest, or – if she had returned from the theatre by now – Armande herself, the chambermaid and the valet-footman Provençal hurried to St Eustache, the parish church. Here two of the clergy on duty, the Abbés Lenfant and Lechat, declined firmly and repeatedly to bestir themselves. Eventually a third priest, the Abbé Paysant, yielded to the entreaties of Molière's brother-in-law Jean Aubry des Carrières, who had sped out on the servants' return, arriving with the Viaticum a few moments after Molière had breathed his last. According to La Grange his time was not long.

> His efforts were so great that a vein burst in his lung. Finding himself in this condition he turned all his thoughts to heaven. A moment later he lost his speech. Within half-an-hour he was suffocated by the blood pouring from his mouth.

What Armande was doing all this time is not clear. If she had indeed returned home, it would seem likely that she lost her head in the general panic, and may herself have rushed out with Baron or Aubry des Carrières in search of a priest, since she was not at Molière's side when the end came. He did not die alone and unaided nevertheless. Grimarest continues:

> He was assisted by two of the nuns who usually go round collecting alms during Lent, and to whom he had given hospitality. In the last moments of his life they rendered him all the spiritual succour one might expect of their charity, and he displayed all the feelings of a good Christian and all the resignation due to the will of God. Finally he gave up his soul in the arms of these two good sisters; the blood which poured from his mouth in abundance choked him. Thus, when his wife and Baron returned, they found him dead.
>
> I have thought it my duty to enter into these details concerning the death of Molière in order to dispel, for the public's benefit, several stories circulating on this occasion. He died on Friday, the seventeenth of February of the year 1673, aged 53; regretted by all men of letters, by the Court, and by the public.

The inaction of the clergy of St Eustache has caused much ink to flow. The reconciliation of stage-players approaching death was a normal routine of the period and a pastoral obligation on call. Unless Molière's stupid manservant was to blame, the two priests of St Eustache obviously acted in defiance of their duty. If they regarded Molière as an enemy of religion, as they seemingly did, all the more urgent was the acceptance, while there was yet time, of his surrender. He was not, of course, an enemy at any time. Indifferent in these matters all his life, he had never brandished impiety in the manner of a Cyrano or a Le Vayer. He had always responded generously to charity, public and private, and never failed the questing clergy. The village curé of Auteuil was his close friend. In 1672 he even performed his Easter duties at St Germain-l'Auxerrois. Such at least was Armande's claim. In her anxiety to ensure him the Church's funeral-rites she may have overstated.[1] But there is a rather surprising little piece among Molière's minor poems, tucked away at the end of the 1682 edition, which seems to escape the notice of everybody. Called simply *Vers*, it consists of eight lines to accompany a print by Le Doyen, after Chauveau, representing the lay confraternity known as the Serfs of Our Lady of Charity, established in 1665 by Pope Alexander VII in the church of the *Frères de La Charité-Nôtre-Dame* near the Temple.

> Brisez les tristes fers du honteux esclavage
> Où vous tient du péché le commerce odieux,
> Et venez recevoir le glorious servage
> Que vous tendent les mains de la Reyne des cieux . . .[2]

Undistinguished verse, doubtless. No better than the half-dozen other trifles among which it nestles, it is even less qualifiable as poetry than *La Gloire du Val-de-Grâce*, a long sequence of alexandrines in praise of the beloved Mignard's paintings round the dome of Mansart's great Renaissance-style church on the left bank, built (1645–65) by the Queen Mother Anne of Austria in thanksgiving for the birth of a long-delayed heir.

> Digne fruit de vingt ans de travaus somptueüs,
> Auguste bastiment, temple majestueüs,
> Dont le dome superbe, élevé dans la nuë,
> Pare du grand Paris la magnifique veuë . . .
> Dy-nous, fameux mignard, par qui te sont versées
> Les charmantes beautez de tes nobles pensées?[3]

[1] It was possible. Unlike the majority of the secular clergy of France, the mendicant Orders often waived the unwritten law for stage-players on demand.

[2] 'Break the dismal fetters of the shameful slavery in which you are held by the odious traffic of sin, and come, accept the glorious servitude offered you at the hands of the Queen of Heaven.'

[3] 'Worthy fruit of twenty years of sumptuous labour! August pile, majestic temple, whose superb dome, lifted in the clouds, enhances the splendid vista of our great Paris! . . . Tell us, famous Mignard — by whom art thou inspired with the charming beauties of thy noble conceptions?'

A comparison some time later between the arts of oil-painting and fresco rescues this performance from total banality; a few of its lines have been almost universally damned as execrable. Mignard's *nobles pensées*, like the architects', were inspired by the Roman Baroque, some of the splendours of which they duly transferred from the banks of Tiber to those of Seine.[1] What of the *pensées* behind those eight lines of devotion composed by Molière for Le Doyen's print? Sincere? A hasty gesture replying to charges of irreligion? They are at any rate unique in Molière's achievement, and in her anxiety to prove her husband a last-moment penitent Armande may have quoted them more than once.

Anxiety was not unjustified. The senior priest of St Eustache, quoting Canon Law, declined to bury an unshriven excommunicate in consecrated ground. At once Armande appealed in writing to Harlay de Chanvalon, Archbishop of Paris. Her petition stressed the facts that before the end Molière had shown every sign of penitence and desire to die a good Christian, that he had repeatedly asked for the last Sacraments, that two of his parish clergy had refused to respond, and that in all the bustle and confusion the Abbé Paysant arrived too late. There was no doubt of a final act of contrition. Having done this, Armande hastened to St Germain-en-Laye, taking the curé of Auteuil with her, and threw herself in distress at the feet of Louis XIV.[2] The King, after gently reminding her that it was not his business, conveyed to the Archbishop his wish that Molière should if possible be accorded a funeral calculated to evoke 'no gossip or scandal', and his Grace accordingly, and with reluctance, gave Molière the benefit of the doubt and authorized a religious ceremony 'without pomp'. On Tuesday, February 21st, the cortège left the house in the Rue de Richelieu. Three priests in black copes preceded four minor clerics bearing Molière's coffin on a bier covered by the richly-embroidered pall of the Company of Master Upholsterers of Paris and

[1] In the building of the Val-de-Grâce Mansart was assisted by Lemercier, Lemuet and Leduc. The dome decorated by Mignard, a smaller reproduction of that of St Peter's at Rome, was justly famous at the time.

[2] Her alleged cry to Louis: 'If my husband was a criminal, it was Your Majesty who authorized his crimes!' may be accepted with due reserve.

escorted by six of the *Enfants Bleus*, orphan-boys in blue gowns employed on such occasions, carrying lighted candles in silver candlesticks. Behind the coffin walked La Fontaine, Boileau, Mignard, and Chapelle, each with a lighted candle, and followed by a number of footmen, also bearing lights. The rear of the procession to the cemetery of St Joseph, serving the parish of St Eustache, was brought up by the greater part of a considerable crowd which had been surging round the house and terrifying Armande in her shattered state. She seems to have feared a riot, or even an attack. Advised to scatter a hundred pistoles in alms from an upper window, begging the mob's prayers for her husband's soul, she did so, and calmed down.

So the body of Jean-Baptiste Poquelin, *dit* Molière, was consigned to the tomb. Where this was nobody knows, though La Grange says it stood 'a foot above ground'. The cemetery was built over at the beginning of the last century, and the Rue Saint-Joseph off the Rue Réaumur is now its only memorial. Like the dust of Rabelais, and the little Dauphin Louis XVII, and many more of the historic dead, the dust of Molière has dissolved, so to speak, into thin air. A macabre and typically Parisian sequel is worth recording.

In 1792 the Revolutionary sector of Molière-La Fontaine deputed a couple of commissaries to exhume the bodies of these two great friends, popularly believed to lie side by side in the cemetery of St Joseph, and to transfer them to the Musée des Monuments Français. The parish registers of St Eustache could have informed them that La Fontaine was buried in the Innocents cemetery. However, after digging up, from under the cross of St Joseph's cemetery, an oak coffin which they took to be La Fontaine's, the commissaries proceeded to a distant corner and chose apparently haphazard, from an assortment of skulls, bones, and débris there collected, a set looking like Molière's; there was in fact a rival tradition that he was buried, or perhaps reburied, in the unconsecrated ground reserved for infants dying at birth and unbaptized. Having at any rate collected what they came for, the two commissaries, who may have been drunk, duly removed the alleged remains to the Museum, whence in 1818 they were transferred to the vast cemetery of Père Lachaise. Before this final transference occurred a mildly comic scene which would have diverted Molière. Among the spectators was a perfervid Gascon dramatist, one Cailhava d'Estandoux, a member of the Institute vowed to the lifelong cultus of Molière, whose *Dépit Amoureux* he had himself rewritten in five acts. Seizing both skulls, by permission, the Gascon pressed them to his throbbing breast. Then, replacing the skull said to be La Fontaine's and kissing the one attributed to Molière, he decorated its brow with a headband inscribed by himself with one of the master's lines –

C'ert un homme qui . . . ah! un homme, un homme enfin![1]

– and handed it back ('Alas poor Yorick!') in tears. The same immortal skulls and bones rest today in their twin mausoleums by Alexandre Lenoir at Père Lachaise.

Weightier funereal tributes than that of the ebullient d'Estandoux were paid to Molière by contemporaries. Those of Boileau and La Fontaine may be read in their collected works. The theme that the stage had lost another Plautus and another Terence is unavoidable, and incidentally true.

Ten years later Fontenelle included in his *Dialogues des Morts* a discussion in the underworld between Molière and Paracelsus, designed chiefly, in Fontenelle's velvety, feline manner, to undermine belief in *des mystères ridicules*; Christianity to begin with. However, he allows Molière the last word on the theatre. Arrogant Doctor Paracelsus cannot conceive what use there can be for such nonsense as the Comedy. 'I venture to predict,' retorts Molière, 'that my comedies will outlast your own sublime works. Fashions change. The productions of the mind have no higher destiny than that of costume. . . . I am perfectly aware of what revolutions in the Empire of Letters can be. I guarantee the survival of my plays in spite of them, for a reason well known to me. Anyone about to paint for posterity must paint fools.'

For all such bouquets, no scrap of Molière's handwriting is preserved, barring two or three signatures on contracts or receipts; one of these, confirming a contract of Baron's, presented

[1] 'This is a man who . . . ah! a man! A man, anyway.'

by the elder Dumas to the Comédie-Française, hangs framed in the *Foyer des Artistes*. What became of the manuscripts of the plays, used by La Grange for his 'definitive' edition of 1682, is not known. When last heard of in 1699, seven years after La Grange's death, they were in the possession of Armande. Possibly her cook, like the housemaid who lit the fire with the opening manuscript chapters of Carlyle's *French Revolution*, had a use for waste-paper.

CHAPTER FIVE

And Armande?

Ordering a handsome stone for her husband's tomb – during the ferocious winter of a couple of years later she had the bizarre and kindly inspiration of ordering a large fire to be kept alight on it day and night for the poor of the quarter, and one may wonder what had become of this stone by 1792 – she returned to work three days after the funeral, when *Le Misantrope* was revived with La Grange as Alceste. On March 3rd she played Angélique in *Le Malade Imaginaire* to La Thorillière's Argan; something of an ordeal for Molière's widow, since La Thorillière industriously reproduced Molière's make-up and delivery, but professionally speaking all in the day's work. The company had its living to earn. Molière himself had taken only one day off for his father's obsequies. Armande was now, with the invaluable La Grange at her elbow, responsible for its entire welfare.

She was to be glad of La Grange very soon. An alarming and even disastrous situation developed after the Easter recess of 1673. While the Palais-Royal theatre was closed during the holidays, emissaries of the Hôtel de Bourgogne set busily to work, and Baron, La Thorillière, and a couple of others changed allegiance. Almost immediately afterwards the remainder of the Palais-Royal troop found itself in the street. The insatiable Lully, who still owed Armande the 11,000 livres Molière had lent him three years previously, had decided that the Palais-Royal was the ideal theatre for his new opera. He got his way as usual with Louis XIV, and Armande and La Grange were forced in desperation to approach the Hôtel de Bourgogne with an offer of amalgamation. This had already been proposed by the Hôtel, and Armande had scornfully refused. It was now her and La Grange's turn to be shown the door.

In this crisis a theatre became suddenly available in the Rue Guénégaud, off the Quai de Conti; an excellent house, quite new, fitted with the latest stage devices by the Marquis de Sourdéac. The comedians of the Marais, long since left high and dry when fashion deserted their quarter, also had their eye on it, and immediate action was imperative. Forcing Lully to repay his debt, Armande and La Grange were able to foil the Marais and secure the lease of the Rue Guénégaud theatre for 30,000 livres just in time. The Marais players, now facing extinction, offered to amalgamate. Terms were agreed, an ordinance signed by Colbert, the Minister, on June 23rd, authorized them, and on July 9th a strongly-reinforced company under Armande and La Grange opened with a Molière season in the Rue Guénégaud.

That this issue was not a total success was no fault of La Grange's. Armande was not a business-woman like her sister, or perhaps mother, and her temperament was quite unsuited to cope with the troubles which soon broke out in the Rue Guénégaud. To defiance of her orders, jealousies, bickerings, and feuds were soon added attempts by De Sourdéac and his business associate, Champéron, to interfere with the direction, and even to lay hands on the box-office receipts, and Armande had at length to take legal action. The menace from the Hôtel de Bourgogne on the other hand was vastly reduced from the day when La Grange lured its eminent tragedienne, Mlle Champmeslé, over to the Rue Guénégaud. On October 21st, 1680, finally, by royal decree, the Hôtel de Bourgogne joined the Marais and the Rue Guénégaud, and the Comédie-Française was born. This signal feat was likewise entirely La Grange's. Long before this Armande had transferred the entire business management to him and returned to the motley, playing second lead to La Champmeslé till her retirement in 1694.

Armande's fortunes after Molière's death are thus linked

firmly with those of the admirable Charles Varlet de La
Grange, who saved the company at least twice and left it a
national institution. It is easy to overlook the virtues of La
Grange, most modest of men. On the stage he was by all accounts one of the best-graced *jeunes premiers* imaginable,
developing such roles as that of Cléonte in *Le Bourgeosis Gentilhomme* and Clitandre in *Les Femmes Sçavantes* into character-
studies of the utmost finesse, mingling youthful brio with perfect manners and the most chivalrous tenderness. He too was
fortunate. As with Armande, his roles were tailored by
Molière like a suit from Savile Row. He more than repaid his
director by bureaucratic efficiency and loyal integrity, combined with a self-effacement not common in men of his trade.
Whatever La Grange's continued services to Armande under
the new regime, nevertheless, she did her best to deserve them.
It was her money which was at stake for the most part, and the
change in Armande on assuming responsibility is quite remarkable. Conquering caprice, she is seen to be putting her company's welfare foremost even to the extent of stepping gracefully down into permanent second place when the tragedy-
queen Champmeslé sweeps on the scene. From 1673 onwards it
is necessary to revise one's entire opinion of Armande, as no doubt
her contemporaries did likewise; even, to some extent, in the
world of the theatre. Kisses exchanged in public with her rivals
and charged normally with 'dreadful meaning', as Barrie said of
actresses' embraces – compare the kisses exchanged by Wimble-
don tennis-queens over the net of the Central Court – would be
still more chilling a spectacle for the onlooker henceforth.

Two unpleasant contretemps diversified her early years of
widowhood. The first, in 1675, is of a quaintly Molièresque
pattern, though it is doubtful if it amused Armande at the
time. A certain M. de Lescot, one-time President of the Parlement of Grenoble, a notorious playboy and rake about town,
fell violently desirous of her from the other side of the footlights in the Rue Guénégaud and hired a professional *intrigante*,
one Mme Ledoux, to achieve his ends. The incident bears one
or two fantastic resemblances to the Diamond Necklace imbroglio which a hundred years later was to do poor innocent

Marie-Antoinette such irreparable harm and to bring the Crown of France to the dust. The tool selected by the woman Ledoux to help pluck a wealthy pigeon was a prostitute named La Tourelle, an almost perfect physical replica of Armande, and M. de Lescot was soon congratulating himself. Though sworn to prudence and secrecy by his supposed conquest, passion and vanity at length overcame legal judgment and he burst one night into Armande's dressing-room at the theatre, amorous and, undoubtedly, drunk. Duly rebuffed, M. de Lescot turned furious and abusive, finally snatching Armande's necklace and shouting that he had given it to her. She then called the police and he was arrested. On October 17, 1675, an order of the Parlement of Paris sentenced the pre-Madame de la Motte and the pre-d'Oliva of the little plot to a double whipping, one to be administered outside the gates of the Châtelet prison and the other outside Mlle Molière's house,[1] and banishment from Paris for three years. The pre-Rohan, the dashing magistrate their dupe, got off more lightly than the stupid Cardinal in 1786, being merely ordered to make a full apology to Mlle Molière in the presence of witnesses.

A few months later a more grievous vexation was in store for Armande. A certain Sieur Guichard, an impresario enjoying high protection, coveted the direction of the Opera, now held by Lully, and allegedly tried to poison him. An enquiry was opened. Among the witnesses called by Lully was Armande, on whom, among others, Guichard launched a monstrous attack in print forthwith, not merely reviving the old incest-*motif* ('her husband's orphan and her father's widow . . .'), but describing Armande as a universal prostitute before marriage and a public adulteress ever since, *la plus infâme de toutes les infâmes*. On February 27th, 1676, the court of enquiry found the accusation of attempted poisoning justified and ordered Guichard to pay a total of 4,200 livres in damages and costs and to make a full apology to Mlle Molière, with a prosecution for his printer. Two months later Guichard was able to have

---

[1] This was a house in the Rue de Seine called the Hôtel d'Arras, occupied by Madeleine's sister Geneviève and her husband, Jean Aubry des Carrières, and shared by Armande for four years after Molière's death.

this ruling quashed on appeal, thanks to pressure in high quarters. Armande's feelings, though she was only indirectly concerned, may be well imagined.

It must have been partly for protection's sake that, in May 1677, 'La Molière' married again, evoking thereby a chorus of reprobation from critics of a later age somewhat resembling that which greeted Mrs Thrale when she married Piozzi. Her new husband was an actor of no great standing and of agreeable disposition named François Guérin d'Estriché. It may be noted that Armande's contemporaries did not carry on about 'treason to a glorious name', perhaps because the apotheosis of Molière had not yet begun. As Mme Guérin, Armande was to enjoy twenty-three years of contented domesticity, the poison-blast of *La Fameuse Comédienne* in 1688 notwithstanding, and to bear Guérin, a year after marriage, a son who loved and long outlived her.

She continued her career meanwhile, quitting the stage, as observed already, at Easter 1694, at the age of fifty-two, which for most leading ladies would be relative adolescence. The comely country-house at Meudon where she spent nearly all the rest of her life was still in existence in the Rue des Pierres until the outbreak of World War I at least; a perfect 'period' piece, with a garden of shady alleys and a *berceau* of vines. Armande died nevertheless in her Paris house, No. 4 Rue de Touraine, now Rue Dupuytren, near the Odéon. It was standing in the 1930's; it may be there still.

The only cloud on Armande's new domesticity seems to have been Esprit-Madeleine Poquelin, her daughter by Molière, who had some of the business instinct of her aunt – or possibly grandmother – Madeleine and her grandfather Poquelin. On coming of age Esprit-Madeleine quarrelled with her mother over the accounts of ten years of upbringing, brought an action, and on gaining control of her financial affairs left the Guérins and lived apart thenceforth. At forty she married a man of good family and no fortune, one Claude de Rachel, Sieur de Montalant, twenty years her senior, and died, childless, in 1723. Esprit-Madeleine is said to have been tall, well-made, unbeautiful, cultivated, and agreeable, and to have lived all her life surrounded by some of her father's belongings, furniture and pictures and books, from the house in the Rue de Richelieu. Since Molière died when Esprit-Madeleine was nine years old, her reminiscences of summer nights at Auteuil would hardly have been of much value to a biographer. One may be permitted to regret that posterity has thereby lost a glimpse, if only one, of Jean de La Fontaine, Nicolas Boileau-Despréaux and Jean Racine playing the fool by moonlight.

From a thick brown contemporary fog of envy, hatred, and calumny Armande Poquelin-Molière, *née* Béjart, emerges as an element in Molière's achievement by no means to be underrated; a petulant and frivolous coquette mated to a sombre, jealous, extremely trying genius, and undoubtedly responsible for half his triumphs. As Étienne Gilson has observed, the artist can love not only as a man but as an artist. 'He needs some sort of emotion or passion for the liberation of his creative power. . . . It does not always need to be accompanied by carnal satisfaction. Its lasting properties are indeed often enhanced if this is denied to it.'[1] Such was the stimulant supplied by Dante's Beatrice, Petrarch's Laura, Heine's Camille, Wagner's Mathilde, Goethe's Christiane, and Baudelaire's 'black Venus', who led him such a life.

> O métamorphose mystique
> De tous mes sens fondus en un!
> Son haleine fait la musique,
> Comme sa voix fait le parfum . . .

The grim deduction – the keener the suffering, the better the style – can hardly be evaded. Molière's finest work was certainly done during the five years of separation. When he and Armande lived and fought together he produced nothing comparable with *Le Misantrope*, which required more than ordinary pain. It was Armande's function, perhaps, to be the grain of sand which produces the pearl, and when her function was over she settled down, as we perceive, with a nice mediocre mate and lived happily ever after. If Molière was *cocufié* as much as they say, François Guérin d'Estriché could go to sleep all his married life with a quiet mind. One sees Armande in her final

---

[1] *Dante Philosophe*, 1946.

years as a quiet, rather prim elderly lady in black, devoted to gardening – she had part of the courtyard of the house in the Rue de Seine unpaved and planted with grass and flowers by arrangement with Geneviève Béjart, as an *acte de location* of 1673 records – and good works, and highly critical of the Modern Girl.

Armande Guérin d'Estriché died on November 30th, 1700, in her fifty-ninth year. On her son's testimony, she alwaysspoke of Molière with admiration and respect, but there is no mention of Molière in her death-certificate. No bust of Armande by Houdon adorns the foyer of the Comédie-Française. It may seem to many that she well deserves one.

Book VII

CHAPTER ONE

'Who, do you think, has been the greatest writer of my reign?'
Louis XIV asked Boileau some years after Molière's death.
'Molière, Sir,' answered the loyal Boileau. 'I had not thought
so myself', said the King pensively. 'But, of course,' he added,
'you know more about these things than I do.'

He continued not to think so. Louis' own choice, which
posterity has largely confirmed, would undoubtedly be Racine.
Apart from a long friendship which does honour to both men,
Louis was well able to recognize that whereas Molière is great,
Racine is incomparable, though, as with Dryden and Pope, his
precedence or otherwise over the surly, arrogant, and magnificent Corneille, his elder, will probably never be settled.

What all that splendid company revolving like planets round
the Sun King – Corneille, Racine, Molière, La Fontaine,
Bossuet, Fénélon, Boileau, La Bruyère, perhaps even acid aris-
tocrats like La Rochefoucauld and Saint-Simon – derived from
Louis' presence on the French throne is sufficiently known.
Hard as the King drove him, Molière owed Louis more than
any of them, perhaps, save Racine, of whom the by no means
negligible Désiré Nisard remarked in the 1870's that 'born only
a year before his King, gifted like him with the rarest qualities
of mind and body, sharing likewise that "great air" of which
Saint-Simon speaks, Racine was linked with Louis XIV in a
species of fraternity. . . . Louis appears in almost every Racinian
drama'.[1] Molière, though Louis undoubtedly had high esteem
and personal liking for him, was not on the same footing. The
two men stood in Louis' estimation, one might judge, as a
Wodehouse and a Henry James stand today in the estimation
of a connoisseur of prose responsive to both; a matter of

[1] *Histoire de la Littérature Française*, II, 7.

degree. Yet it is to be noted (Saint-Simon records it) that amid the trials and disillusion of his concluding years, some time after Lully's death, it was to Molière that Louis XIV turned again for refreshment. Though by this time he was weary of the theatre, and a single act of any new play was usually enough for him, the ageing Louis would sit through a comedy of Molière's with almost the same zest as he had done forty or fifty years earlier. A not insignificant curiosity of this last phase is recorded in Dangeau's memoirs. The King took a fancy to staging occasional private performances of some of Molière's comedies himself, using the Court musicians and drilling them apparently into quite presentable actors.

But Louis XIV never placed Molière on the same level as Racine, or for that matter Corneille. Nor, to do him justice, did Molière himself, though to judge the sincerity or otherwise of his publicly-expressed admiration for both his eminent fellow-craftsmen – especially Corneille, 'my master, the foremost of dramatists' – is of course impossible.[1] His private opinion may, as happens occasionally in the world of letters and art, have differed. Each of these supreme artists in tragedy trespassed on Molière's preserves with conspicuous success. Most of Corneille's comedy *Le Menteur* (1643), the study of a pathological liar, is extremely amusing, even if Corneille lifted the best scene, with contemporary aplomb, from the Spanish dramatist Ruiz de Alarcón. Nobody at the first night of Racine's comedy *Les Plaideurs* (1668), again, approved the show more warmly than Moliere, whom one may venture to glimpse applauding from his box, perhaps with hands at the same high ecstatic altitude which is *de rigueur* for stage celebrities applauding their rivals from the stalls today. Magnanimity, considering what Racine had done to Molière three years previously, could hardly be better demonstrated. Yet for any observer who has mingled with the retinue of Melpomene and Thalia to any extent a prickly doubt persists.

[1] Another remark of Molière's on Corneille has a slightly more authentic ring: 'My old friend Corneille has a familiar who inspires him with the finest verse in the world. Sometimes it leaves him to shift for himself. He then fares very badly.'

For one thing Molière could envy Corneille and Racine equally. They stirred up the normal enmities successful artists incur, but they never had to face the kind of trouble Molière created for himself by plunging into waters too deep for him.

Pascal is an arresting but hardly a sympathetic type. Native frigidity plus a talent for physics plus the Jansenist *mystique* make a solution to turn the reddest litmus blue. But when Pascal agrees with Bossuet their reflections on the contemporary Comedy are worth pondering. And they certainly agree on Molière, though Pascal does not mention or quote him. 'Of all the diversions that the world has invented,' says Pascal in the *Pensées*, speaking of perils to the spiritual life, 'there is none to be feared more than the Comedy.'[1] He is dealing exclusively with its effect as an aphrodisiac, to illustrate which he might have drawn on at least three of Molière's comedies. From the message of *La Princess d'Élide* in particular anyone overlooking the good manners and the strict decorum, at least in public, of Louis XIV's Court might be forgiven for imagining a Versailles turned for a fortnight into the groves of Paphos. It was left to Bossuet, now Bishop of Meaux, to develop Pascal's theme in *Maximes et Refléxions sur la Comédie* thirty years later. An appreciative letter from the Latin of a priest, one Père Caffaro, had been used by Edmé Boursault, Molière's old antagonist of the Hôtel de Bourgogne, to preface a newly-published collection of his printed plays. To find a clerk in Holy Orders alleging that the contemporary French stage displays nothing contrary to good morals takes Messire Jacques-Bénigne's breath away. 'So we have to pass as decent the impieties and infamies of which Molière's comedies are full?' he demands on recovery. He is of course aware of the argument that the cleaned-up French stage of the 1690's presents love only as 'an innocent inclination towards beauty, ending in the conjugal knot'. Very well, says Bossuet:

[1] Part II, Art. XVII, 75.

Then at least, in accordance with these principles, we should rid a Christian milieu of the debaucheries of which the Italian Comedy is full, even in our time, and which one sees served up again raw in the plays of Molière. We should reprobate those speeches in which this austere censor of long *canons*, this grave reformer of the expressions and grimaces of our *précieuses*, exposes to the full light of day the advantages of an infamous tolerance in husbands, and incites wives to shameful vengeance on their jealous mates.

Thence to score a real point:

He has enabled our age to perceive what one can expect of the morality of a theatre which attacks only the absurdities of this world, leaving it meanwhile all its corruptions. Posterity will learn no doubt of the end of this actor-poet, who while playing in his *Malade Imaginaire*, or else his *Médecin Par Force* (Bossuet means *Le Médecin Malgré Luy*), received the final stroke of the malady from which he died a few hours afterwards; passing from the japes of the stage, amid which he nearly gave up his last breath, to the tribunal of Him who said, 'Woe to you that laugh, for you shall weep!'

The heroic love of Corneille's Cid comes under Bossuet's lash likewise, most unfairly. We may observe that then as nearly always, ecclesiastical views on the theatre differed. It would be interesting to have had Bossuet's opinion of a brilliant and exemplary confrère in Holy Orders flourishing earlier in the same century – the Spanish monk, Maestro Fray Gabriel de Téllez, otherwise Tirso de Molina, with his four hundred (no less) racy satiric comedies, his fifty or more sacred dramas, *autos sacramentales*, and other stage-works in prose and verse, including the immortal *Burlador de Sevilla* and, incidentally, at least one far more expert onslaught on religious hypocrisy than Molière's. Though he had probably never heard of the Spaniard, Bossuet's protest was undoubtedly extra-acidulated by the fact, appearing in Boursault's preface, that the priest who so scandalized him belonged to an Italian Renaissance congregation known as the Clerks Regular, or Theatines. Their Parisian community had lately (1688) received a rap from the sombre La Bruyère in *Les Caractères* for giving 'theatrical' recitals of oratorio and other sacred music in their fashionable church on the Quai des Théatins, today the Quai Voltaire.[1]

[1] 'Theatine' has no connection with 'theatre'.

These Italians! . . . Fortunately for them, the Eagle of Meaux was not their diocesan.

The ancient issue raised once more by Bossuet, namely whether the theatre is or may be an instrument for evil, was discussed a century later, we may recall, by another great moralist. Thus Dr Samuel Johnson in 1775, as reported by Boswell, on a celebrated test-case:

> *The Beggar's Opera*, and the common question whether it was pernicious in its effects, having been introduced – JOHNSON. 'As to this matter, which has been very much contested, I myself am of opinion that more influence has been ascribed to the Beggar's Opera, than it in reality ever had; for I do not believe that any man was ever made a rogue by being present at its representation. At the same time I do not deny that it may have had some influence, by making the character of a rogue familiar, and in some degree pleasing.' Then collecting himself, as it were, to give a heavy stroke: 'There is in it such a *labefactation* of all principles, as may be injurious to morality.'

The operative and detestable word, therefore, is 'glamour'. Gay's Prince Charming of the High Toby is certainly brimful of it. Surveying Molière's *racaille*, on the other hand, one is rather surprised to find how unglamorous his professional rascals are. No youthful ambition is liable to be fired, no maiden heart is likely to be shattered by a Mascarille, a Sbrigani, or a Scapin. The charms of a Nérine or a Frosine are negligible. Issuing from a performance of *Les Fourberies*, only an exceptional type will go home and put his father in a bag, though Cléante's insolence to Harpagon might admittedly have some effect on the impressionable young nowadays. It can justly be said that in this respect all Molière's loose characters put together cannot compete with a single Macheath; hence to enjoy their antics entails very little risk of Dr Johnson's 'labefactation'. The typical Molièresque thug is in fact strictly comic. Gay's is a hero of romance.

Johnson is rarely wrong on a commonsense issue. The influence of the theatre for bad can, as he opined, be easily exaggerated. Among the *alumni* of the Newgate Calendar, that improving work, is a young ruffian named Joseph Powis, who, midway through a sequence of robberies and housebreakings, went to see *The Beggar's Opera*, then enjoying its initial run. So far from being beglamorized young Powis was, he said, 'greatly shocked at the appearance of Macheath on the stage in fetters, and could not forbear reflecting what might be his own future fate'. It is true that after a swift recovery he resumed business and was duly hanged at Tyburn, aged 22. But his reaction to the play, if authentic, would have gratified Dr Johnson, if not Mr Gay.

No doubt the secular theatre has little influence for good either, even when 'good' can be stretched to embrace social or political upheavals of, morally speaking, very mixed inspiration. During periods of public excitement it may echo a few current slogans and glamorize a few contemporary illusions, but that is about all. The destructive qualities of *Le Barbier de Seville* and even more its successor, *Le Mariage de Figaro*, have been absurdly magnified. In the latter comedy long furry ears in a later age have even heard 'the first clang of the tocsins of '89'.[1] Actually Beaumarchais and his actors bear about as much responsibility for the storming of the Bastille as Mme du Deffand's lapdog. Without doubt Figaro's insolence towards what Beaumarchais calls *la disconvenance sociale* appealed as amusingly to the jaded French high society of the 1780's as to its social inferiors. 'Nobility, fortune, rank, places – what have you done to deserve so much? You merely gave yourself the trouble of being born.' Such quips from the famous monologue in the park, addressed to an absent Count Almaviva, were on every fashionable lip at a period when the urge to *s'encanailler* was seizing Europe's aristocracy at large. To hail Figaro on this account as a nuncio of bloody revolution and a protomartyr of Democracy is to read history backwards and sideways. The same applies probably to every other character in secular drama for whom similar claims have been made. Charged with subversive intent over the supper-table by giggling smart women, some of whose heads were due to fall within the decade, Beaumarchais, no demagogue, must have laughed

[1] *Le Mariage de Figaro* was produced in 1784, having its first Court performance, after many refusals by Louis XVI to indulge his wife, at Versailles in September of that year.

politely, perhaps quoting the curiously inauspicious last lines of *Le Mariage de Figaro*, a satiric song about the French nation:

Qu'on l'opprime, il peste, il crie,
Il s'agit en cent façons;
Tout finit par des chansons.[1]

A little old nursery-rhyme could likewise have served him. It can serve any man of the theatre at any time – was it not Henri Ghéon who said it should be inscribed on every actor's tomb?

Les marionnettes font, font, font
Trois petits tours et puis s'en vont[2]

Whatever allure, therefore, the voices of Armande Béjart or La Grange may have lent some too-luscious line of Molière's evaporated with the candle-smoke and is certainly not recaptured in a printed page. As for the effect on an audience, neither Pascal nor Bossuet frequented the theatre, we may recall. Neither of them, in fact, was in a position to assess what is nowadays called 'listener-reaction'. With their many and outstanding virtues, these great men had a further handicap. Each lacked a sense of humour, Bossuet particularly. One would certainly not go to Molière for moral instruction, as Faguet said, but it is possible to exaggerate his coefficient of harm. Compared with the brutish obscenity of the English Restoration stage, indeed, everything he wrote seems beautiful and blameless, and compared with the theatre of an age in which a play about a group of incestuous semi-morons in the American backwoods could run for three years, anything contemporary critics called raw in Molière seems the daintiest of bread and butter. A modern Bossuet, having taken a psychology course at his seminary, would be in better control of his thunder.

And the spell of Molière continues. His best plays radiate an eternal vitality and offer a concentrated richness peculiar to them alone. 'When you play a Molière part,' remarked the late

---

[1] 'If oppressed it swears, it screams, it bestirs itself in a hundred different ways . . . and everything ends in song.'
[2] 'The marionettes, they mop, they mow,
Twirl three times, and off they go.'

Louis Jouvet, most highly-graced of modern French comedy-actors, 'it *nourishes* you.'

This nourishment the audience shares. The repast is of the finest *cuisine bourgeoise*, perfectly prepared, cooked, and served, and conceals no exotic surprises or shocks. Molière is a cornucopia of shrewdly amusing lines and situations, but he does not indulge in wit for wit's sake. His finest gentlemen emit no recurring flashes of brilliance like the fine gentlemen of Congreve or Wilde ('one of those men who have no enemies, but are greatly disliked by their friends' – Molière has nothing coming within miles of this, and for that matter who has?). And if he lacks the diamond-wit of Congreve, his only comparable contemporary, Molière is far kinder than Congreve to his audience. Whatever he may ask it to swallow, natural bonhomie prevents his exploitation of such a grossly unfair trick as, for example, the one in Act V of *The Double Dealer* in which the villain, talking loudly to himself in a gallery, is overheard, as luck would have it, by his host and benefactor, one of the persons against whom he is plotting:

MASKWELL: O, there is a Secret burns within this Breast, which should it once blaze forth, would ruin all, consume my honest Character, and brand me with the Name of Villain!

LORD TOUCHWOOD: (*aside*) Ha!

MASKWELL: Why do I love! Yet Heaven and my waking Conscience (etc., etc., etc.)

The stage conventions of the period allowed this kind of cruelty, but Molière is too decent to take advantage of it. Even a Tartufe never soliloquizes aloud. This assurance that the playwright is our friend and does not despise or wish to hurt us is very comforting in an age in which so many playwrights, M. Sartre for example, barely trouble to hide their anger and contempt. The kindliness of Molière towards the cash-customers is most certainly part of his enduring spell. We realize from the beginning that he is on our side.

Some ultra-preposterous situation in a Molière comedy which in print may bore or irritate turns out to be perfectly natural and extremely laughable on the stage; for which, after all, and not the library, it was written. And so fully do some of his leading characters live on the stage that they continue doing so after curtain-fall and never really die. We know or feel that Alceste behind his high park-walls in the Cevennes is still impossible, brooding over an incurable wound, infuriated by rustic villainy as by that of the Court, shunned by his neighbours, a most unhappy man. We know or feel that Célimène is still queen of her little circle, and finding (like Ninon de l'Enclos at 70) the adoration of the young nice but a trifle tiring – but after all what is not? Her mirror may have become an enemy at morning, but at night she is Célimène still. Orgon is cured of his special kind of foolishness and now suspects nearly everybody of hypocrisy, including the Archbishop of Paris. Tartufe, when last heard of, was at Dieppe, awaiting transportation to Louisiana after forging a pious old dowager's will in the provinces; chained with the ladies of the same convoy, perhaps, is Nérine of *Monsieur de Pourceaugnac*, and possibly Manon Lescaut as well. Sbrigani is at Marseilles, serving a long sentence in his Majesty's galleys and branded with the fleur-de-lys in three places. All the young married lovers are happy, except, perchance, Isabelle of *L'Escole des Maris*, whose gift for Boccaccian intrigue is surely ominous? Harpagon lives alone, crooning to his casket and haunted by a shabby old hag named Frosine, who terrifies him . . .

In what Léon Daudet used to call 'the Stupid Nineteenth', when the deification of Molière was at its height ('He is truly formed in the image of God,' wrote a fantastic art-critic of 1847, one M. Thoré, urging expectant French mothers to furnish their bedrooms with Molière's portrait as Greek women did with statues of heroes and gladiators), the master critic Sainte-Beuve devoted one of his *Nouveaux Lundis* to a panegyric of the master of comedy.[1] Discounting one or two bravura-passages due to what might politely be styled 'coincidence of progressive ideologies', it is an admirable summing-up of reasons for loving Molière, the more so because it admits the strong counter-pull of his two great contemporary rivals of the

[1] Vol. V, 1863.

stage. To love and cleave to Corneille, says Sainte-Beuve, is an excellent thing. One takes one's place thereby in a world of great and noble souls, being at the same time compelled, amid all the grandeur and sublimity, to accept a certain amount of pomposity, over-emphasis, and heroism round every corner. You prefer Racine? Sainte-Beuve congratulates you. To love Racine is to love elegance and grace and nature and sensibility and passion of the most moving and exalted kind; but is it not also to accept a certain conventional beauty, a certain languishing softness and sweetness, a certain exclusive and excessive refinement of delicacy? Does not love for Racine bring with it the risk of acquiring too much of *ce qu'on appelle en France le goût, et qui rend si dégoûtés?* Then again there is Boileau. Though nobody can love Boileau, he is a judge of sovereign equity who hailed Molière as the greatest poet of Louis XIV's reign. And finally there is La Fontaine, who is Sainte-Beuve's eyes shares all Molière's gifts, together with certain weaknesses of style which one does not find in 'the virile and simple genius, the master of masters'. Perhaps one cannot separate these two, concludes Sainte-Beuve; they must be loved together.

Thus the greatest of French critics, himself a Molièresque character whose betrayal of Victor Hugo in his home-circle ('*Vil drôle!* . . .') not a little resembles that of a Tartufe cuckolding a Sganarelle. But with the possible exception of Matthew Arnold no professional critic of his fellows is entirely free from human frailties, and with this charitable reflection one may drop the curtain.

Index